FORGET KATHMANDU

~

'What distinguishes this book from mainstream history books is its stance: the Elegy revisits Nepali history from the point of view of a history-dweller rather than a history-broker… It is at once a celebration of the power of the literary monologue and a cry of outrage at the reality in which the…Nepali state and society are trapped.'—*Nepali Times*

['Manjushree's] prose exudes vigour and charm… Writing with a lot of candour, emotion and passion, [she] innovatively mixes reportage, travel writing, memoir and history to come up with a compelling tale of her country.'—*Sahara Time*

'It is important for the world at large, and India in particular, to listen to the voice of Manjushree Thapa, for even if she does not indicate a way out of [Nepal's] impasse, she speaks with knowledge, insight and a healthy scepticism about her country's travails. She emerges from these pages as a sensitive, passionate and sophisticated witness to a phase in Nepal's history.' —*Seminar*

'Thapa gives a splendid brief history of Nepal… Her analysis is astute and her observations often wry and illuminating.'
—*The Indian Express*

'Manjushree Thapa is the best kind of chronicler because she breaks down conventional modes of how history should be recorded: she acts, by turns, as reporter, activist, analyst and archivist, employing the techniques of each discipline. What makes *Forget Kathmandu* unforgettable is its courageous personal voice… Thapa is both passionately involved and coolly sardonic.'
—*Business Standard*

~

By the same author:

FICTION
Seasons of Flight
The Tutor of History
Tilled Earth: Stories

NON-FICTION
A Boy from Siklis: The Life and Times of Chandra Gurung
Mustang Bhot in Fragments
The Lives We Have Lost: Essays and Opinions on Nepal

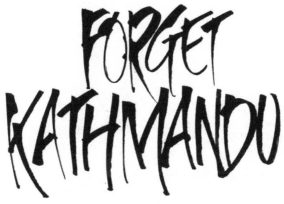

FORGET KATHMANDU

An Elegy for Democracy

MANJUSHREE THAPA

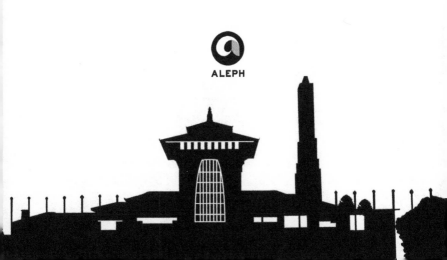

ALEPH

ALEPH BOOK COMPANY
An independent publishing firm
promoted by *Rupa Publications India*

Published in 2013 by
Aleph Book Company
7/16 Ansari Road, Daryaganj
New Delhi 110 002

First published in India
by Penguin Books India 2005

ISBN: 978-93-82277-00-2

1 3 5 7 9 10 8 6 4 2

For sale in South Asia (Bangladesh, Bhutan,
India, the Maldives, Nepal, Pakistan and Sri
Lanka) only.

To Khushwant Singh—for his honesty

History is a collection of found objects washed up through time. Goods, ideas, personalities surface towards us, then sink away. Some we hook out, others we ignore, and as the pattern changes, so does the meaning. We cannot rely on the facts. Time, which returns everything, changes everything.

—JEANNETTE WINTERSON

CONTENTS

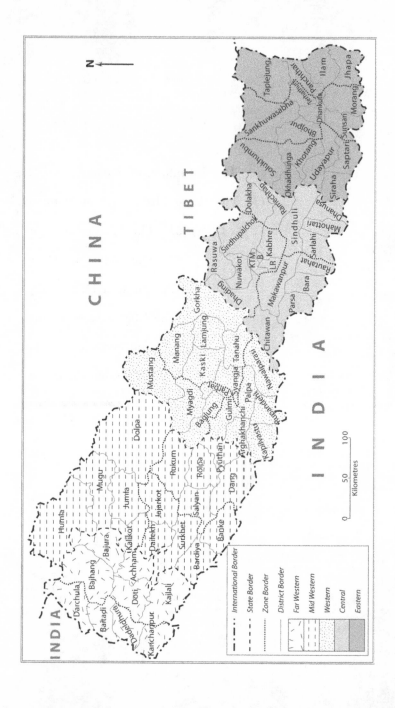

Introduction | READING NEPAL

When, in June 2001, King Birendra Bir Bikram Shah and his family were killed in a massacre at the Narayanhiti royal palace, the world took new notice of Nepal. Soon thereafter, the country plunged into chaos. The Maoist insurgency and government counter-insurgency on the way since 1996 suddenly escalated. We lost thousands of lives to war. Thousands of ordinary people were orphaned and widowed, hundreds of thousands were displaced from their towns and villages, and incidences of maiming, rape, unlawful detention, extortion, kidnapping, child conscription and disappearances rose rapidly. Parliamentary democracy—won late, in 1990—was lost to a gradual, staggered coup that began in October 2002, and culminated in February 2005, with a military takeover by King Gyanendra Bir Bikram Shah.

In this period it wasn't easy for Nepalis to trace what was going wrong, because so much was. And those who live in the thick of events more easily experience them than understand them. Like many of my compatriots, I have often found myself wondering: What the hell? Yet if we in Nepal were unable to understand our present, so too was the rest of the world—or those segments of the rest of the world that were paying us any attention. The last anyone knew, this was a pre-political idyll, a Himalayan Shangri-La good for trekking and mountaineering and budget mysticism. Suddenly, the news out of here jarred: Maoists? In this day and age? In a Hindu kingdom full of simple hill folk? The events in Nepal mystified the world, including Nepalis.

The truth is that this is a complicated country, its 26 million people an intricate social tangle. Best estimates have ninety-odd caste and ethnic nationalities living in the country's 1,50,000 square kilometres (less than 20 per cent of which is arable), speaking seventy-one languages and dialects, and observing Hindu, Buddhist, animist, Muslim, Sikh or Christian rites, or, more and more, eschewing god. There is no such thing as a typical Nepali. Each caste and ethnic nationality has its own class divides, hierarchies and patriarchies. Each has its own origin myths, its own history and its own particular relationship to state power in Kathmandu. People's political affiliations swing from communist to Hindu fundamentalist. All this makes the country difficult to decipher.

It has not helped that honest scholarship here was censored until 1990, when the 'People's Movement'—led by the then underground political parties—overthrew the Panchayat system of absolute monarchy. When my generation of thirty-somethings was growing up, anyone who strayed from the government line risked being branded an 'anti-national element'. People spoke evasively, in broad generalizations, resorting to adages and clichés that sounded catchy but meant little. Ferreting out the truth was next to impossible.

The legacy of this censorship has stayed with us. Long after 1990, our school textbooks continued to teach old, discredited histories that glorified our rulers and made no mention of the people. Our national myths were not revised. We remained in the courtier-like habit of fawning over authority—though secretly we also lacked faith in authority. Veering unstably from traditional belief systems to secular, scientific rationalism and back, we remained a society where more theories abounded than facts. Inevitably, many of these were conspiracy theories.

Of course, democracy brought in much change after 1990. Under a democratic polity that allowed uncensored discourse, intellectual enquiry began in earnest. Nepalis began to contest old national myths and to replace them with new truths—or at least with pertinent questions. The private media boomed after 1990, and books began to be published at an unprecedented rate. Every day there were scores of talks, seminars and debates in Kathmandu. The city's tea shops, restaurants and bars were abuzz with punditry. Nepali society was in a state of intellectual ferment.

Yet, in the cacophony of public discourse, statements of significance were easily drowned out by time-pass chatter. Public understanding still lagged behind events—especially at times of crisis.

And crises abounded. After the massacre of the king, his son the crown prince—the alleged murderer, himself with a bullet in his head—became king for a bizarre if brief reign, all of it spent while he was comatose. Upon his death, his uncle, Gyanendra Bir Bikram Shah, ascended to the throne.

Gyanendra Bir Bikram Shah was never, even as a prince, much liked. He has become more unpopular after, in response to a constitutional crisis in October 2002, he fired the elected prime minister and assumed direct control over the government. The legality of his takeover was hotly debated. Royalists claimed that the constitution drafted in 1990 allowed the king to rule directly in the case of a crisis. Yet many lawyers, including some who helped frame the constitution, argued that the king had overstretched the powers granted him. His rule, they said, was not legitimate.

Nevertheless, in part because of the backing he received from the diplomatic and aid communities, he retained his hold. On 1 February 2005 he further consolidated his rule when he effected a full-scale military coup, appointing himself the 'chairman' of a new right-wing cabinet and suspending all civil liberties and most constitutional remedies. He deployed the Royal Nepal Army to arrest and intimidate democratic political activists, journalists and human rights workers. And democratic institutions—such as the private media—came under systematic attack.

After that, the country continued its downward spiral. Because of the Maoist insurgency, it became impossible to hold local elections. Since October 2002 all we had had was a king, a royal cabinet, an army and a bureaucracy, all operating in what amounted to a constitutional never-never land. The political parties that had brought us democracy in 1990—the Nepali Congress Party (alternatively Nepali Congress or just Congress) and the Communist Party of Nepal (Unified Marxist Leninist) (alternatively CPN(UML) or just UML)—had lost much credibility. From 1990 right to the 2001 royal palace massacre, their leaders had often sacrificed the greater good to make selfish power grabs. Using the Maoist insurgency as an excuse, they had curtailed many democratic rights and precipitated a constitutional crisis, enabling King Gyanendra's staggered coup. After October 2002 they variously decried the revival of the monarchy and sought the king's favour to gain entry to his royal cabinet. Only after the February 2005 military takeover were they jolted into their senses.

Sobered, they began then to call for the restoration of 'full' democracy. Yet it was uncertain whether they could reform, regroup and wrest sovereignty back from the king and military. This, as the Communist Party of Nepal (Maoist) continued to rally the countryside for revolution...

Both absolute monarchy and Maoism were unappealing alternatives to most Nepalis. There had been such hope for progress when democracy was won in 1990. Since then, things went so wrong so fast, it felt as though we could not stop and gain control over our next move. The most obvious trajectories were all leading to military options. When democrats asked each other, 'What now?' no easy answer came to mind. We were caught in a quandary, a muddle.

I wrote this book in the thick of events, as a personal effort to work my way out of this muddle. Like many Nepalis, I had grown tired of what Edward Said has called the perplexity of living. As our democracy floundered, many of us who were not members of the political parties began to wonder what we should be doing to help save it. My own decision was to record what happened, to write what it has been like to watch democracy come, and slip away.

I am not a historian, yet in parts of this book I have written history—if history can be as trifling as the private search of a writer. It should not be. I have written too personally for that. What has resulted is a mongrel of historiography, reportage, travel writing and journal writing. You could call it a book on bad politics, spanning the founding of Nepal in 1768 to the events that led up to the abolition of the monarchy in 2008.

Part of the challenge of writing this book was to keep up with events, which kept outpacing the narrative. Weeks after its release came King Gyanendra's February 2005 military coup, and the revocation of all political, civil and human rights, including freedom of speech. Telephone lines were cut, satellite television was censored, and the country was forcibly cut off from the rest of the world. I left Nepal so that I might write in favour of democracy without fear. Many other dissidents soon gathered in India, while others chose to stay in Nepal and go underground, or to openly defy what they saw as a rogue regime.

Since then the king's rule has been overthrown peacefully through a second People's Movement, the Maoists have ended their insurgency and entered a peace process monitored by India and the United Nations, elections have been held for a Constituent Assembly, the monarchy has been abolished altogether, and the country has launched on an ambitious exercise of remaking itself, drafting a new constitution.

Like all peace processes, Nepal's has been imperfect, yet it has offered some hope that we might make democracy work for us at last. This book was written in grief, in mourning, as an elegy for Nepal's short-lived democracy, but in hope of its resuscitation, its revival. Let us hope that no such elegy ever need be written again.

THE COUP
THAT DID NOT
HAPPEN

DIPENDRA DIDN'T DO IT?

It was nearing 10.30 p.m. on 1 June 2001, when some friends and I were making our way through Kathmandu's tourist district, Thamel, where we came to escape our daily lives, to seek out some fun in the sparkle of lights and the hush of shadows. The trekking season was over, but a few late backpackers were roaming the streets, dressed in garish hippy garb. The restaurants and bars were throbbing with reggae, pop, hip hop and electronic music.

We were subdued, having just finished a 'goodbye-and-have-a-good-baby' dinner. A friend of mine was pregnant, and she and her husband had decided, on a hormone-driven whim, to have the baby in the United States. They were leaving in a few days' time.

'We had to go to the doctor's office three times to take an ultrasound test,' my friend had said over dinner, explaining their decision. 'Everyone has caesareans here because the doctors make more money off surgery than natural birth.' The final straw had been a three-day general shutdown, a bandh, called by the main opposition party in Parliament, demanding the prime minister's resignation. The bandh was zealously enforced by party cadres: No cars or buses were allowed to operate in Kathmandu, and shops and offices were forced shut. Even ambulances were attacked. Trapped inside their apartment for three long days, my friend and her husband saw themselves walking to the hospital on the day of delivery, and they decided: No.

Thamel lay a block from the Narayanhiti royal palace. We parted at its edge, the husband and wife walking to their car, and I to mine with another friend, whom I had promised to drop off at his home.

I took a shortcut through the narrow, hemmed-in lanes of old Kathmandu, past the ancient Hanuman Dhoka palace. At daytime these streets were jammed with pedestrians, but now they were empty. It felt a bit like sacrilege to drive amid the temples; the sheen of a car jarred badly with their intimate brickwork and handmade feel. Beyond a well known Ganesh shrine, I entered a row of concrete block houses constructed in the modern pillar style that is the cheapest—and ugliest—to build.

My friend was a Nepali visiting from Seattle, where he had settled. Two years back he had opened a factory here to export brassware to the US, only to fall into debt. 'No one works here, no one makes an effort,' he said as we crossed the Bishnumati River into the Chhauni neighbourhood. 'No one's serious about anything they do.' Investing in Nepal, he said, had been the biggest mistake of his life.

After dropping him off, I drove home along the road past the army hospital, then turned onto a wider boulevard. Even at 11 p.m., there was a stream of traffic here, the recent craze for oversized Prados and Pajeros manifested in sleek blurs of metal and chrome. It was easy to forget at this time that Kathmandu was more of a sleepy town than a city: The municipality had yet to name the streets, so we still said such things as, 'I live in the yellow house behind the peepul tree northeast of the junction, between a sweetmeat shop and a blue gate.' But after 1990, an influx of migrants from the countryside had begun to give Kathmandu a bustling, big-city air. Neon lights and backlit billboards lined the boulevard, and ads for Shikhar cigarettes blinked in the sky. The tinny sound of Nepali pop wafted out of the windows of cheap dance restaurants. Inside, young women from the countryside, working under the protection of hooligans or the police or both, would be catering to their clients' mass-market fantasies. Taxis idled along the boulevard in anticipation of cash-happy drunks.

My phone rang at four in the morning. I answered it warily, and what I heard sounded like a hoax: 'The king and queen are dead.'

It was a friend who would not call me casually. I sat up. 'What?'

He sounded weak with panic. 'The crown prince started an argument about his marriage. He shot them. They're dead.'

I assumed that he had fallen prey to a prank, and asked, 'Are you all right?'

'Then he shot himself. It's on the BBC.'

I turned to the window. It was dark outside. The night was completely silent. I told my friend I'd find out more and call him back. When I put down the receiver, the phone rang again. It was another friend: 'Have you heard?'

'Is it true?'

'I don't know.'

I called someone, he called someone, someone called me, and everyone asked everyone, 'Have you heard?' A few people had: Crown Prince Dipendra had gunned down his family.

Suddenly my hands began to tremble. Because Kathmandu was so small, everyone lived close to the Narayanhiti palace; the massacre felt very close by. I rushed down and turned on the television. The BBC was reporting that up to nine members of the royal family had been killed. I realized that my friends and I had been dining just one block away at the time. Then I'd driven to Chhauni, the site of the army hospital where the bodies had reportedly been taken. Had I passed ambulances on the road? Had I simply not noticed them?

I had seen King Birendra on the road a few days back, as he drove to the annual Bhoto Jatra festival. A convoy had led the way. The king had looked at ease in the driver's seat of his Mercedes-Benz. A few cars behind was the crown prince, driving his Pajero. He had grown obese in the past few years. He tended towards a poor fashion sense, favouring a scruffy beard, florid caps, red jackets—that sort of thing; but that day he had looked sharp. I had noticed that. Yet I had felt pity for him. Wasn't he too old to be herding around with his parents? At thirty, shouldn't he be leading a life of his own?

Was that why he had killed his family—out of frustration?

Or were these just rumours to cover up the truth? These doubts sprang up immediately, because in the last few years, every six months or so, all of Kathmandu would be shaken by rumours: *The king's going to take over on Monday—I heard it from a close palace source!* Or: *The army's declaring martial law on Tuesday! They're forcing the king to go along!* Parliamentary democracy, won only a decade ago, had ground to dysfunction due to the Maoist insurgency. And people had lost faith in the democratic political parties, all extremely disorganized and faction-ridden. Royalists had begun to openly call for the restoration of an absolute monarchy. Even lifelong democrats were beginning to feel that democracy had failed in Nepal, and a coup of some kind was inevitable. The king would take over any day now, or the army would, or some faction of the royal palace allied with some faction of the army.

As the sun rose, casting an aura of normality over the day, I remained glued to the television, flitting between the BBC, CNN, Star TV and Zee, which were uniformly reporting that a weekly family gathering at the palace had led to a dispute over the crown prince's choice of bride, and the prince had gone on a shooting spree. Nine were dead, including the king and queen and their two younger children. There was no word on the crown prince's condition.

None of the Nepali newspapers came that morning. The private FM stations—of which there were seven in Kathmandu— did not broadcast any morning news, and eventually they all halted transmission. The satellite TV entertainment channels had all been blocked—apparently in mourning, though it felt like in censorship. The state media offered no news: Radio Nepal was playing dirges, and Nepal Television was flashing pictures of the Pashupatinath temple, one of the four must-visit pilgrimage sites for South Asia's Shiva devotees. This felt like a sick insiders' joke, for Nepalis widely laugh off the monarchy's shadowy powers with the refrain: 'Only Lord Pashupatinath knows what holds this country together.'

Everyone wanted to know what had happened at the palace, and beyond that, to understand the massacre's political fallout—how would this affect democracy? The 1990 constitution had curtailed the powers of the king, yet it was believed that the army's top brass operated in strict loyalty to the monarch. King Birendra, a dove by nature, was thought to have kept the army out of the state's counter-insurgency effort. Whoever replaced him might be more hawkish, people feared. And once the army went into action, there was no saying where its generals would lead it. The chief of the army staff was openly disdainful of the political parties.

Everyone also wanted to know whether the crown prince had survived the massacre, and if so, whether he would inherit the throne. Or would Prince Gyanendra, the elder of King Birendra's two brothers? Gyanendra had once been king before, at the age of three, in 1950-51, when his grandfather King Tribhuvan had gone into exile in India, leaving only him behind. The boy-king had been stripped of the crown upon his grandfather's return three months later. People felt that he had always aspired to return to the throne. As an adult, he had gained the undesirable reputation of misusing his royal privileges for business gains in tea estates and tobacco companies and a five-star hotel. Rumours, never substantiated, also linked him to idol theft and drug-smuggling rings. His post as chairman of a conservation trust loaned him international prestige; but even as he hosted glittering fundraising galas, the Nepali public looked at him askance. Some believed that he and a secretive, tight-knit clique of conservatives had been urging King Birendra to end democracy and take back absolute power.

My family home was in old Baneswor, a crowded, ungainly maze of asphalt lanes and pillar-system buildings that embodied the middle-class aspiration for a house in Kathmandu. As the international TV news channels started to repeat themselves, and as I exhausted my stock of people to call, I began to feel isolated in the house. I wanted to be out in the city. I wanted to be among friends.

I called a friend who lived nearby, and the two of us met on the street and made our way along the fetid, garbage-choked banks of the Dhobi Khola to visit a couple who shared the same neighbourhood. The couple's apartment gave off the inviting, open-door aura of rural homes, and people just dropped by to chat. Usually bursting with plans, all that the husband and wife could do that day was fiddle with the television and radio dials. 'Can you believe he killed his whole family?' We all exchanged banalities. 'Then he shot himself. It all sounds so—unreal.' 'Who's the army source talking to the international media? It sounds like a prepared statement to me.'

The husband went out and returned with a copy of *Samacharpatra*, which had issued a late-morning edition on the massacre. The front page carried colour pictures of the king and queen, their daughter, Princess Shruti, and their younger son, Prince Nirajan. The story told us little more than that they had been killed. King Birendra had lost weight after a heart attack some years back, but he looked stately in the picture, flashing his usual serene smile. The queen was dolled-up, but the beauty of her early years had been lost to corpulence. Princess Shruti had a pleasant face, and Prince Nirajan's features were still boyish. It occurred to me, through my shock at their gruesome deaths, that these had all been very ordinary individuals fulfilling—with varying degrees of success—the roles that history had landed them.

The BBC finally reported that Crown Prince Dipendra was alive, albeit in a critical condition. Someone phoned the apartment and said that Prince Gyanendra was being brought back from Pokhara in a helicopter. 'Why wasn't he at the family gathering?' the caller asked. 'If it was a family dinner, why was he away in Pokhara? He did it, I tell you, he did it. He killed his brother.'

A series of telephone calls followed. We asked each other, 'Where was Paras during the shoot-out?' More unpopular than Prince Gyanendra was his son, Prince Paras. In August 2000, he had been driving his father's official Pajero when he ran over, fatally, a singer named Praveen Gurung. He had topped this off by rushing to the police station to warn the duty officer, at gunpoint, not to report the accident.

Prince Paras had a pattern of trouble. Just weeks before that incident, he had manhandled the driver of a three-wheel tempo after running into the tempo. Before that, in October 1999, he had hit a police officer in the eye with the butt of a machine gun when his car was stopped during a general shutdown. Kathmandu's elite society buzzed with stories of him inciting fights at one or another disco in Thamel.

When he ran over the singer, though, the private media—emboldened by a decade of democracy—had taken up the story. Student activists had started a signature campaign demanding that he be stripped of royal immunity. Though the singer's family had refused to pursue the matter, the issue had eventually reached Parliament. 'This is murder and this is not the first time that Paras Shah has been involved in a murder,' a member of Parliament had said in the Upper House.

People did not like this side of the royal family. While King Birendra and Crown Prince Dipendra were seen as the family's good eggs, Prince Gyanendra and his son were seen as its bad eggs. Now the good eggs had apparently all died, while the bad eggs had survived unscathed.

When the BBC and Star TV momentarily retracted their original stories, saying that they were awaiting confirmation that Crown Prince Dipendra had gone on a rampage over his choice of bride, people crowed: 'See?'

The next caller said, 'It wasn't Dipendra at all.' The telephone circuits jammed with speculation. Up to eighty people had been shot at the palace, someone said. There was a stream of blood in the palace compound. The wounded had already been sent abroad for treatment. No, they were in the army hospital; doctors from all over the city had been summoned there. Dipendra was dead. No, Dipendra was alive. He was in a coma. He was brain-dead. He would be our king.

At three that afternoon, seventeen hours after the massacre and eleven hours after the BBC's first unconfirmed reports on it, the ministry of home affairs announced that King Birendra, Queen Aishwarya, Princess Shruti and Prince Nirajan had 'passed on to the heavenly realms'. The sentence construction was passive; there was no mention of culpability or cause of death, and it was as though they had all, by coincidence, died of natural causes. No word was given on the other victims. No mention was made of the crown prince. Neither did the government offer information on whether the massacre would be investigated.

Fifteen minutes later came another announcement: The funeral cortège for the royal family was to begin in an hour.

(But why so fast, my friends and I asked each other. Shouldn't the bodies be kept for investigation?) Government employees were to attend in appropriate attire, which meant daura-suruwal for men, and saris for women, and—because leather was not allowed in Hindu rites—black cloth shoes. Male government employees were required to shave off their hair in the style of Hindu mourning (even if they were not Hindu). The public was invited to pay respects, and the cortège's route was laid out.

That evening, tens of thousands of people thronged the streets, waiting for the cortège. There was disquiet all around, for we did not know whether we were witnessing a family tragedy or something more political, more sinister, like a coup.

My friends and I stood at the Gyaneswor intersection, balancing on a raised sidewalk, as all around us people craned for a view from windows and balconies of houses. The crowd included all types—elderly men, middle-aged housewives in flower-patterned nightgowns, young men sporting baggy shorts, public figures conferring in tight circles, entire families holding on to each other. A number of young men had shaved off their hair in mourning. Night fell as we all waited.

The funeral cortège, when it came, was lit by the flares of high-wattage battery lamps. An army band marched at the head, playing a traditional march. Next came a caravan of cloth-covered bodies laid out on bamboo stretchers, each carried on the shoulders of shaven-haired men of the priestly Bahun caste, who looked, from their notable brawn, like soldiers. A few plaintive voices cried out, 'Long live King Birendra.'

From my vantage point I couldn't make out the bodies, and presumed that the first one was King Birendra's. His face was obscured by flowers, and red abhir powder. Queen Aishwarya's body lay inside an ornate palanquin that had borne her into the palace as a bride. The bodies of their two younger children followed, also covered by wreaths and flowers. Then there were official cars belonging to the prime minister and other government officials, followed by an army contingent glancing about warily. Someone next to me said that the prime minister had been mobbed earlier by crowds demanding to know what had happened. In the process his car had been stoned.

In the darkness the sound of the funeral march faded, and the flash and pop of cameras subsided. The crowd disbanded, feeling lost, and made its way through the winding streets, exchanging stray observations: 'The windshield of the prime minister's car was cracked.' 'The king looked like he was smiling.' There were also irate voices: 'But *what* actually happened?' 'Did Dipendra *really* kill them all?' Then a voice rasped harshly in the night: 'This may be the last king whose funeral procession is worth watching. Let's go to the ghats.'

Those heading to the Pashupatinath temple's cremation grounds turned east at a major intersection. My friends and I parted there, heading back to our homes. I walked quickly; the cremation was to be aired on a twenty-minute delayed telecast on state-run Nepal Television.

But when I got home, I found I didn't want to watch it. All day long we had been shut out of the news by the government, and this one broadcast seemed a paltry concession. Nothing, after all, could be learned from seeing the bodies of the royal family members burn; we already knew that they were dead. Instead of telling us what had happened, or analysing the massacre's political implications for the country, the government was only allowing us to watch the death rites. Sitting before the television set, I felt manipulated.

Instead I switched on Radio Sagarmatha, an FM community station, and listened to the BBC Nepal Service—the most reliable source of news at a time of crisis. Then I couldn't resist turning on the television.

There was a macabre pull to the images on the screen. At the cremation ghats by the Bagmati River lay four wooden pyres. The army conducted a salute as the brawny Bahuns carried the royal family's bodies around each pyre three times before setting them down. In the course, one of the queen's arms dangled loose, her wrist decked with red glass bangles. Close-up shots of her face showed that the left half had been reconstructed; a fake eye jutted out at a cubist angle. The king's mouth was pulled back in a gruesome grin. Princess Shruti, a wife and mother of two girls, had a beautiful, serene face; in death she looked like her mother had as a young bride. Prince Nirajan's body dragged on the ground as the Bahuns struggled to circle his pyre. The astrological chart of each person was torn and scattered into the foul and polluted, yet sacred, Bagmati River. The banks of the river had been shored up so that there would be enough water to wash these scraps away.

Each pyre was lit by members of the royal family, and the kindling quickly caught fire. The grim-faced Bahuns in charge of completing the cremation poked at the bodies and added ghiu to feed the flames. The royal family looked like just so much evidence being destroyed.

Through all this, the television anchorwoman offered a choked, halting commentary on how dearly beloved the royal family had been. She named government officials as the camera panned over them, and explained the more intricate aspects of the Hindu rites. Prince Gyanendra, in a white military uniform, was standing near his brother's pyre, frowning crossly and occasionally snapping at those around him. The anchorwoman explained that he was grief-stricken. She did not mention, let alone explain, the crown prince's absence from the funeral. Nor did she say who would be named the next king.

THE FATALISTS AND THE CONSPIRACY THEORISTS

I woke up the next day in a panic about all that remained unsaid, and raring to go. But where? I had no mind to stop and think. It felt as though terrible things were afoot, and I needed to prepare for them. I had to do *something*.

This rush to do something, anything, was quickly thwarted by the sheer lack of news. No statements had been made by government authorities. Not a peep was heard from the Royal Palace Secretariat or the Royal State Council, the two offices responsible for palace matters.

Finally, in a terse mid-morning announcement on Radio Nepal, the chairman of the Royal State Council, Keshar Jung Rayamajhi, announced that Dipendra Bir Bikram Shah had been named the king. As the new monarch was 'unable to discharge his duties', he said, his uncle Prince Gyanendra had been appointed his regent. With this the radio went back to broadcasting dirges.

What the hell? How could an alleged murderer be named the king? And all the rumours were that he was brain-dead. We had an alleged murderer king with possible brain damage: What kind of addle-headed Royal State Council would wish that upon the country?

The phones began to ring off the hook.

'It's custom,' the more contemplative said. 'The only way the Royal State Council can bypass someone who's in line is if it declares him physically or mentally unfit to be king.'

'He killed his whole family. Isn't that grounds to prove he's mentally unfit?'

'What if he wasn't the one who killed his family? What if it was a coup?'

'But he's brain-dead.'

'That's just a rumour. He'll be fine.'

Everyone's logic was getting tied into knots. More than thirty-six hours after the massacre, the government hadn't actually blamed the crown prince—now king—for the massacre. And so the reign of rumour and speculation began, and I, like everyone I knew, fell under its sway.

'It was fated all along—it was written in the stars,' went one strain of the rumours that took over our days. 'The Shah dynasty wasn't fated to continue beyond the tenth king.' Once, long, long ago, Nepal's first king, Prithvi Narayan Shah, had apparently met the deity Gorakh Nath, who had taken up the guise of an ascetic. To test the king's loyalty, Gorakh Nath had offered him some curd that he had vomited. If the king had eaten the vomited curd, his dynasty would have ruled for ever and ever. But he tossed it aside, and some fell on his feet, meaning that his dynasty would only rule for ten generations—one generation per toe. Dipendra was the eleventh Shah king. 'This is the end of the entire Shah line,' said one brand of fatalists. Another brand agreed that the massacre was fated all along, but they were referring to Dipendra's star-crossed love life. It was widely known that sundry astrologers, soothsayers, palmists and tantric holy men preyed off the psychological weaknesses of the deeply superstitious royal family. It was also known that one astrologer had told Dipendra that if he were to marry before his thirty-fifth birthday, his father would die. Dipendra, now thirty, had a long-time girlfriend. 'Dipendra married her a few days ago in a secret ceremony,' I heard some people say. 'He got sick of waiting. That's why the massacre happened. That's why the poor king had to die.'

Those were the fatalists. They subscribed to one or another 'lone nut' theory: The crown prince, and the crown prince alone, was culpable for the massacre. On why, they differed. While some were simply superstitious, others were more matter-of-fact. Queen Aishwarya and the crown prince's girlfriend both came from the same extended family that had ruled Nepal from the 1850s to 1951. But there was a rivalry between the queen's line of Ranas and the girlfriend's line of Ranas: the girlfriend's line had tricked an uncle from the queen's line into abdicating his power several generations ago. The queen had forbidden the crown prince from marrying his girlfriend. This was what had driven the prince to murder.

There were plenty of other lone-nut theories. There was, many people said, insanity in the Shah dynasty. The nineteenth-century kings Rajendra Bikram Shah and Surendra Bikram Shah had both been notoriously unstable. People said to each other, 'There were several crazy kings. Remember?'

Nobody could quite; the Shah dynasty had a long and obscure past that few paid close attention to. But yes, it sounded plausible that the crown prince might have been insane.

Still, most people refused these lone-nut theories, because the massacre felt too politically charged. The majority became conspiracy theorists. 'They're just pretending Dipendra is alive so that it won't look too obvious that this is a coup,' one conspiracy theorist said to me over the phone. 'Gyanendra's using him as a buffer so that it looks like he was unwillingly thrust into power.' This person even thought that rumours about Dipendra's inauspicious marriage charts had been spread years before, in order to frame Dipendra for this massacre: 'This coup was years in the planning. He's very, very shrewd, that Gyanendra.'

Several others echoed the same mistrust of Prince Gyanendra. 'They did it, Gyane and his son Paras.' Gyanendra had wanted power badly enough to kill for it, they said. And Paras had colluded with his father; he had locked everyone in the room that they were meeting in just before the shootings began. 'Just watch, once Dipendra dies, they'll declare an army curfew to burn his body, and they'll do it without conducting an autopsy.

They'll destroy all the evidence.'

Quite a number speculated on the involvement of the army. 'The army chief was in the palace that night. He drove one of the royals home himself. He's behind all this—this is an army coup in disguise.'

The most ambitious of the conspiracy theorists concluded that the American CIA was behind the massacre—they wanted a king who was more hawkish than Birendra had been—or that India's RAW was, or even Pakistan's ISI. Peaceable King Birendra had been killed so that a warmonger could become the king. This was the kind of thing the CIA, especially, did all over the world—remember Chile?

Nobody could quite. But yes, it sounded plausible that the CIA might have done something.

'WE DON'T NEED A MURDERER KING'

The next day I was back at the apartment of the husband and wife. The lives we'd all been leading till the massacre had fallen by the wayside. We flitted between all the news channels we could find, scrounging for the latest. India's Star TV and Zee TV kept getting blocked at any mention that the Nepalis did not believe that their crown prince—now their king—had been culpable. Baffled by this scepticism, the international media explained that the Nepalis were a deeply religious people and looked upon their king as an incarnation of Vishnu. Therefore we could not conceive that any king—or even a future king—might be capable of such a crime.

Having succumbed to self-censorship, the Nepali media was equally unhelpful, and so the people around us became the only source of information. An acquaintance, his hair freshly shaven off, dropped by to talk about the mood on the streets. 'Everyone's shaving their hair,' he said. 'Bald boys have already started protesting on the streets. No one thinks Dipendra did it.'

The fresh rumours that morning were: Dr Upendra Devkota, the neurosurgeon who had treated King Birendra and his family, had disappeared. Hundreds had died at the royal palace. The cremation ghats had been in flames all night, with the pyres of all the slain palace guards. The army was ready to split into factions supporting and opposing Regent Gyanendra.

Beneath these rumours lay a quieter concern. If it were true, as word still had it, that Dipendra—it was hard to remember that he was now the king—was being kept alive artificially on a ventilator, then his death could be announced at any moment. Along with this announcement would come news of Regent Gyanendra's ascension to the throne. No one was ready for this.

Not even the government. At 11 a.m., Star TV became the first to announce King Dipendra's death, seven hours after the fact. (The death had taken place at 3.45 a.m.) A later announcement informed the public that preparations were being made for the cremation, and for Regent Gyanendra's ascension as king.

My friends and I felt a sudden urge to go out onto the streets, to find out what was going on. As we put on our shoes and gathered our bags, we heard a distant boom in the sky, and then another, and another, all in time. It was the start of the thirty-three-cannon salute for an ascension to the throne. The government had waited till Gyanendra's ascension was under way before announcing it to the public. We were deliberately being shut out of the news. Without any plan in mind, we rushed out onto the narrow alleyways, towards the wider main street. All around us, people were pouring out of their houses, overtaken, it seemed, by the same urge to be part of what was happening. Everyone was heading north in the direction of the Narayanhiti royal palace. A light rain was pattering, and I stopped at a shop to buy an umbrella. The shopkeeper, listening to dirges on the radio, shrugged when I asked what he thought. 'He killed his own brother to become king. Who cares what happens now?'

The Dillibazaar road was thronged with people standing by shuttered shopfronts, looking east down a long slope, towards the route that the new king was taking from the Hanuman Dhoka palace, the site of his ascension to the throne, to the Narayanhiti royal palace where he would presumably now live. A haze of smoke and tear gas floated above the skyline. A band of young men with shaven heads materialized behind us and marched ahead, shouting, '*Bhai marna paindaina, hatyara raja chaindaina*'— You can't kill your brother, we don't need a murderer king—and '*Hamro raja hamro desh, pranbhanda pyaro chha*'—Our king and our country are dearer to us than our lives. From the sides, groups of bystanders clapped and hooted.

At an intersection we ran into an acquaintance who was raging to enter into battle, a middle-aged housewife with the gold-laden get-up and portliness of Kathmandu's home-owning classes. She said, 'None of the men of my house wanted to go out, and how could I, a lone woman, go by myself? Now that I've met you I'll go with you.' She tucked the end of her sari in at the waist. 'How can anyone stay home at a time like this? A brother-killer is trying to become our king. We've got to stop him from entering the royal palace!'

We headed east, buoyed by the crowd. I remembered watching from the sides of these streets during the 1990 People's Movement, when activists had demonstrated, rooted and rioted for democracy. The roads had the same disorderly feel now. People were crammed at the windows of all the houses, looking out in anticipation as crowds continued to gather but without any leadership, without any organization and without any sense of what was to happen. At the junction of Bagh Bazaar the crowd suddenly dispersed, unsure whether to head towards Hanuman Dhoka or towards Narayanhiti. A band of chary-eyed riot police were watching from the sides, outnumbered but vigilant. A thin man slipped among my friends, saying, 'Don't go any further. The army is using tear gas to clear the route. And it's not like the tear gas the police use, it's more powerful.'

He easily convinced us to back away. For a while we milled about aimlessly, talking to perfect strangers, the way one does at times of crisis: 'Gyanendra's already reached the palace.' 'They're preparing to cremate Dipendra—without performing any autopsy or forensics.' 'They'll have to declare a curfew to get his body to the cremation ghats.'

A few more groups of bald-headed men and boys rushed past us in the direction of the Narayanhiti palace. They looked flushed and defiant. Each group carried a Nepali flag, and chanted slogans against the new king: '*Bhai marna paindaina, hatyara raja chaindaina.*'

'Who's organizing these groups?' I asked a friend. 'Are any of the parties involved?'

A man slipped among us, turned slightly away but listening alertly. When I looked directly at him, he slipped away, much in the style of a plain-clothes informer.

Other groups of young men and boys came into view, wave after wave. Their slogans were unambiguous: 'Gyane thief, leave the country.' A few slogans were also hurled the way of Prime Minister G. P. Koirala. There was an air of recklessness all around. These young men seemed, almost, to be marching to their deaths.

It became clear that my friends and I weren't going to join them. And it felt fatuous to just stand around and watch. So we ducked into the house of a poet who lived close by. His family was watching the delayed broadcast of the new king's ascension to the throne. With shock, we gaped at footage of Gyanendra, his face pulled down in a habitual grimace, sitting with the monarch's plumed, emerald-drop crown on his head. He sat askew on the throne, looking completely out of place. Government officials dropped coins at the new king's feet in a traditional show of respect. Then King Gyanendra was shown stepping onto a carriage—minding his head, for his crown was unstable—and being driven past silent, gawking crowds. The demonstrations taking place all over Kathmandu had been carefully edited out.

Then the electricity went off, and we were spared any more of that footage.

We went to the balcony to watch the crowds on the streets. By now there were thousands of young men—and many women—all around. Smoke from burned rubber tyres was visible from the rooftop. The city looked aflame.

On the neighbouring rooftop was a low-level member of the opposition party. Were his party's cadres organizing any of these demonstrations, one of my friends asked. The man shook his head, a little wistfully. 'Our leaders told us not to.' He added, 'They say the Maoists are behind these demonstrations. You'd better go home. The government's going to crack down.'

My friends and I heeded his warning and left the poet's house, skirting the demonstrators. As we passed a shop we heard on the radio that a shoot-on-sight curfew had been imposed in less than half an hour. A man nearby broke into a trot.

Dissatisfied by the haste with which King Dipendra's body was going to be cremated, people felled trees along the road to the ghat and burned tyres, hoping to obstruct the army convoy on its way to the Pashupatinath temple. But only a few dared to defy the shoot-on-sight curfew. In the end most people watched helplessly on television as the man everyone had seen grow up before their eyes, the man who had been the country's king for a day, was put to flames. With him went his entire family, and much evidence about the massacre.

A kind of depression crept over me that night. In many ways Nepal was still traditional, yet it was far more modern than it—in such incidents as these rushed cremations—appeared to be. The international media was reporting that it was a Hindu rite to cremate the bodies so quickly. Nepalis knew this was patently untrue. All citizens who died in unnatural circumstances had the right to an autopsy. Word had it—and this was later confirmed—that the Nepali government had turned down several offers of forensics specialists from foreign embassies. As far as the public knew, no autopsies had been performed. Would anyone ever conduct ballistics tests? Or even a proper investigation? Already, it seemed that there would never be any conclusive proof as to what had happened.

In a brief televised address to the nation later that evening, a sombre King Gyanendra sat before photographs of his dead brother and nephew, and mourned his lost relatives. He said that the massacre had occurred due to 'a sudden explosion of an automatic weapon'. Then he said that he had appointed a three-man committee to investigate the massacre and submit a report on it within three days.

A sudden explosion? A report on a massacre within just three days when there was almost no evidence left?

'Jaya Nepal,' the king said, concluding his address in the traditional way of the Shah monarchs. 'May Lord Pashupatinath protect us all.'

There was a blackout that night, and the lights went out all over the city. From my family home I looked onto the inky cityscape, the buildings and streets indecipherable, alien, unknown. In the past four days we had had three kings. And after this one? King Paras.

I thought of my pregnant friend and her husband, planning to leave in a few days' time. I was glad for them. I envied them. A great restlessness overtook me. I stayed up late, listening to the cries of a few people defying the curfew orders, and an occasional burst of firecrackers, tear gas and firearms.

THE POLITICS OF THE SPECTACLE

A week later Nepalis had resumed their everyday lives, but psychologically everyone was lingering. The media, returning to normal, ran stories on the widespread belief that Crown Prince Dipendra was innocent. An early *Kathmandu Post* report read:

> No one in the country is ready to believe that...Dipendra opened fire during a dinner at the Royal Palace on the evening of June 1, as initially stated by different foreign media and then by some local media as well.
>
> 'As I knew him he was a gem of a person and it is impossible to believe that he did all this,' said Diwakar Golchha, a prominent businessman, when asked if he believed it was the Crown Prince who shot his family members...
>
> 'This is a conspiracy, I don't believe the things the people are saying,' said Purna Shrestha, a carpenter from Bansbari. 'I cannot even believe that King Birendra is dead,' he added.
>
> 'It is indeed a conspiracy of a great magnitude, the royal family has become a victim of that,' said Netra Basnet, a political enthusiast from Dolakha district now in Kathmandu. 'But if the political parties go on acting like they have been doing then I am convinced that the nation itself will be the victim of [another] unexpected incident like this one.'
>
> 'This is a foreign move to bring instability and break national unity,' said Laxmi Prasad Kharel, a lecturer in Amrit Science College.

The three-man investigation committee appointed by the new king had, however, run into hitches. One day after its formation, a member had withdrawn, questioning its legality. The deputy prime minister had clarified that the new king hadn't, as it had appeared, appointed the committee on his own: Prime Minister G. P. Koirala had advised him to do so, based on a cabinet recommendation. The member nevertheless refused to reconsider his decision. So the committee now consisted of two men: the Speaker of the House and the Chief Justice of the Supreme Court.

This mix-up had served to remind everyone that the country had, after all, a government—and a democratic one at that—independent of the monarchy. In retrospect, it became inexplicable that the prime minister, deputy prime minister and the entire Parliament had been completely silent following the massacre. If the leaders of the democratic political parties had any doubts about the new king, they had put them aside. One by one they showed up on Nepal Television urging Nepalis to unite behind the monarchy at this tragic hour. Reading prepared speeches denouncing those who questioned the new king as 'irresponsible troublemakers', they evoked memories of the days before democracy, when the autocratic Panchayat government used to denounce these same individuals as 'anti-national elements' or 'nefarious elements trying to destabilize the country'. A decade on, these political leaders were using similar terms to denounce others who opposed the monarchy.

The Maoists, by contrast, were quick to try and capitalize on mass disaffection. An early Maoist press release expressed concern for the lack of post-mortems of the massacre victims, and stated that the killings had been carried out by right-wing and anti-national forces (a term that, in their code language, described King Gyanendra). 'To think that King Birendra's patriotic stand and liberal political ideology were not the reason for the royals' deaths would be greatly misleading,' the Maoist press release said.

The public mistrusted the new king, but found itself bereft of any democratic leadership. Not wanting to play into Maoist schemes, people stopped organizing street demonstrations and instead took to other, more subversive means of dissent. Primarily, they indulged in increasingly elaborate conspiracy theories. It was said that anywhere from five to eight commandos had done the killing that night, all wearing masks resembling the crown prince. Some survivors of the massacre had claimed that Crown Prince Dipendra had no expression on his face as he shot his father dead, his cap was pulled low and he was wearing gloves—so obviously he had been impersonated. Reports came from all over Kathmandu that people had seen—with their *own eyes*—Dipendra driving very, very fast on the night of the massacre. There had been, as it were, several crown princes on the loose. Obviously, the crown prince had been poisoned, then killed in his room, people whispered, and highly trained commandos had dressed up as him and killed everyone. Who these commandos were, where they had come from, nobody could say.

Mass sympathy towards Dipendra grew. Suddenly, everyone felt they knew and loved him deeply. Many men who had refused to shave off their hair at King Birendra's death were moved to do so when his son died. By now bald heads were everywhere. (It helped that barbers were offering their services for free.) Even staunch advocates of republicanism lined up for hours to sign condolence books at the Narayanhiti palace. Neighbourhood clubs set up copycat condolence books, and impromptu shrines popped up in street corners, attracting heaps of incense and bouquets. Pictures of the slain royal family sold furiously off the shelves of photo studios.

There was not a little hysteria in all this. Word had it that four months before the massacre, a stone idol of the Bhimeswor

deity in Dolakha District, in the hills east of Kathmandu, had
produced beads of sweat to warn the country of some kind
of disaster. At this year's annual Machhendranath festival, too,
there had been bad omens. For a few days after the massacre,
rumours spread that the water at a reserve tank in the Mata
Tirtha neighbourhood had been poisoned with cyanide, and all
Kathmandu convulsed in a scare.

All these were not mere expressions of love for the slain
royal family, they were also a challenge to the new king. The
authorities understood these subversive undercurrents. And so it
was that policemen arrested street-side vendors hawking pictures
of Kings Birendra and Dipendra.

We found out only later that the police were entitled to make
arbitrary arrests by this time. Three days after the massacre, while
the country was in shock, and while the media had shut down—
when no one was looking, so to speak—the cabinet had passed
a Public Security Ordinance that granted officials of the ministry
of home affairs the power to arrest or detain anyone suspected
of acting against 'national unity' or 'national security'.

This was not the first time since 1990 that the government
had tried to curtail democratic rights. Citing the Maoist insurgency,
it had twice tabled similar bills: the rights to free expression and
assembly were, apparently, making it difficult to fight the Maoists.
Both bills had failed to garner two-thirds of the votes in Parliament.
This time, the government had bypassed Parliament altogether.

Immediately after the ordinance was passed, the minister for
information and communications appealed to the media not to
publish news and opinions that 'harmed Nepal's nationality'. The
police raided a few newspaper offices, and in some smaller towns,
officials of the ministry of home affairs began vetting newspapers
before they went to press. Books were seized from street-side stalls

and public meetings were forcibly disbanded. Security check posts sprang up all over Kathmandu, and pedestrians were subjected to body searches. Many teenage boys were jailed for merely loitering about looking thuggish.

Alarms were raised a week after the massacre with the arrest of Yubaraj Ghimire, the editor of the biggest national daily, *Kantipur*, along with the paper's publisher and managing director. Ostensibly, this was for publishing an article by a Maoist leader urging the army not to support the monarchy. Yet the paper had published such articles before. Why were things different now?

Was this a coup?

The political quandaries facing the country before the massacre—and the multiple crises looming now—proved of little interest to the international media, who had descended upon Kathmandu to scoop the story of the duty-bound crown prince and his forbidden love (helpfully for the cameras, Dipendra's girlfriend was a stunning beauty). Team after team could be seen tromping through the city saddled down with cameras, microphones, tripods and recorders. As they saw it, the massacre had taken place against a romantic medieval background. But for the Nepali people, it had taken place in a field charged with politics.

Despite their divergent approaches, the international media and the Nepali media alike attended with keen interest a press conference held a week after the massacre by the first eyewitness to go public. Rajiv Shahi, an army captain, was married to a niece of King Birendra's who had survived the massacre. The press conference took place at the army hospital, where he was convalescing.

Shahi appeared before the cameras wearing an intense, concentrated expression that suggested that he was still in shock. His shaved head gave him a fiery look, as did his grey T-shirt with 'Om' emblazoned across the chest. With great efficiency, he first mapped out the drawing room in the Narayanhiti palace where the royal family had gathered on 1 June—an L-shaped hall with a bar and billiards table to one side and a sitting area to another. He then explained that the crown prince had been heavily intoxicated by eight that night, tripping and slurring his speech. Shahi, along with Prince Paras and Prince Nirajan, had escorted the crown prince to his room.

Shortly afterwards, the crown prince had returned to the drawing room dressed in battle fatigues. He was toting more than one firearm, among them an M16 and an MP5. He shot indiscriminately at family members, going in and out of the room. Shahi did not see the crown prince during the first round of shots, but he saw King Birendra lying prone on the ground, bleeding at the neck. He rushed to staunch the flow of blood with his coat. Prince Paras had played a heroic role at one point, begging the crown prince to spare himself and the younger relatives. To this request the crown prince had complied without a word. Through all this, the security aides-de-camp, or ADCs, were in a separate part of the building, Shahi said. This was why they had not intervened in time. In the third round of shootings, the crown prince returned to shoot his father, to make sure that he was dead. Shahi hid behind a couch. He eventually managed to flee the room by climbing out a window. He found four ADCs and told them to call ambulances and doctors.

One of the Nepali journalists asked, 'Why did the crown prince do it?'

Shahi said he wasn't sure, but he was sure that Crown Prince Dipendra was the murderer.

A spate of questions followed, and Shahi, looking startled, mumbled that he would not entertain questions. But the journalists pressed on, till Shahi stormed out, leaving the cameras to linger on the white board marked with lines, squares and arrows.

Conspiracy theorists immediately said the press conference had been staged in order to lead the investigation committee, due to begin its work the next day. They were now convinced the committee would say exactly what Shahi had said, which was also what the unnamed army source had been saying all along. The investigation was part of a cover-up.

Eleven days after King Birendra's death, a saiyya daan or bed-donation ceremony was held to help his soul cut its links with the material trappings of this life and pass on to the next. Most Nepalis had never heard of the ceremony before; it had last been performed in 1972, after the death of King Birendra's father. It was observed only for kings. It would now be televised for the first time.

The ceremony began with the selection of a katto priest, who would receive donations of King Birendra's belongings. Durga Prasad Sapkota, the chosen priest, was a skeletal seventy-five-year-old. He was shown on Nepal Television sitting contentedly on a double bed that had been donated to him. Then he was shown tucking into a ritual meal of eighty-four dishes, one of which was prepared of the flesh of a freshly sacrificed goat and, according to myth, laced with the bone marrow of the dead king. Or with the king's brain tissue. Or with his ashes from the funeral pyre. Or with his ground-up bones. Nobody knew exactly what. Sapkota looked serene enough eating the meat, throwing away his high caste (for the priestly Bahun castes are not supposed to eat meat). Afterwards the old man donned a gold-flecked daura suruwal, and, bizarrely, put on King Birendra's eyeglasses, with large square black frames. He had also been donated the dead king's briefcase and walking stick.

Government officials, including Prime Minister G. P. Koirala, the Speaker of the House, the Chief Justice (but shouldn't these two have been conducting their investigation?) and top police and army officials watched as Sapkota finally put on a golden paper-cut-out crown—a replica of King Birendra's crown—and clambered onto the back of a waiting elephant. Amid gaping crowds, he was taken across the Bagmati River. The soul of King Birendra was thus symbolically exorcized from the valley.

The entire event was ridiculous. Not just the ceremony, but the breathlessly orientalist coverage it received the world over: We looked, suddenly, like the medieval kingdom that the outside world saw us as. True, Nepal was by constitution a Hindu kingdom, but its spirit after 1990 had been decidedly secular. Right now, for example, people didn't want Hindu rituals; they wanted scientific evidence for the truth about the massacre. They wanted to regain their lost civil liberties. And they wanted political direction. The international media preferred to overlook all this in favour of the fey cultural antics of a dying order, antics that confirmed, in their minds, that Nepal was indeed a Shangri-La.

Two days later, the saiyya daan ceremony was repeated for King Dipendra. But by this time, twenty-first-century chinks had appeared in the rite's medieval facade. Nepali human rights activists had vocally questioned the upholding of caste in a state ritual. Government officials ignored this objection but issued denials that any dish in the eighty-four-course meal was laced with any—as they euphemistically called it—'polluted substances'.

A second elderly Bahun-caste priest, Devi Prasad Acharya, was selected to be King Dipendra's katto priest. Wearing another paper-cut-out crown and Dipendra's hideous-funky wraparound sunglasses, he too climbed onto an elephant to join Sapkota on the far edge of town. On the way to the site of the saiyya daan ceremony, his elephant had managed to kill a pregnant woman: Following a local superstition that this would bear her a boy child, she had run beneath the animal, only to be trampled by it.

In less picturesque parts of town, editor Yubaraj Ghimire and his colleagues at *Kantipur* were released after widespread outcry over their jailing. Kathmandu had picked itself up off the ground, and returned to its usual heady debates. Journalists, lawyers and civil rights groups were openly criticizing the newly passed Public Security Ordinance. Kathmandu's intellectuals rallied for civil liberties. Even the most moderate people were predicting the end of the monarchy—or the beginning of the end of the monarchy.

It was a bracing time. Was Nepal ready to do away with the monarchy? Vestiges of our feudal past were embedded everywhere—even in the democratic constitution of 1990—and ancient ways of thinking still patterned our everyday behaviour. But suddenly it seemed possible that the country might shrug off the scraps and relics of that past. It seemed possible that this massacre, this coup—a coup that apparently had not happened— might yet coalesce into a left/liberal movement for a republican Nepal.

But there was no time to dwell on this thought, for the investigation committee submitted its report on the massacre.

AND THE TRUTH ELUDES US

At the press conference in a dingy hall at Parliament House, Speaker of the House Taranath Ranabhat and Chief Justice of the Supreme Court Keshab Prasad Upadhyay sat behind a spread of guns, facing the most intense scrutiny of their lives. Lights, cameras and microphones hemmed them in from all sides. Exactly two weeks had passed since the massacre.

The Chief Justice tried to read out their findings, but his voice was drowned out by the scrapes and shuffles of the journalists in the room. The Speaker then took over this task.

Taranath Ranabhat had till then attracted little attention for his work. The Parliament he had served in since 1999 had been largely paralysed by daily bickering between the ruling and opposition parties. In the last session he had several times been surrounded at the rostrum by angry, sometimes violent, opposition members sloganeering against Prime Minister G. P. Koirala, who was facing corruption charges. Several times the Speaker had ended the day's proceedings within ten minutes. His most controversial move had been to continue proceedings after every single opposition member of Parliament walked out in a boycott of the whole session.

As he began to read the investigation's summary report, Ranabhat's face took on the look of an evil aunt telling ghost stories to terrified children.

The crown prince and his family had met on the evening of 1 June for a weekly family gathering, he said. They met in the large drawing room of the building complex that the crown prince lived in, within the Narayanhiti royal palace. 'Apparently there is such a thing as a billiards table,' he said. The drawing room had one of these, off to a side.

At around 7 p.m., the crown prince drove over to fetch the Queen Mother, who lived in a nearby building. By 7.30 p.m. he had returned to the drawing room, and was playing billiards, working through his second peg of Famous Grouse. By this time, twenty-five other guests had settled around the drawing room and a smaller side room.

Soon, however, the crown prince was unable to stand on his feet. Assuming he was drunk, Prince Nirajan, Rajiv Shahi, Prince Paras and Princess Shruti's husband escorted him to his bedroom. Once they returned to join the rest of the family downstairs, at around 8 p.m., the crown prince phoned his ADC Gajendra Bohora and asked for 'a special kind of cigarette prepared with a mixture of hashish and another unnamed black substance'.

Ranabhat paused after reading this part, and gave everyone a significant look. These cigarettes were dispatched via an orderly, who in turn gave them not to the crown prince, but to Prince Paras, who was in the drawing room.

Ranabhat then skipped to the crown prince phoning his girlfriend, Devyani Rana, from his bedroom. His mobile phone record showed that he had called her twice, at 8.12 and at 8.19 p.m. Convalescing in Delhi after the massacre, Devyani Rana had testified that the crown prince's speech that night had been especially slurred. Worried, she had at 8.25 p.m. phoned his ADC Gajendra Bohora and another ADC, urging them to check in on the crown prince. They had dispatched the crown prince's orderly and his nurse to his bedroom.

Entering the room, the orderly and the nurse found the crown prince prone on the floor, straining to undo his shirt. Once he got the shirt off, he went to an attached bathroom, and the orderly and nurse heard him retching. In a while he returned to the bedroom and told them to go to away. At 8.39 p.m., he called Devyani Rana again, and said, 'I'm about to sleep now, good night. We'll talk tomorrow.'

Sometime after this, the crown prince put on battle fatigues and left his bedroom armed with two rifles and a revolver. Assuming that he was going out, his orderly, at the door, asked if he needed his emergency bag, and was told, 'It's not necessary.' Downstairs, a palace 'boy' standing next to the alcove with the billiards table saw the crown prince enter the drawing room.

First the crown prince fired at the ceiling with a 9mm MP5K automatic sub-machine gun, said Ranabhat. Then he fired at his father. Then he moved back, tossed a twelve-bore SPAS 12L French SPA gun towards a stairway near the building complex's garden, and re-entered the drawing room, this time aiming a 5.56-calibre Colt M16 A2 rifle at his father. He shot again, hitting several other family members as well. Again he moved back to the door, then returned a third time, shooting. Then he left via the garden.

At this point, a female figure in a red sari (presumably his mother, Queen Aishwarya) was seen chasing him through the garden. The body of Prince Nirajan was later found in the garden, and Queen Aishwarya's body was found on the stairs to the crown prince's bedroom.

Only after the shooting ended did the ADCs, in a separate room of the building complex, break through the glass doors of the drawing room. Ten members of the royal family lay dead or mortally wounded. Evacuations began at once. The crown prince was eventually found shot in the head—and gurgling for breath—near a bridge by a pond in the garden. He was wearing black leather gloves, black army boots, a combat jacket and trousers, black stockings and a camouflage vest. There was a 9mm Glock pistol and some empty cartridges in the water nearby.

Those listening closely could already pick holes in the report: It did not, for example, say where the crown prince might have found the 9mm pistol or the cartridge cases found in the pond beside him. He had not been carrying this gun when he came into the drawing room. Neither did the report clarify whether the crown prince had shot himself using this pistol or whether someone else had shot him. Similarly, it offered no explanation as to who owned another—unfired—9mm Glock pistol found in the billiards hall.

Ranabhat simply said that the M16, and weapons resembling the two other guns that the crown prince had carried into the drawing room, had been checked out from the armoury at the royal palace. According to the ADC Gajendra Bohora, they had been in the crown prince's possession. Ranabhat mentioned that the crown prince was used to having free access to the armoury, and he also said that one Glock pistol had been issued in Prince Nirajan's name.

In addition to the four immediate members of the royal ramily, five others had died that night: Princess Shanti Rajyalaksmi Singh, Princess Sharada Rajyalaksmi Shah, Princess Jayanti Rajyalaksmi Shah, Kumar Khadka Bikram Shah and Dhirendra Shah. Their deaths had been caused by bullet wounds, Ranabhat said, concluding his report. Then he looked up, appearing pleased to have finished. For the benefit of foreign journalists in the room, he also read the entire report in his halting English.

Then, to everyone's surprise, he stood up and strode over to the table with all the evidence, pointing at the weapons collected from the royal palace grounds. The Chief Justice hung back judiciously at this point, surveying his colleague through narrowed eyes.

The Nepali journalists in the room could not help but bait the Speaker. A cameraman called out, 'We can't see the guns from here, Sir. Can you pick one up?'

Ranabhat obliged, lifting the rifle.

'Turn this way, Sir. This way.'

'Like this?' The Speaker lifted the rifle above his head and posed for the shots. Then he put it down and posed with another rifle, smiling gamely.

All around him, Nepali journalists egged him on:

'This way, Sir.'

'One shot here.'

At one point, the Speaker aimed a sub-machine gun at the journalists and playfully called out, 'I'll shoot you!'

Some journalists gasped, but one remained collected enough to ask: 'Who shot the crown prince, Sir? Did he shoot himself?'

Ranabhat shrugged. 'God knows.' Then he added: A bullet had been fired into the crown prince's head from the left side. Again he paused to give everyone a significant look. He did not say, but it was soon discovered that the crown prince had been right-handed.

Then the Speaker suddenly seemed to remember himself. He returned to his seat and refused to answer any more questions, ending the press conference.

With atypical efficiency, the government instantly posted the investigation committee's full report, in Nepali, on the Internet. I, like many others, quickly downloaded it.

Its first section concerned the investigation committee's formation and mandate; it was easily skimmed. The second part mapped out the massacre site and listed the objects found there: coats, caps and eyeglasses, blood-like stains, cigarette holders and lighters and stubs, other personal effects and an array of firearms, bullets and magazines. Among these were the M16 rifle and the MP5K sub-machine gun that the crown prince was said to have used. The twelve-bore gun that he had reportedly tossed into the garden was also listed here. In addition, a loaded 9mm Glock pistol had been found, still in its holster, as well as another 9mm pistol and three magazines, and a number of shells and magazines. All this was consistent with the Speaker's report.

The committee then interviewed survivors, starting with King Gyanendra's wife, Komal Rajyalaksmi Shah (who was also Queen Aishwarya's sister, as Queen Aishwarya and her two sisters had married King Birendra and his two brothers). The new queen was in the hospital, convalescing from a bullet wound that had reportedly just missed her right lung. Displaying great sensitivity, the two-man committee limited their interrogation to one question:

'Keeping in mind Your Majesty's health condition, would it be possible for Your Majesty to provide some information to this committee about this incident?'

Queen Komal replied: 'I was also at the family gathering organized at Tribhuvan Sadan that day. I heard that His Highness the Crown Prince went to sleep a little early. After a while there was the noise of a bullet being fired, and that bullet struck the ceiling. After that I saw a bullet strike His Majesty King Birendra on the right side of his neck. Kumar Gorakh and Kumar Khadka were also struck by bullets. After that I too was hit from the back, and I fell. I found it hard to breathe at that point. Shanti Rajyalaksmi fell on top of me and her blood was on my head. I heard Rajiv and Paras shout for the wounded to be evacuated. Because Shanti had fallen on top of me, I couldn't see anything else.'

The committee showed the same consideration to the other massacre survivors, all severely traumatized and in mourning. The next interview consisted of only these questions:

1. We have come before Your Highness in the process of discovering the facts about the event that took place at the royal palace on 1 June.

2. Whatever information you have, Your Highness.

3. Your Highnesses were in the small room, the small drawing room?

The answers were brief and uninformative.

The interview that piqued the most interest was that of Prince Paras. It consisted of a freewheeling stream-of-consciousness narrative that began with his arrival at the gathering:

'Mother, me, my younger sister and [wife] Himani got there a little late. We got there at around 7.40, and when we arrived, the crown prince looked uh…as though he had had some cocktails. [He said] *So, what will you have?* I decided to have a Coke. *You're only having Coke! I'm having whisky*, he said. By then he already seemed gone, he was acting quite drunk.'

Prince Paras continued, 'Uh…what we started to talk about

was, there has been talk about this wedding. *I, I also spoke to Mother. I spoke to Grandmother also, and both of them said no. On Sunday I'll speak to Father,* he said. That's what we were talking about, and then it was eight o'clock.'

Prince Paras said that after all the guests had arrived, the crown prince began to look very intoxicated. 'He lay down as though extremely drunk, he fell asleep as though he had fainted. He slept right there on the floor. I, Gorakh, Nirajan and Rajiv picked him up: *Your Highness, not here…*'

They carried him to his bedroom, put him in bed, turned off the lights and came back downstairs to rejoin the gathering. Prince Paras reported, 'His Majesty the King had just taken his drink. We haven't even said cheers, he has just taken his drink, in the middle of this—now we were to one side in a corner, hajoor, we didn't see the crown prince come in.' He said that the younger family members usually sat in a corner at such gatherings. 'And I hadn't seen anyone come in there, the first time I found out he had come was…I found out after the first gun went off. It made a blasting sound, about three rounds have been fired. As soon as he entered, three rounds were fired. One is up, one is straight.

'His Majesty the King had just said, *What are you doing,* when one blast here and another blast here. His Majesty the King slumped over. I and Doctor Rajiv [Shahi] were next to each other. We both ran over. Doctor Rajiv was able to reach His Majesty, hajoor, but Princess Shova wouldn't let me go, she said, *Don't go anywhere, stay right here.* There I turned back and told all our younger sisters and everyone to lie down. There are already the sounds of explosions. Saying, *Everyone lie down,* I kept everyone out of the line of fire…'

As Paras was helping relatives seek shelter, the crown prince entered the room once again. 'What I saw, hajoor, I saw him shoot His Majesty the King. I saw him shoot [his uncle] Prince Dhirendra when he went up saying, *Baba, you done enough damage.* When he went back the second time, what Prince Dhirendra said was, *You done damage.* While he says this, another banging shot hit here. Either one or two… I can't remember clearly. He fell. Prince Dhirendra fell, as soon as he fell then other people fell, one after another, I can't really say after that.'

What Prince Paras did remember clearly were the weapons that the crown prince had used, but his account did not tally with that of the report. The crown prince first came into the room shooting an automatic weapon, an MP5, Paras said. 'Then he went out, then came back in again, then he tossed aside that small weapon MP5, the weapon that His Majesty the King picked up. He picked up that weapon. Princess Shova came and took that weapon, she also took out the magazine. She put it there on the floor. Now what she thought was, there's probably only that one [gun]. But even I had seen [the crown prince] carrying others. He was carrying three others. There were four weapons. One was a gun, a handgun, on the left side. The handgun was on the left side. In his right pocket was an MP5. He was toting a shotgun and an M16, those are automatic.'

He went on to describe the crown prince leaving, then returning a third time. This time, he went to a corner, and came into direct view of Prince Paras and the younger members of the royal family. Paras pleaded for their lives: '*What are you doing, hajoor…* I made the request…*what are you doing please…go away.* I said to older brother, *What are you doing, we…here…it's just us, please…* One by one he looked at everyone and he left and went outside, and that's when we knew he had not shot us.'

After that, Paras busied himself, trying to rescue his wounded relatives. When the sound of bullets ended, the crown prince's ADC arrived, saying, 'He shot himself, he shot himself.'

Asked about the crown prince's possible motives for the massacre, Paras said, 'It was the marriage, hajoor. As far as I can tell, it's the marriage. This began last year, at the time of the birthday celebration... There were those against versus those for [the marriage]. Now his younger brother and I were always for [the marriage]. We were people who did whatever our older brother bade... Now Rajiv the doctor was [also] for, but Shruti, Gorakh and other younger brothers were against the marriage. I feel that this is the main issue. This is the main issue.'

The investigation committee asked: Had the issue of marriage come up that night?

'As I told you earlier, as soon as I got there, what he said to me was, *I spoke to Mother, I also spoke to Grandmother, it won't go ahead. I'm having a meeting with Father on Sunday, I'll speak then,* that's all he told me.'

And was his mood good that evening?

'It was like he was drunk. His mood was very good. None of us had thought that something like that could happen. Like he was joking a lot, he was making everyone laugh while he was downstairs.'

At the end of the interview Prince Paras expressed his regret that whatever he had done that evening had been too little.

In his interview, Prince Paras made no mention of the laced cigarettes that he had been given to pass on to the crown prince. The two-man committee found out about these in a later interview with the crown prince's ADC Gajendra Bohora, who said that the cigarettes had been laced with ganja. According to Bohora, they were prepared by an orderly at the royal palace, Ram Krishna KC.

When the two-man committee interviewed Ram Krishna KC, he admitted in a garbled fashion, 'I...cigarettes now there was a special…substance in the cigarettes.'

What special substance, the committee asked.

'Ganja,' he said. 'He had said to bring cigarettes with ganja. And so, once I reached the main door of the billiard hall, I gave them to His Highness Paras. I didn't go in.'

The committee asked, 'Which door? The door on the eastern side? How many did you take?'

'The big door. There were five or six [cigarettes]…'

'Who used to make them? What was put in them?'

'We made them ourselves. It's made with a mixture of ganja and tobacco.'

When asked if ganja was all the cigarettes had besides tobacco, Ram Krishna said, 'There would be ganja and some other black substance that they brought. I would have to mix and fill them.'

'Who brought that, from where?'

'It would just be there.'

The two-man committee helpfully asked, '"There" meaning in the bedroom, maybe?'

The orderly replied, 'It would be there, it would be in the bedroom.'

'You recognized the ganja? You didn't recognize the black? How much black would have to be put in?'

'It depended. It depended on the cigarette.'

'How much ganja and how much black was put in one cigarette stick?'

'Well that… He had given them beforehand… That tobacco and the other thing would all be mixed in together.'

Speaking in a bureaucratese lingo replete with passive sentences, the two-man committee then asked, 'Would the colour of the black be recognizable if seen now? Was it fully black or a little purplish?'

The orderly replied with a swarm of oo's—a Nepali term

roughly meaning 'that thing': 'I don't know the full oo. That too not always; every now and then at the time of a oo…'

'On that day, which was it?' the committee asked, as the report became increasingly unintelligible. 'Was it an oo with black, or with the other?'

'There was black mixed in and also the other. Both types.'

In an attempt at clarity, the committee asked, 'You took it and gave it to His Highness Paras. When you gave it to His Highness Paras you had come because [the cigarettes] had been asked for by His Highness the Crown Prince. Did you or did you not say that it was you who reached it there?'

'It's not possible for me to say that. I went to oo there and sat down. I was about to go directly, but His Highness Paras came, laughing. I had them in my hand. I gave them. And then His Highness Paras took them and went.'

The investigation committee never went back to check with Paras whether he had delivered the laced cigarettes to Crown Prince Dipendra. If he had done so, this would have occurred in a span of twenty-odd minutes: From his bedroom, Dipendra had phoned for the cigarettes at 8.19 p.m. Twenty minutes later, at 8.39, he had placed his last call to Devyani Rana, saying that he was going to sleep. It was soon after this, according to all accounts, that he came out of his room dressed in military fatigues. When, in these twenty-odd minutes, had Paras taken him the cigarettes? And what had he seen if he had done so? The two-man committee did not ask.

The committee went on to question government officials, security personnel and doctors on other aspects of the massacre. What their report did reveal was what a shambles the government was in at the time. Prime Minister G. P. Koirala was phoned two and a half hours after the massacre by the chairperson of the

Royal State Council, Dr Keshar Jung Rayamajhi, and told that the king had suffered a serious heart attack. Soon afterwards, an official from the Royal Palace Secretariat came to fetch him to the Narayanhiti palace, where he was briefed. Only then did he discover that the king had been shot. From there he rushed to the hospital, where he found Dr Rayamajhi waiting.

'When I asked him what happened,' the prime minister said to the investigators, 'he too didn't know… It was known that bullets had struck and so on, but nothing else. There was no one to ask; I only recognized Dr Rayamajhi there. People were running this way and that; as for the doctors, they were all busy upstairs. I kept sitting there. I just sat there; I didn't receive any information about what was going on, how things were.'

He was told that a helicopter had been dispatched to fetch Prince Gyanendra from Pokhara, where he had been that night, but that bad weather had forced the helicopter to return. The prime minister suggested that it return to pick him up somewhere off the road, where it was safe to land. Then, as he testified, he just waited: 'After this the Chief Justice came to the upper room. The Speaker of the House also came. The others also all arrived, and we were sitting around in confusion about what had happened. I don't know anything other than this.'

By contrast, the chief of the army staff, Prajwalla Sumshere Jung Bahadur Rana, had promptly arrived at the hospital, conferred with the surviving members of the royal family, and dispatched the helicopter to Pokhara. Curiously, he spent most of his interview with the investigation committee explaining that he was not responsible for security in the grounds of the Narayanhiti palace. The ADCs and palace security staff were originally selected by the Royal Nepal Army, true. But once they were at the palace, they were appointed and promoted directly by palace officials. The army chief was adamant: 'The palace's security does not belong to the army.'

The two-hundred-page report detailed medical reports on everyone's cause of death, and descriptions of wounds, and also a list of bloodstain results—though it was not clear which stains belonged to whom. Post-mortems had not been performed on the bodies, in contradiction to the usual legal practice in homicide cases; simple medical tests had sufficed. Forensic tests had only gone as far as to identify, by blood type, the blood on the crown prince's fatigues—which could have belonged either to him or to Queen Aishwarya, both of whom had type-B blood. Fingerprinting had been carried out, but no prints were found on the weapons involved, or on the staircase to the crown prince's bedroom, or on any other tested surface.

The two-man committee ended the report with a largely senseless discussion with a psychologist on what incited people to violence. 'Taking one's personality to be good is called *positive thinking*,' the psychologist explained to them. 'Taking one's personality to be bad is called *negative thinking*...' The report ended with a list of some of the narcotics that exist in this world—cocaine, amphetamine, LSD, cannabis—in an apparent attempt to identify the black substance in the crown prince's laced cigarettes.

That was that. So inconclusive was the report that it left the Nepali people free to choose whatever they wished to believe. And this was what we did.

For a few months, rumours floated that a vial of Dipendra's blood had been saved, and it would prove conclusively that he had been intoxicated that night. Nothing ever came of this. Eventually the building complex where the massacre took place was razed to the ground because it caused the Queen Mother so much grief to see it every day.

More than three years have passed since the massacre and

its investigation. Yet, when Nepalis turn to each other now and ask, 'So what do *you* think really happened?'—understanding at once that we are talking about the massacre—we still do not know what we believe.

One man I know always begins by blaming King Gyanendra. 'I think Gyane did it,' he says in a whisper, and lays out all the evidence that supports his case: How could someone who was throwing up, sick on whisky (as Dipendra had allegedly been) execute people so precisely twenty minutes later? How could he have dressed in military fatigues if he had been so drunk that he struggled even to take his shirt off? How would he have tied his shoelaces? And why would he have worn gloves? To leave no trace of his fingerprints? That made no sense. Why had his face been expressionless, as some eyewitnesses had claimed, if that weren't a mask? Why hadn't any of the ADCs and palace guards stopped the killings, when the shots were heard all around the neighbourhood? The man who had killed the royal family was obviously a masked gunman, concludes the man—a highly trained commando of some kind.

Then, to be fair, he admits that his case does sound quite far-fetched. His 'Gyane' would have had to be ruthless enough to kill his own brothers and relatives, organized enough to do so without being discovered, shrewd enough to steer the international media and investigation committee in his favour and wily enough to fool or intimidate every last eyewitness. His 'Gyane' would have had to plan this massacre for years. The prospect that the present king (or anyone, for that matter) might be so maniacal depresses the man. Besides, there is not a shred of evidence supporting a single conspiracy theory: The required tests were never performed, and the physical evidence was disposed of.

The man eventually backs down. 'It could have been Dipendra,' he concedes. 'The royals are inscrutable. Maybe Dipendra was insane all along. Or it could have been the army. Maybe some faction of the army wanted Birendra out, and forced poor King Gyanendra to suffer this terrible personal loss. How sad for our new king. Imagine losing both brothers in one night!' He goes on, 'Some people say the CIA was involved. Or RAW or ISI. Who knows? Nothing is impossible.'

When trying to take a position—a reasonable position, one that we can defend in our most dispassionate moments—most Nepalis will conclude that we just don't know what happened on the night of 1 June 2001. We lost the truth; we lost our history. We are left to recount anecdotes and stories, to content ourselves with myth.

THE
HISTORY
EXHIBIT

THE GREAT UNIFIER UNIFIES
HIMSELF A NATION

There is a kind of person in Nepal, likely but not necessarily of college education, who carries the nation's history in the mind. Tapping into arcane knowledge of events that took place fifty or a hundred years ago, he or she backs all pronouncements on current events with historical evidence—or the most solid evidence available, given how poorly our past has been recorded.

Another kind of person passes the days in a lost-in-the-trenches daze about the present moment, piecing together shards of history and references and facts, none of which comes together to offer the overall picture, the panoramic overview, the concise analysis, the meaning of it all. This person is haunted by the realization that much knowledge is incomplete in Nepal, that the truth has been lost many times to speculation and can easily be lost again.

I am the latter kind of person. After the massacre at the royal palace, garbled thoughts about the past jammed my mind, making me feel: I *know* all this, because something like this has happened before. Exactly what had happened before, I couldn't say. But I *felt* I did, at some deep subconscious level, *know*. Didn't some Shah king kill his own brother, way back when? Or maybe it was the later Rana rulers who were always knocking off their family members. Hadn't some regent queen engineered a massacre?

I can blame no one for my stupidity. It is however true that those of us who grew up in the 1970s received very partial history lessons. The Panchayat system of 'indigenous' (meaning 'lack of') democracy under an absolute king had implemented the nationalistic New Education Policy. Government-issue textbooks urged schoolchildren to feel a heated one-nation-under-a-Shah-king pride. Because the present king's eleventh predecessor had unified himself a nation, we were now in possession of our unique identities as Nepalis. For this we were beholden to the Shah dynasty.

I was a dull child. But even dull children can pick up on adult prevarication, and the ra-ra nationalism of our textbooks felt forced to me. It was too breathless, this celebration of the Shahs, too blown up and out of proportion. Nepal was, after all, one of the poorest countries of the world. True, our very own Sagarmatha himal—Mount Everest—was the world's tallest mountain, but the Shah dynasty had not, as far as I could tell, contributed to its height. Siddhartha Gautam, later to become the Buddha, had been born in present-day Nepal, but back in 566 BCE his birthplace fell in the Sakya kingdom. Our textbooks insisted that in all of South Asia, Nepal alone had never been colonized; so cowed were the British by us that they had recruited our Gurkha troops. But no one told us that the Gurkhas were, in fact, lesser paid, dispensable mercenary soldiers.

The jingoism of the Panchayat era rang false. There was no hiding the glaring fact that we were (in the idiom of the day) backward and underdeveloped. We lagged far behind the rest of the world, where, I had come to understand from the rare, coveted comic books that circulated among the children of the bourgeoisie, humankind would soon strap rocket propellers to their backs and zoom off to jet-age offices. We, meanwhile, were sacrificing goats at the temples.

Growing up, we became aware of other, less obvious but equally untenable 'truths' of the day. For example, Nepal was said by our textbooks to be a nation of four castes and thirty-six ethnic nationalities. In reality, though, just three groups ruled the country.

The Chettri caste, including the Shahs's Thakuri sub-caste and the Ranas, controlled the palace, the court and the military. The Bahun caste, as royal priests and preceptors, held religious authority. The Newars—the ethnic group indigenous to Kathmandu—held key posts in administration. Everywhere in power were the Chettris, Bahuns and Newars, and a few rare members of the remaining ninety-odd caste and ethnic nationalities. Women, too, were almost invisible in the government. More than 90 per cent of the country's population, therefore, found no representation at all.

Falsehood results in a loss of faith; state-sanctioned falsehood results in a loss of faith in the state. As we grew up, it became obvious that we were not a peace-loving Hindu nation of poor but happy villagers smiling for the benefit of passing trekkers. The People's Movement, which restored democracy in 1990, allowed us to manifest ourselves as a real country with real politics. Yet, because all through the past our historians had been barred from writing true histories, even in 1990 we didn't quite know who we were.

About the ruling Shah dynasty we were ambivalent. On balance, the Shahs had behaved badly during the three-decade Panchayat era, which began in 1960 when the present king's father ended Nepal's first experiment with democracy. After 1990, many of us felt that we had an unremarkable royal family, several of whose members overindulged in drugs and drink (and sometimes brawled at discos, ran over people with their cars and sometimes, according to widespread rumours, smuggled idols), but on the positive side, the monarch's powers had been curtailed by the new constitution. King Birendra Bir Bikram Shah was himself an affable man, and his son, Crown Prince Dipendra, looked much the same, and one of their ancestors had, after all, unified Nepal. Besides, the tourism industry profited by telling the rest of the world that we worshipped our king as an incarnation of Vishnu, and that we were the mythical Shangri-La, so why be prickly and demand a republic? Why not accommodate, and in sentimental moments even celebrate, the fact that we have someone, anyone, to hold up as a symbol of our nation, such as it is?

This was what we felt, till the massacre at the palace prompted most of us to examine our views on the monarchy, and seek some clarity.

The National History Museum stands near the army hospital in Kathmandu's Chhauni neighbourhood. After the Narayanhiti massacre, I visited the museum to see what wisdom it would yield. Entering the gate, I was met by a machine-gun nozzle sticking out of a sandbagged trench. A soldier in the trench eyed me closely as I paid the five-rupee entry fee, suddenly feeling delinquent, as though I were planning an assault of some kind.

I ventured past an unkempt garden to three buildings that had an air of defeat about them. In the one that housed the history exhibit, four gallery attendants were lounging in the foyer, gossiping. Since the museum grounds' soil was very fertile—I heard them say as I entered—soldiers were digging up sackfuls to supply to the gardens of the army brass. 'If you mix some dung into the soil, your flowerpot will teem with greens,' one man said with a strange passion as I took in two cannon manufactured in Nepal in the mid-nineteenth century, and the first Radio Nepal transmitter, a clunky contraption bearing the label 'Chicago Telephone & Radio Co. Ltd. Bombay Calcutta Lucknow Lahore New Delhi'.

From there I headed upstairs, to the exhibit proper. It began with a life-size diorama of primitive man clad in a cotton loincloth, spearing a beast that looked like a mix of wolf and boar. Nearby were ancient pottery shards, including a pot from Jerusalem donated by the government of Israel. A moth-eaten hand-drawn map of Nepal covered one wall, its villages summarily marked 'Village'. Nothing was explained about its significance. Beyond that began a mind-numbing display of swords, bows, shields, arrows, sickles, cannon and knives of varying kinds and sizes: khukuris, machete-like khadkas, sword-like khudas and arrow-headed kataris. They were classified by whom they had belonged to: 'Personal Weapons of HM the Great King Prithvi Narayan Shah', 'Personal Weapons of Ranajit Malla', 'Weapons Seized at Nuwakot, 1744 CE', 'Weapons of Kalu Pandey', 'Toy Cannon of HM King Rana Bahadur Shah', 'Leather Cannon Seized in the First War against Tibet'...

I walked on, overtaken by a choked, inarticulate sense of our exceedingly martial past, till I found a plastic chair that I could sit on, brooding.

The chair was positioned before a gallery of portraits of the Shah kings, most of which were painted by the mid-twentieth-century artist Amar Chitrakar. The artist had endowed the country's first king, the Great Unifier Prithvi Narayan Shah, with the solemn, world-weary expression of someone who had done too much too fast, and was not pleased by the thought that he might have to keep up his pace.

What a man this king must have been! From 1743 on he served as the king of Gorkha, now a district in west Nepal. His old palace still stands there, a humble building perched atop a steep, fortress-like hill. The walls are adorned with only the starkest of woodwork, and the rooms are dark and cramped. The hill on which the palace stands is almost its most impressive feature. It is hard to believe that it housed Nepal's most successful kings.

The Shah kings had ruled here for two centuries before Prithvi Narayan Shah, variously identifying themselves to be Rajput or Khan or Shah in origin, allying themselves with the powers of the times in the subcontinent. By Prithvi Narayan Shah's time—he was the tenth king of the line—they had decided that they were Thakuri Chettris, meaning that they belonged to the Thakuri sub-caste of the Chettri, or warrior caste. They spoke the Khas tongue, the precursor of the Nepali language, and they ruled over an area inhabited largely by people of Magar ethnic nationality.

In the mid-eighteenth century, the Himalayan belt, including present-day Nepal, was a scattering of tiny hill kingdoms, constantly warring with each other. The British East India Company was governing Bengal, and competing colonial powers were breaking apart what remained of the Mughal Empire in present-day Pakistan, India and Bangladesh. To the north of the Himalayan belt, the Qing dynasty was flourishing in China and Tibet. Gorkha's immediate neighbours to the west were a cluster of twenty-four kingdoms. Further west lay another cluster of twenty-two kingdoms. Prithvi Narayan Shah defeated many of these and other nearby kingdoms, and then, audaciously, set his sights further east, on Nepal valley, or present-day Kathmandu.

Nepal valley was at the time one of the Himalayan belt's richest kingdoms. As far back as 700 BCE, the Kirant rulers—of unknown origins—had ruled here, leaving a few scant traces in the shrines they established: Swayambhu, Gujeswori, Pashupatinath, Boudhhanath and Namuda Buddha. Around 250 BCE, the Mauryan emperor Ashoka had sent emissaries here to build the four Buddhist stupas of Patan. The valley had then fallen under the rule of the Licchavi kings (who ruled from 205 to 879 CE or from 400 to 750 CE, depending on different history books). The Licchavi kings patronized the Shiva cult of the Pashupatinath temple, and built four major Narayan shrines—Changu Narayan, Bisankhu Narayan, Shesh Narayan and Ichangu Narayan—as well as the sleeping stone Vishnu of Budhanilkantha. Stone tablets with Lichhavi-era inscriptions are still scattered around the valley today.

For reasons unknown, the Lichhavis's power waned after the eighth century. Little is known of the rulers who followed. By 1200, however, the valley had come under the rule of the Malla kings, who were ethnically Newar in origin, and who had their own language, now alternatively called Newari or Nepal-bhasa. By 1482, the Malla kings had established three independent kingdoms, called Kantipur (now Kathmandu), Patan (still called Patan) and Bhadgaon (now Bhaktapur).

To understand how audacious it was for Prithvi Narayan Shah to covet Nepal valley, one need only contrast the humble palace of the Shahs in Gorkha with the old palace of Kantipur, Hanuman Dhoka, home to the last Malla king, Jayaprakash Malla. Hanuman Dhoka is a sprawling medieval palace. Beyond a gate guarded by an idol of the monkey god Hanuman lies a courtyard decked with stone carvings and gilded water taps. To one side looms a shrine that only the kings' families were—and still are— meant to enter, its tiered pagoda roof topped by a temple finial. Through the courtyard is a maze of other courtyards that open into interconnected rooms, halls, chambers, vestibules. At the end of the innermost courtyard is a circular Hanuman temple with a five-tiered pagoda roof.

Just as impressive as Hanuman Dhoka is the temple complex that it stands in, which also dates back to Malla times. In this complex are the Taleju Bhawani temple, built in 1576, and the even older Tarani Devi temple. The nearby Jagannath temple to Vishnu dates back to the seventeenth century, as does the Gopinath shrine. In the same complex is an octagonal temple with brick plinths, Chasin Dega, a Vishnu shrine built in 1649. Directly south of Hanuman Dhoka is Kumari Bahal, where a young girl designated as a virgin goddess, a kumari, still lives. To the west, on nine brick plinths, is the 1692 Maiju Dewal temple. Further off in the Maru Tole neighbourhood are the

Narayan temple of 1690, the Kastamandap building of 1620 and the Mahadev shrine which predates both by over a century. The Dhansa building, with elaborately carved lattice windows, dates back to 1673.

Nepal valley's other two kingdoms of Patan and old Bhadgaon were no less impressive.

And yet in 1768 the scrappy hill king of Gorkha defeated the Malla kings. The general explanation is that the three Malla kings bickered a lot among themselves, which made them vulnerable to outside attacks. And the Gorkha king was ambitious. Before laying siege to Nepal valley he went to Benares in India to buy muskets. There he observed the ascendant power of the British East India Company, and became inflamed with expansionist passions of his own.

Prithvi Narayan Shah began his siege on Nepal valley by capturing nearby fortresses and blockading the Tibet and India trade routes, which were vital for Nepal valley's survival. The British East India Company dispatched some troops to aid Jayaprakash Malla, but the Gorkha king's siege continued unabated. Six months later, Prithvi Narayan Shah launched his final battle on the day of Indra Jatra, a festival that had been celebrated in the valley since the tenth century (and is still celebrated). A Newar friend of mine sometimes laughs, a little bitterly and in earnest, that his urbane people were vanquished by us—coarse hill folk—through unfair means: 'We were so drunk at the festival, all we could do was flick peas at you guys.' The more zealous of Prithvi Narayan Shah's soldiers cut off the noses of the local inhabitants after their victory.

Once Kantipur fell, Patan followed, and eventually Bhadgaon was won. Prithvi Narayan Shah expelled all foreigners from the valley—including a Capuchin mission that had been set up in 1715—and shifted his court from the hilltop palace in Gorkha to the palace of Hanuman Dhoka. Kathmandu became the seat of the emerging nation of Nepal.

At the National History Museum, next to the portrait of Prithvi Narayan Shah hangs a portrait of his son, the second king, Pratap Singh Shah. And next to that are portraits of all the other kings—Rana Bahadur, Girwanyuddha, Rajendra, Surendra, Prithvi, Tribhuvan, Mahendra, Birendra, all in a row, all donning the diamond and emerald-drop Shah crown with bird of paradise plumes spouting, fountain-style, off the top. Dressed in full regalia—their chests gleaming with sashes and medals that they had awarded themselves—they stand, sceptre in hand, before their red-and-gold throne.

Watching them, it felt as though I had entered my childhood textbooks, in which one glorious king made way for another in a tidy succession. The reality was far more treacherous.

THE AGE OF THE REGENT QUEENS

After Prithvi Narayan Shah died in 1775, Nepal was ruled for the next seventy years by kings who were either underage, inept, insane, or all three. They and their fierce regent queens played unending power games with the Chettri-caste courtiers of the Thapa, Pandey and Basnyat clans, in what amounted to a bad show all around:

The second king of Nepal, Pratap Singh Shah, died of natural causes after two years on the throne. His son Rana Bahadur Shah was crowned in 1777 at the age of two and a half. The boy-king's mother served as the regent queen for eight years— till the boy-king's uncle imprisoned her on charges of having sexual relations with her minister. He killed the minister for good measure, and went on to serve as regent prince himself for the next nine years. Both regents had continued Nepal's east- and westward expansion. Testing boundaries to the north, the regent prince twice invaded Tibet, leading Nepali troops into battle against Chinese forces dispatched from Beijing.

In 1794 King Rana Bahadur Shah wrested sovereignty from his unwilling uncle, two years after coming of age. He promptly imprisoned his uncle, who later died in mysterious circumstances in jail.

At first Rana Bahadur Shah looked like a capable king. But, as the story goes, he fell prey to the wrong kind of woman. While his first wife was childless, his second wife had given him several sons. Yet it was an illegitimate son born of a Bahun-caste concubine named Kantivati that the king wanted as his successor. So, within three years of becoming the king, he abdicated in favour of his illegitimate son Girwanyuddha Shah. His first wife became the infant-king's regent queen. (Sadly for the abdicated king, his beloved concubine died not long after this.)

Already the country had had six kings and regents. This brisk rate of turnover continued:

Because he was a half-caste, Girwanyuddha Shah was never allowed to rule directly. When the abdicated king went into exile in Benares, his first wife, who had served as the regent queen till then, went with him. And so his second wife became the new regent queen. Rivalries developed between the courts of the two queens. The new regent queen favoured courtiers of the Pandey clan, while her predecessor had favoured Thapa-clan courtiers.

During the second queen's regency, the British East India Company sent its first resident, Captain W. O. Knox, to Kathmandu in 1802 for a four-year stay. Around this time Rana Bahadur Shah decided he didn't like being in Benares, so far from the throne he had given up, and he played on the favours of the British to return from exile. Upon his return he killed his second wife's head minister, or mukhtiyar, Damodar Pandey, so that he could himself serve as her mukhtiyar. He then reinstated his first wife as the regent queen. Until, that is, he exiled her on suspicions of political disloyalty and got himself a third wife, a teenage girl, Lalita Tripurasundari, who then became the regent queen to the still underage half-caste king Girwanyuddha Shah. The abdicated-king-cum-mukhtiyar was killed in a family spat in 1806. There are questions as to his sanity.

The court was in considerable disarray by now, but brutality helped the Shahs to ward off threats to their power. The murder, maiming and torture of criminals had been practised earlier as well, but in this period government servants found guilty of crimes had their hands cut off, had heated metal put in their mouths, and were fed excreta or ritually polluted food and drink like pork and alcohol. Those who bad-mouthed the king lost their tongues. To ascertain guilt in civil suits, both the accuser and the accused were subjected to tests of endurance; for instance, they were tossed into rivers, and whoever survived was considered innocent.

Yet the country was the largest it would ever be, a long, craggy sliver stretching from Kumaon and Garhwal (now in India) in the west to Sikkim (also in India now) in the east. Greater Nepal. A map has flooded the market nowadays—I saw it first in a grain shop, then in an office and then at the houses of friends—and it brags of a country one-third larger than present-day Nepal. That was Nepal at its expansionist height.

There are no portraits of Lalita Tripurasundari in the museum's history exhibit. But in the art exhibit, in another building, stands a black stone sculpture of her seated in a posture of supplication, in the style of royal patrons before a temple. It is an uncommonly fine sculpture, the folds of her sari snaking delicately along her smooth body and her oval features expressing great serenity.

She ruled, remarkably, for twenty-six years as the regent queen. She was skilled, despite her youth, at managing the intrigues of the Thapa, Pandey and Basnyat clan courtiers, who were forever wrangling for power. It also helped that she had a very loyal mukhtiyar, Bhimsen Thapa, who put more than ninety people to death to consolidate her power, among these fifteen of her late husband's wives and concubines.

At the time, the British were hemming Nepal. In 1814, Bhimsen Thapa instigated a war against them in Saran and Gorakhpur in present-day India. The defeat that Nepal suffered ended Nepal's expansion. The 1816 Treaty of Sugauli ceded Kumaon, Garhwal and Sikkim to the British, along with a portion of the fertile Tarai plains in the south. Nepal also agreed to host a permanent British residency in Kathmandu and to recruit Nepali soldiers to the Gurkha battalions of the British army.

King Girwanyuddha Shah's reign ended with his death in the year of this treaty. His son, the fifth king, Rajendra Bikram Shah, was only two years old at the time, and so Lalita Tripurasundari continued as the regent queen. Her mukhtiyar Bhimsen Thapa modernized the army and reformed the civil administration, delineating district borders, assessing land taxes, improving the postal system, setting up courts of law and building a few roads and bridges. When Lalita Tripurasundari died in 1832, Bhimsen Thapa built in her memory the minaret-like tower that still stands in Kathmandu today, called Dharahara. Soon after her death he was jailed by the next mukhtiyar, a Pandey. (By now the Thapas and Pandeys had been at each others' throats for generations.) In jail, Bhimsen Thapa killed himself after hearing that his wife had been paraded naked in public. (She had not been.)

Now I feel that it was not entirely my fault that I could not, as a schoolchild, keep the Shah kings straight. They were clearly a convoluted lot, and their court intrigues all resembled each other in sometimes gruesome, sometimes tiresome ways:

The fifth king, Rajendra Bikram Shah, had been king for sixteen years before becoming sovereign upon Lalita Tripurasundari's death. But he proved an ineffectual ruler, displaying a trait that no king is forgiven for: He was weak (some historians say he was insane). Fierce queens ran roughshod over his court—his elder and younger wives formed rival factions backed, respectively, by Pandey and Thapa courtiers. To make matters worse, his son, Crown Prince Surendra Bikram Shah (who most historians also agree was mad), began pressing him to abdicate and hand him the crown.

All this proved too much for Rajendra Bikram Shah. To put an end to the bickering in his family, he named his younger wife, Rajyalaksmi, his *own* regent in 1843. She duly executed her rival queen's Pandey courtiers and brought her favoured Thapas into the court. The (mad) crown prince, born of the elder queen's loins, waged a bitter struggle to prevent his stepmother from deposing him in favour of her own son. The king—officially powerless—meanwhile dithered, sometimes backing his wife and sometimes his son.

Eventually, Regent Queen Rajyalaksmi decided to slay her mukhtiyar, though he was a Thapa whom she had hand-picked, because he was plotting against her with the (mad) crown prince. The mukhtiyar's own nephew, General Jung Bahadur Kunwar, shot him dead. Remarkably, till now only a few mukhtiyars serving the Shah courts had ever died a natural death, yet someone always stepped up to become the next mukhtiyar. A relative of the Shahs stepped up this time.

But another crisis ensued as soon as the new mukhtiyar formed his council of ministers. Gagan Singh, a favourite of Regent Queen Rajyalaksmi—some say he was her lover—was

denied a post. She immediately set about demanding a position
for him. Enough is enough, thought the (officially powerless) king.
He had the regent queen's favourite—her (purported) lover—
assassinated. Or maybe not. Maybe the (mad) crown prince was
behind Gagan Singh's assassination, or maybe the new mukhtiyar
was, or maybe General Jung Bahadur Kunwar was. We do not
know. What we do know is that Gagan Singh's murder sparked
a massacre—the kot parwa, the massacre at the armoury—which
was decisive to the turns the country then took.

The year was 1846. Regent Queen Rajyalaksmi was at the
Hanuman Dhoka palace when she heard that Gagan Singh had
been killed. In a rage, she summoned all court officials to the
palace's armoury, or kot. General Jung Bahadur Kunwar arrived
first, with his five brothers and three regiments in tow. Some take
this to mean that he was prepared for the massacre that ensued.
Others think he was simply prepared for all contingencies.

Following General Jung Bahadur Kunwar's advice, the regent
queen ordered the arrest and execution of a Pandey courtier,
accusing him of having killed Gagan Singh. However, the man
charged with executing him refused to follow her order. The king
also pleaded for reason: No one must be executed without a trial,
he said, but of course he was officially powerless. In desperation
he left the palace and went to the mukhtiyar's residence. In a
move that keeps historians guessing, he then went to the British
residency, perhaps to seek advice, perhaps to seek shelter. He
was denied entry by the officer in charge. It was past midnight
at the time.

As for the mukhtiyar, he rushed over to Hanuman Dhoka,
where General Jung Bahadur Kunwar advised him to support
the regent queen's execution orders. The mukhtiyar refused. At
this point, the story goes, the crazed Regent Queen Rajyalaksmi
lunged at the Pandey courtier to kill him herself, but the mukhtiyar

intervened. And then, we are told by what scrappy records exist, 'the massacre happened'. Historians do not know who began it. As the regent queen strode away in a huff, there was, apparently, a sudden firing. A bloody sword battle followed. At the end the mukhtiyar lay dead, along with at least fifty-five other court officials.

The kot parwa. The main lesson we learned from it as schoolchildren was that kings should not be weak; they should not give women power. Tales have it that the (officially powerless) king returned to Hanuman Dhoka past midnight to see a stream of blood in the gutters. The next day began an exodus of 6,000 members of the courtier families. Entire lineages were displaced as the Thapas and Pandeys and Basnyats and other Chettri-caste families of the court fled Kathmandu in fear for their lives.

And so it was that another Chettri-caste clan rose to power: the Kunwars. Renaming themselves Ranas, they captured power over the Shah kings and ruled Nepal for the next hundred-odd years.

THE GILDED AGE OF THE
MAHARAJA-CUM-PRIME-MINISTERS

In the mid-nineteenth century, the world beyond the peaks and waters of Nepal was fast transforming. The industrial revolution had dotted Europe with steam and coal engines, trains, lights, factories, urban centres and slums. Liberal democracy, socialism, communism and anarchism were simmering as capital shifted labourers from the countryside to the city, and from one nation to another. Karl Marx had written *Das Kapital*, and the Revolutions of 1848 had enfranchised at least Europe's bourgeoisie. The empires were entrenched in Asia, Africa and parts of the Americas. China was battling onslaughts from Britain, Russia and Japan. The British Raj was at its peak in India.

In Nepal, the mad Surendra Bikram Shah had become the sixth king following the massacre at the armoury. He was heavily dependent on his new mukhtiyar, General Jung Bahadur Kunwar, a dashing figure who, according to the first British woman to live in Nepal, spent most of his efforts 'devising new uniforms'. This was the same general who had killed his uncle for Regent Queen Rajyalaksmi and won her favour. He had a way with the royals: In years past, he had performed many amusing antics for the new king. At his behest, he had jumped into the Trishuli River, northeast of Kathmandu, on horseback, from a height of eighty feet. He had followed this up by jumping into a deep well to delight the insane king. According to legend, he had also leaped off the Dharahara minaret with parasols to cushion his landing.

Jung Bahadur Kunwar is shown in the portrait gallery of the National History Museum as a slight man with a wispy beard and a passionate, feral look in his eyes. On his head is the elaborate Rana crown, a copy of the Shah crown, but with an added cluster of emeralds, like a bunch of grapes, off to one side, which makes the crown's wearer look a bit daft. He was not yet thirty when he became the mukhtiyar in 1846.

He was not without his foes. Surviving an attempt on his life by loyalists of the deposed regent queen, Rajyalaksmi, he exiled her, then quelled an uprising by the (officially powerless) former king and arrested him. Four years on, his hold over Surendra Bikram Shah's court was so strong that he could, without fear of being ousted, set out on a journey across the seas, to England.

This was a momentous decision. The 'Belaayat voyage', as this trip is known—England being Belaayat in the Nepali tongue—was Nepal's tryst with Empire. A report in the *Morning Post* proclaimed Jung Bahadur Kunwar to be 'the first Hindoo of high caste' to visit England. In fact he was the first truly powerful functionary from South Asia to do so. It added to his appeal that by this time he was no longer a mere mukhtiyar: He had adopted the title of 'Pradhan Mantri', a literal translation of the English 'Prime Minister', which sounded so much more credible abroad. He had also risen above his common Kunwar roots by adopting the fanciful surname 'Rana', which sounded just as Muslim—just as exotically Mughal—as 'Shah'. He had also upgraded himself to princeling status, gaining, by the time of the Belaayat voyage, the hefty title 'Srimad Rajkumar Kumaratmaj Sri Prime Minister and Commander-in-Chief General Jung Bahadur Kunwar Ranaji'.

There were twenty-five people in the troupe accompanying him to England. First they went to Patna in present-day India, hunting tigers and deer and capturing elephants along the way. Belaayat's influence was everywhere in India. A Nepali document of the journey survives—though the identity of its author is uncertain—and the chronicler noted down all that struck him, observations such as 'Toasting is a custom at British banquets.' The Nepali troupe toured Calcutta's city centre, surveying the waterworks and examining weaving machines, bottle-manufacturing plants, mints for rupees and paisa coins. Proper Hindus, they also made a pilgrimage to the Jagannath temple in Puri, which remains a major draw for the Nepali royal family even today.

The voyage's chronicler describes the steamship 'Hatan'—the SS *Haddington*—which the troupe boarded in Calcutta as being three hundred feet long, seventy-five feet wide and seven stories high. The ship's management impressed the chronicler: All duties are performed without instruction, he wrote. Everyone has his or her own bed, and meals are served three times a day. He, of landlocked origins, was fascinated by the wide sea: 'There was no mountain, no tree nor bush, no land to be seen. The sun rose out of the water and sank back into it,' he wrote.

Jung Bahadur Kunwar Rana proved just as much of a curiosity to the British on board as they proved to the chronicler. Decked in fine silks and velvets, the prime minister spent his days touring the decks, taking in the sea air, shooting bottles and dazzling others with his striking mien. As per Hindu custom, he always ate alone—away from polluting non-Hindus—and this piqued much curiosity. This Nepali dignitary—but what was he: prime minister, commander-in-chief, an ambassador, royalty?—was a most exotic oriental: For all his high ranking he milked cows, which were on board along with herds of billy goats, sheep and horses.

The SS *Haddington* sailed past Madras, Ceylon and Aden to Egypt, all amid gun salutes, celebrations, parades and stops at sites of interest. From the Suez the troupe went overland to Alexandria, and from there they sailed along the Nile till they were back at sea. There they boarded the SS *Ripon* and proceeded past Malta and Gibraltar—Gibraltar becoming 'Jivapur' in the chronicler's notes.

On 26 May 1850, 'His Excellency General Jung Bahadoor Koorman Ranagee, Prime Minister and Commander-in-Chief of the kingdom of Nepaul'—as the *Morning Post* dubbed him—arrived in Southampton, called 'Sautanghat' by the Nepali chronicler. Many finely dressed ladies graced the crowd that cheered his arrival. This, at least, is what the Nepali chronicler noticed. The *Morning Post* fixed on other details: 'The Ambassador declined to go to any Southampton hotel unless he could have it entirely to himself. This arose from religious scruples, lest any food prepared for Christians should be mixed with his own.' The Nepali chronicler was stunned by the affluence of Belaayat's citizenry: 'Not one bad-looking or undernourished individual was to be seen.' The *Morning Post* was struck by the disparity among the Nepalis: 'The servants of the embassy were evidently of the lowest caste; some were meanly and miserably clad, many of them without shoes, and their clothing formed a striking contrast to the magnificent costume of the chiefs.'

From Southampton the Nepali troupe took the train to

London, where they settled into 'Rijavant Karij'—Richmond
Terrace—close to the river Thames. They examined such marvels
as water piped in copper pipes, tap systems, charcoal engines
and heaters and charcoal mines, and timber yards. 'The English
have made fire, water and wind their slaves.' This, apparently, was
Jung Bahadur Kunwar Rana's response to technological progress.
The chronicler made more painstaking observations. Everyone in
Belaayat carries a watch, he noted: 'Getting dressed, eating, keeping
appointments, sleeping, getting up or going out—everything is
determined by the clock.' He wrote of the police stations; he wrote
of the shops. High-level officers told Jung Bahadur Kunwar Rana,
'No person as distinguished as yourself has ever come here from
Hindustan,' and the chronicler wrote this down. He documented
evening parties, bands and feasts. This was a country, he observed,
upon which Laksmi, the goddess of wealth, had smiled.

The chronicler also wrote about government. There was a
constitution, and this constitution decreed the limits of power,
even the limits of the monarch's power: 'The sovereign cannot
confiscate anybody's property, punish anyone, resort to violence
or insult, nor hand out and cancel appointments at his own
pleasure, as if he were absolute master of his own resources.' In
Belaayat there was a prime minister on whose recommendation
the sovereign must act. There was a commander-in-chief to head
the army. There was a Parliament, about which the chronicler
wrote: 'The Parament council does not tolerate wrongdoing on
anyone's part. They can even replace the sovereign. If the Prime
Minister offends, they can dismiss him. If the Commander-in-
Chief offends, they can replace him. Be he lord, duke, general,
colonel or anything else, a man's rank is of no account if he
does wrong.' Common people also had responsibilities, he noted,
and there was a system of administration.

Jung Bahadur Kunwar Rana met with Queen Victoria several

times, the first time at an official welcoming audience before
royal family members and government officials. He was later
invited to observe the queen granting audience to nobles. The
third meeting took place at a soirée, in a fine drawing room
where a band was playing. As the Nepali troupe watched, the
British danced, and even the queen joined in—asking as she did
so whether Jung Bahadur Kunwar Rana approved. We might
speculate that he did not. The chronicler, for his part, was startled:
'Some of the officials and their wives danced, some walked
about and others remained seated. They paid no attention to
differences of rank, ignoring all questions of precedence. Such
was the entertainment.'

Jung Bahadur Kunwar Rana's fourth meeting with Queen
Victoria took place when she invited him to a dance performed
by women 'as beautiful as heavenly nymphs'. The final meeting
between them took place just before he left Britain. By then
Jung Bahadur Kunwar Rana had made a splash in British high
society. The *Times* wrote: 'The Nepaulese Princes continue to
form one of the most brilliant cynosures of the day. They are,
certainly, going through the London season in style; while, as for
diamonds, the brilliant eruption appears to take new forms and
still more glittering features every time the Oriental Magnets
appear in public.' The *Edinburgh News* wrote: 'He wore a superb
oriental costume consisting of a robe or tunic of rich blue cloth
or velvet, trimmed with gold lace. His cap, which fitted closely,
was of white silk and glittered with pearls and diamonds, loops
of emerald coloured stones hanging in front, while a long feather
of the Bird of Paradise waved in the air.'

What do we bring back from a visit abroad? In addition to
attending parties in Belaayat, the Nepali troupe visited shipworks
in Plymouth, and went to Birmingham to observe the smelting
of metals, iron and glass, and to see the manufacture of cannon,

rifles, bullets and ammunitions. In London they took in the theatre, and Vauxhall's acrobats, performers, food stalls, archery, card games and amusements. They marvelled at hot-air balloons, horse dances and horse races, promenades and walks.

From England Jung Bahadur Kunwar Rana proceeded to France. 'Seeing this city of Paris is like being on Mount Kailash,' wrote the dazzled chronicler upon reaching the seat of the revolution that was inspiring the world to democracy. (This visit took place during Louis Napoleon's reign as the president of the Second Republic, just two years before he declared himself Emperor, as his uncle Napoleon Bonaparte had been.) The Nepali troupe visited Fontainebleu and Versailles, and went on to Marseilles. There, they impressed the French by attending not just operas but also their rehearsals. And they astounded their hosts by killing goats in their hotel. Jung Bahadur Kunwar Rana's chastity, too, was noted by *L'Illustration*, as was his compulsive gambling: 'Whether out of indifference or bashfulness he has stubbornly refused all the seductive offers made to him... What innocents these Oriental travellers are! To come to Paris only to see the Academy, to milk heifers and participate in the Lottery! The Napaulese ambassador has invested ten thousand (i.e. four hundred pounds) in the eight-million-franc lottery.' The reporter was duly gratified when Jung Bahadur Kunwar Rana finally broke down and presented an opera performer two diamond bracelets.

And then it was back to Nepal—via Aden and Bombay, with a pilgrimage to Dwarakanath in Gujarat, on to Ceylon, with a pilgrimage to Ramnath temple in Tamil Nadu, then through Calcutta. In Benares, Jung Bahadur Kunwar Rana took a wife— one of eventually more than thirty wives—and returned to Nepal through the forests of Chitwan, not without getting in a little hunting on the way.

Inspired by the Napoleonic code, Jung Bahadur Kunwar Rana immediately ordered the task of codifying Nepali law, resulting in the promulgation, in 1853, of the Muluki Ain or the 'Law of the Country', the basis for Nepali law today. He also applied himself, singularly, to capturing power over the king. To do this he married his son to a princess, setting off a spate of Shah-Rana intermarriage that lasts to this day. In 1854 he convinced the king (who was, remember, mad) to declare him the 'Maharaja' of Kaski and Lamjung Districts, and to grant him the power to overrule even the king in politics and diplomacy. The 'Maharaja' title was an entirely new concoction. The Shah kings were considered sri panch, or five-titled—as in Sri Sri Sri Sri Sri Surendra Bikram Shah (the English equivalent would be Mr Mr Mr Mr Mr). The Maharajas were given sri teen, or three-titled status, as in Sri Sri Sri (Mr Mr Mr). The new title gave Jung Bahadur Kunwar Rana a personal income of 2,00,000 rupees a year. It was to pass to his sons upon his death.

In a separate decree, the king decided that the Rana family would also, from now on, inherit the prime minister's post. This post would, however, pass not from father to son but from brother to brother. (This helped the Rana family to widen its power base.) And so began the monarchy-within-a-monarchy of Rana rule.

Jung Bahadur Kunwar Rana momentarily relinquished his prime minister's post to his brother, after leading Nepal into a war with Tibet, which Nepal lost. When the brother died, another brother became the prime minister. But after that, Jung Bahadur Kunwar Rana manoeuvred his way back, serving as the maharaja-cum-prime minister—who also controlled the military and the treasury—for the remaining twenty years of his life.

One lesson the maharaja had learned from his Belaayat voyage was that the British could prop him up. He regularly told on the (mad) king to the British resident, conveying gossip about his liaisons with stable boys and his moody suicide threats. When the resident persisted in viewing the maharaja as a pretender to the throne, Jung Bahadur Kunwar Rana led Nepali troops to battle in the 1857 Sepoy Rebellion in Lucknow and Gorakhpur, in present-day India, helping the British to quell the uprising. In return, the British conceded to Nepal some territories they had earlier won.

British recognition secured, the maharaja settled back in his lavish British-colonial-style palace in Thapathali—which has been truncated into bits by his inheritors—and began to tinker with the brother-to-brother roll of succession for the prime minister's post, inserting favourite sons and nephews into line. To consolidate his dynasty's power, he also married two of his daughters and a niece to the crown prince.

But death, as it does, loosened his grip on power. The brother who became the next prime minister, Rannodip Singh Kunwar Rana, wanted to inherit Jung Bahadur Kunwar Rana's 'Maharaja' title as well. So he suppressed news of the maharaja's death, sent the crown prince out of town (lest he cry foul) and got the (mad) king to strip Jung Bahadur Kunwar Rana's sons of the Maharaja title, and to bequeath it to him instead. This, the (mad) king did. The Maharaja and prime minister titles were from then on welded together.

The crown prince died suddenly, possibly by poison. Three years later, in 1881, Surendra Bikram Shah also died, having spent thirty years as a king despite, or possibly because of, his madness. His grandson, Prithvi Bir Bikram Shah, became the seventh Shah king. He was, conveniently, just a boy at the time.

Due to the by now extensive intermarriage between the Shahs and the Ranas, the boy-king was also Jung Bahadur Kunwar Rana's grandson—and this made Maharaja Rannodip Singh Kunwar Rana nervous, for he had usurped the Maharaja title from the boy-king's uncles, Jung Bahadur Kunwar Rana's sons. He discovered that these sons were scheming to claim back the title. Adding to the new maharaja's woes, the British were bargaining for greater Gurkha recruitment by withholding recognition of him as the legitimate prime minister.

Even as the maharaja fretted about how to placate the British, he lost his own place: In 1885 he was murdered by his nephews. These were not, as one would expect, the nephews whose Maharaja title he had usurped, but the seventeen sons of Dhir Sumshere Kunwar Rana, who was the youngest of Jung Bahadur Kunwar Rana's five brothers. By murdering their uncle, these seventeen brothers started the second generation of Rana rule.

To monopolize the second generation, the seventeen brothers exiled and killed their cousins, the sons of Jung Bahadur Kunwar Rana, and forever expelled them from the roll of succession. They deleted 'Kunwar' from their names, replacing it with 'Jung Bahadur'. Five of them eventually became maharajas.

The first was Bir Sumshere Jung Bahadur Rana, who spent much time surviving overthrow attempts by his relatives, and exiling his many critics. Not coincidentally, he built Nepal's first jail in 1894; it is known today as the Bhadragoal jail, and has housed many political prisoners over the years.

The concept of 'public works' caught on during this time. The maharaja's slain uncle had opened Durbar School, the first modern school in the country. He topped this by ordering the construction of water pipes in Kathmandu, as well as sewers, the first suspension bridge, a leprosy hospital and a palace school where English was taught. He reorganized land taxes and effected administrative reform. But he mostly set about enriching himself: It is said that in his palaces, Kathmandu's Seto Durbar and Lal Durbar, he kept a harem of five hundred women. The American embassy's sports complex of today, Phohora Durbar, also belonged to him.

He continued the Rana tradition of seeking British support by giving in to demands for greater Gurkha recruitment. In return the British granted him the Knight Grand Commander of the Star of India on Queen Victoria's diamond jubilee. Maharaja Bhim Sumshere Jung Bahadur Rana died of natural causes at the turn of the twentieth century—and this is progress: to have rulers die of natural causes instead of murder.

The next maharaja, Dev Sumshere Jung Bahadur Rana, was said to be a reformer. He opened twenty vernacular schools in a country where education had been limited to the classical Sanskrit language. He encouraged discussion among courtiers, and had public suggestion boxes placed around Kathmandu. He emancipated female slaves in Kaski and Lamjung Districts and in Kathmandu. He also launched *Gorkhapatra*, the country's first newspaper, which at the time published a weekly edition.

He set to work fast, and this is lucky, for three months later his title was snatched away by his brother Chandra Sumshere Jung Bahadur Rana in a bloodless coup—and this too is progress: to have a family coup that does not necessitate bloodshed.

The twentieth century was a year old. The Shah kings were virtual prisoners of the Rana maharajas, kept under strict surveillance at all times. The maharajas themselves were under the increasing control of the British. British histories describe Nepal at this time as a 'quasi-British protectorate'. George Nathaniel Curzon, Viceroy of India, wrote: 'To describe Nepal as an Independent State is not only inconsistent with the views that have…hitherto been entertained…but such a definition might…prove extremely embarrassing.' Nepali historians contest such claims, arguing that the Ranas allowed the British to entertain the illusion that Nepal was 'quasi-British' because the Ranas depended so heavily on them for their own legitimacy within Nepal.

Chandra Sumshere Jung Bahadur Rana is thought to have consulted Viceroy Curzon during the latter's 1901 hunting trip to Chitwan about his plans to depose his brother. Perhaps this was why he was quickly recognized as the legitimate maharaja. He made the most of the British support for him: In 1908 he visited England and received an Order of Knight Grand Cross of the Most Honourable Order of the Bath.

By this time he had already started the construction of his palace, Singha Durbar, the palace of lions. It serves as the seat of Parliament today, reconstructed after an extensive fire in the 1970s. The original structure was an orgy of stucco and plaster, with columns decked with ornate capitals and cornices, and with gay follies, esplanades, pavilions, galleries and arches. The rooms had high ceilings and bay windows, the hallways were vast, the stairways grand and the courtyards large. The palace even boasted a hall bedecked with mirrors, in imitation of Versailles. It is far, far grander than the Hanuman Dhoka palace, and in its day it towered over the mud and brick-and-mortar hovels of ordinary Nepalis in Kathmandu. Five million rupees went into its construction. (Chandra Sumshere Jung Bahadur Rana's family later sold it to the Nepali government for a tidy profit of 15 million.)

Not that the maharaja did nothing for his approximately 6 million subjects. He sent a handful of favoured Nepalis to Japan to study mining, geology, mechanics and industry, and to Assam, India, to learn the British system of accounting. But he also reduced the already small number of schools. He ordered the construction of iron bridges all over the country, fixed the value of the Nepali rupee, reformed the judicial system and delineated the powers of various government offices. He rid all but Kathmandu of the practice of jagir, a policy of parcelling government officials public land. He fixed the market rate of grains, standardizing the rate at which tenant farmers paid taxes. But he also spent much energy devising means to control the fractious Rana clan: He classified them into the 'A', 'B' and 'C' classes. 'A'-class Rana men, of pure birth, were deemed fit to inherit the maharaja's post. 'C'-class Rana men—born of concubines—were not. And the 'B'-class Ranas could always hope.

Meanwhile, the king, Prithvi Bir Bikram Shah, began to try to challenge the power of the maharajas and re-establish the sovereignty of the five-titled Shah dynasty. He died without any success. In 1911 Tribhuvan Bir Bikram Shah was crowned at the age of six as the eighth Shah king. He would later end Rana rule. But at the time the Shah kings posed little threat. The maharaja went on with business as usual, hosting a hunting expedition for King George V, and bringing electricity in 1912, so that Kathmandu's palaces could light up at night.

NO YETI

Global events would finally overrun the rule of the Rana maharajas. Before the First World War, 1,500 Nepali men served annually in the British Gurkhas. By 1918, when the Treaty of Versailles was signed, ending the First World War, up to 1,00,000 Nepali men had served the Allied forces in India, France, Gallipoli, Egypt, Mesopotamia, Palestine and Africa.

A hundred thousand Nepali men beyond the borders of their landlocked kingdom. In Europe they saw the Austro-Hungarian Empire break into nations racked by revolution. They witnessed democracy, Bolshevism and the expanse of the French and British empires. In Africa and the Middle East they saw the re-mapping of nationalities. They met Canadians, Chinese, Africans, Indians,

Australians and New Zealanders.

In the years since Jung Bahadur Kunwar Rana's charmed Belaayat visit, a select few rulers and courtiers had seen the world; in the First World War, ordinary Nepali men—men from the villages—saw what was happening in the rest of the world. The historian Ludwig F. Stiller describes this as 'the first great learning experience for many Nepalese'.

They saw that India was entering into struggle against British rule. The Bengalis had started boycotting British goods, the Indian National Congress was demanding home rule and armed political unrest was on the rise. The religious reforms of the Hindu group Arya Samaj had begun to make an impact even in Nepal, where a particularly conservative school of Hinduism, sanaatan dharma, had for centuries oppressed women and those who were neither of Chettri nor Bahun caste.

The progress in India worried Maharaja Chandra Sumshere Jung Bahadur Rana. Publications emerging from Darjeeling and Calcutta, where many Gurkha soldiers settled, were sometimes openly critical of him. He meted lashings to home-grown troublemakers and exiled them. To appease the masses he began a few reforms. In 1919 Tri Chandra College opened in Kathmandu to prevent Nepalis from picking up politics in Indian colleges. New bridges were built; an electric ropeway was set up from Bhimphedi to Kathmandu. Private motor cars began to run on Kathmandu's roads—after first being carried over the hills and into the valley on the backs of porters. The government built two major irrigation canals and began the construction of a military hospital, a hospital now known as Bir Hospital. But all this was too little and it came too late. For instance, the maharaja abolished the practice of sati, and also slavery—compensating slave-owners in order to do so—but similar practices had been banned in India over a century ago.

One lasting change came from granting farmers ownership rights in 1923; till then, Nepalis enjoyed only the rights of tenants. Suddenly, an economically independent bourgeoisie came into being (and this bourgeoisie would soon foment discontent). Also in 1923, the maharaja got the British to unequivocally acknowledge Nepal's sovereignty in the Treaty of Friendship, a treaty that flooded Kathmandu with foreign imports, resulting in an indebted population but a much enriched maharaja. When Chandra Sumshere Jung Bahadur Rana died in 1929, he left his progeny an inheritance of over 40 million pounds.

Beyond the portrait gallery, the National Museum's history exhibit consists of displays of increasingly sophisticated weapons, including a Thompson sub-machine gun, a VIP gun, a Louis gun, a light machine gun and an anti-tank gun. Not much is explained about how they came to Nepal, and how they had been used. Where had the government acquired chain-mail suits from the eighteenth century? Why not just buy muskets from British India; why manufacture, as the government had in the nineteenth century, the 'Sundari' (or beautiful) rifle and 'Birgun' (or brave-gun) cannon? No explanation is offered.

Wondering darkly how much it could possibly cost to curate the displays in more informative ways, I came upon an Electric Gun, which stopped me in my tracks. It was a tinny horror, a Bride of Frankenstein contraption with exposed wires, levers, poles and barrels poking out in a mangled, wholly unconvincing manner. I stared at it dumbly, imagining an indolent Rana ordering his servants to plug in the gun as the heathens arrived at the gate...

On the museum's top floor was a collection of coins, which I took in as a gallery attendant railed with another attendant against her husband, who had recently brought home a younger wife: 'I have to hide the money in the pillow of my brother-in-law's bed.'

'In your brother-in-law's bed?'

'In my brother-in-law's bed!'

Their voices ricocheted off the walls.

I went from there to the natural history section, and took in a room full of dusty stuffed birds and animals. Briefly, I stopped to study a Nepali flag that had been carried to the moon and back in *Apollo II*. Attached to it was a moon rock bearing a message from Richard Nixon: 'This fragment is a portion of a rock from the Taurus Littrow Valley of the Moon. It is given as a symbol of the unity of human endeavor and carries with it the hope of the American people for a world of peace.'

As I examined the rock, a foreign man—German or Austrian by his accent—came in and went up to a nearby gallery attendant, and asked, in broken English, to see a yeti.

The attendant did not understand him.

'Ye-ti, yet-ee,' the foreign man said.

'He's looking for a yeti,' I said to the attendant in Nepali.

'No yeti,' responded the attendant, surprised.

The man said, 'My guidebook says there is a yeti skin in the museum.'

'No yeti,' the attendant repeated.

'My guidebook says yes.'

'No yeti.'

Out of what seemed like sheer politeness, the attendant then said, 'Anyways we ask the curator,' and led the man outdoors.

I too left the building. My legs were sore. There was no toilet in sight. I did a quick run through the building that housed the Buddhism exhibit—all statues and mandalas—and entered the art collection.

Here I saw a huge marble bust of a portly, mustachioed man wearing the daft Rana crown. The handiwork was excellent. A sign on the back read: 'Ojaswi Rajanya Prithuladhisa His Highness

Maharaja Joodha Sumsher Jung Bahadur Rana, prime minister and supreme commander-in-chief of Nepal—a man of high integrity, scrupulous veracity, indomitable moral courage, irrepressible spirit of nationalism; and, last but not least, an all round reformer who throughout his long and eventful life has been working to give a proper orientation to everything concerned with Nepal and the Nepalese nation;—This art gallery is named after him as the founder and this tablet inscribed as a mark of heartfelt gratitude and deep appreciation of the nation.'

The final display was of temple sculpture and repoussé and lost-wax carvings. The museum spoke nothing of the political struggles that took place in the 1940s, or the experiment with democracy in the 1950s. Missing, too, was the People's Movement that restored democracy to Nepal in 1990. The political parties— the Nepali Congress and the Communist Party of Nepal (Unified Marxist Leninist)—which had governed democratic Nepal—after a fashion—since 1990 were wholly absent. There was nothing on the country's many leaders of social reform, and no mention of our myriad popular uprisings and revolutions. It was as though the Nepali people had not found a place in their country's history.

A SHAH-RANA-PEOPLE SOVEREIGNTY CHART

Dates	*Sovereign Head (Title)*
1768–75	Prithvi Narayan Shah (King)
1775–77	Pratap Singh Shah (King)
1777–85	Rajendralaksmi Shah (Regent Queen)
1785–95	Bahadur Shah (Regent Prince)
1795–99	Rana Bahadur Shah (King)
1799–1800	Rajarajeswori Shah (Regent Queen)
1800–03	Subarnaprabha Shah (Regent Queen)
1803–06	Rajarajeswori Shah (Regent Queen)

1806–32	Lalita Tripurasundari Shah (Regent Queen)
1832–43	Rajendra Bikram Shah (King)
1843–46	Rajyalaksmi Shah (Regent Queen)
1846–49	Surendra Bikram Shah (King)
1849–76	Jung Bahadur Kunwar Rana (Maharaja)
1876–85	Rannodip Singh Kunwar Rana (Maharaja)
1885–1900	Bir Sumshere Jung Bahadur Rana (Maharaja)
1900–01	Dev Sumshere Jung Bahadur Rana (Maharaja)
1901–29	Chandra Sumshere Jung Bahadur Rana (Maharaja)
1929–32	Bhim Sumshere Jung Bahadur Rana (Maharaja)
1932–45	Juddha Sumshere Jung Bahadur Rana (Maharaja)
1945–48	Padma Sumshere Jung Bahadur Rana (Maharaja)
1948–51	Mohan Sumshere Jung Bahadur Rana (Maharaja)
1951–55	Tribhuvan Bir Bikram Shah (King)
1955–59	Mahendra Bir Bikram Shah (King)
1959–59	Bisheswor Prasad Koirala (Prime Minister)
1959–72	Mahendra Bir Bikram Shah (King)
1972–90	Birendra Bir Bikram Shah (King)
1990–91	Krishna Prasad Bhattarai (Prime Minister)
1991–94	Girija Prasad Koirala (Prime Minister)
1994–95	Man Mohan Adhikari (Prime Minister)
1995–96	Sher Bahadur Deuba (Prime Minister)
1996–97	Lokendra Bahadur Chand (Prime Minister)
1997–97	Surya Bahadur Thapa (Prime Minister)
1997–98	Girija Prasad Koirala (Prime Minister)
1998–99	Krishna Prasad Bhattarai (Prime Minister)
1999–2001	Girija Prasad Koirala (Prime Minister)
2001–02	Sher Bahadur Deuba (Prime Minister)
2002–06	Gyanendra Bir Bikram Shah (King)
2006–08	Girija Prasad Koirala (Prime Minister)

The monarchy was abolished in 2008, and Ram Baran Yadav became Nepal's first President.

THE WIND,
THE HAZE

THE ENLIGHTENMENT
BY FITS AND STARTS

Not far from my family home is a street that I think of as 'Construction Avenue', a line of stores that sell building materials. It has recently been named by the municipality, but people still call it the 'Old Baneswor Road', or even the 'Old Airport Road', as it used to be the only road to the airport. Thirty years ago wolves howled in the paddy fields here. Over the 1970s and '80s, and especially in the '90s, migrants from the impoverished countryside poured into Kathmandu in search of opportunities, turning this into one of the densest areas of the city. Now every shop on this road sells a dizzying array of corrugated tin sheets and iron rods, taps and door handles, bathroom tiles, commodes, PVC pipes, glass from India, cans of paint, tube lights, shovels, barbed wire... The street is choked with traffic every morning and evening, and the sidewalks are crammed with vegetable vendors living off the purchases of harried passers-by. Electric and telephone wires press in from above, blocking out the sky, and the entire stretch is arid and treeless. If someone were to plant a sapling on the sidewalk, people would trample it in the rush to get on with their days.

Construction Avenue is probably not what tour operators are thinking of when they describe Kathmandu as a land of 'eternal attraction' where 'pagodas, narrow cobbled lanes, old carved windows and stone shrines are backdrops to the drama of life that continues unhindered'. But sadly for latter-day orientalists, the life of Kathmandu is now found as much in the city's unseemly clutter as in its traditional quarters, with their medieval temples and Rana palaces. In the unseemly clutter live the political leaders, intellectuals, social activists and bourgeoisie who have influenced the course of events in Nepal over the last half century. In the clutter lives our recent past.

In 1929, the sixth maharaja, Bhim Sumshere Jung Bahadur Rana, came to power. The king, Tribhuvan Bir Bikram Shah, was independent-minded, but powerless. However, by this time, the people were beginning to rebel against Rana rule. The Nepali enlightenment had begun.

But, as elsewhere in the world, the enlightenment here took place erratically, staggering ahead, stagnating and at times passing by in a blur. There is a sweep to the term 'enlightenment'. It suggests wide avenues of knowledge, straight lines of rationality. In Nepal, the enlightenment has followed a tortuous path. Sometimes it feels as though it is still on its way here.

The 1920s had seen the rise of anti-Rana sentiment among the Nepalis enlisted in India's Gurkha troops, who were often critical of their own role in suppressing India's freedom movement. Through their publications *Tarun Gorkha*, *Gorkha Sansar* and *Gorkhali*, brought out from Benares, Calcutta, Dehradun and Bombay, where they had settled after the First World War, they began to vent their grievances. Dissidence had also grown within Nepal. Madhav Raj Joshi had openly challenged the orthodoxy of the state-sanctioned sanaatan dharma in favour of the more progressive Arya Samaj school of Hinduism, which promoted widow remarriage, caste equality and education for boys and girls alike. Jaya Prithvi Bahadur Singh had written a provocative treatise on social conduct and political justice. Krishna Lal Adhikari had authored a book on farming, *The Cultivation of Maize*, containing an allusion to foreign dogs, implying that the Ranas were pets kept by the British; the book had been burned and the author jailed for six years. (The construction of new jails throughout Nepal accompanied the rise of dissent.) Poets such as Shambhu Prasad Dhungel, Lekh Nath Poudyal and Juddha Prasad Mishra had begun writing lyrically against political oppression.

The maharaja, who was what we would today call a pot head, responded with a few modest reforms: He set the six-day work week and banned the death penalty in civil cases. But he did not appreciate the growing numbers of freethinkers that the times were spawning. When the social activist Tulsi Mehar introduced Gandhi-style spinning wheels to Nepal, he was arrested. When a group of Kathmandu intellectuals started a public library, they were handed prison sentences, as they had broken a ban on reading (the maharajas found it convenient for their subjects to not study). Members of the revolutionary Prachanda Gorkha Association, formed to end Rana rule by violent means, were sentenced to life in prison and their properties confiscated.

Nevertheless, other dissidents—teachers, lawyers, citizens' rights activists—cropped up from the growing bourgeois class. Even a few Ranas took to nonconformity: One, a general, began to write dramas, becoming known by the pseudonym Balkrishna Sama, a prominent liberal voice of his time.

When Juddha Sumshere Jung Bahadur Rana became the seventh maharaja in 1932, the ferment for bourgeois rights was palpable.

Shukra Raj Joshi, the son of the Arya Samaj activist Madhav Raj Joshi, had met Gandhi and Gandhi's rival, the advocate of armed revolt, Subhas Chandra Bose, in British India. He set up the Nepali Nagarik Adhikar Samiti to demand citizens' rights. In 1936 he gave a public lecture on the Gita and karma yoga, emphasizing the need for a just religion and calling for an end to child marriage. His message, mild by today's standards, earned him six years in jail. But other members of his group continued to speak out.

Another group, called the Ajambari Mat, inspired by Gandhi and the Arya Samaj, was also formed in the 1930s, founded by Newars who opposed the Bahun-caste supremacy in the Hindu hierarchy. The Mahabir School in the Kilha Tole neighbourhood of Kathmandu became a hotbed of bourgeois revolution, as the teachers prepared a syllabus aimed at sparking political consciousness in students.

All this intellectual ferment formed the grounds on which Nepal's first political party established itself in 1940: the Praja Parishad. Founded by Tanka Prasad Acharya, Dasrath Chand, Dharma Bhakta Mathema, Jiv Raj Sharma and Ram Hari Sharma, and with the fiery leader Ganesh Man Singh among its members, the Praja Parishad smuggled in an old duplicator from India and ran off pamphlets against the Ranas. Its members even communicated, via middlemen, with the king, Tribhuvan Bir Bikram Shah, to form an alliance of convenience against Rana rule.

Bolstered by the king's support, the Praja Parishad began to plot the assassination of the entire Rana clan. This was to take place when the Ranas came to visit the king during the autumn-time Tihar festival for a movie screening. The plan was for the king to leave the cinema hall just before a bomb exploded, killing everyone in the hall, including the maharaja and all his successors. Thus would Rana rule end.

But the assassination plot was discovered when an insider snitched. Maharaja Juddha Sumshere Jung Bahadur Rana ordered mass arrests of Praja Parishad members, and placed the insubordinate king under surveillance. He meted life sentences to fourteen members of the party, and sentenced twenty more to long prison terms. Four party members were banished from Kathmandu. For good measure the maharaja also arrested the teachers of the Mahabir School, sentencing some to eighteen years in jail.

Though he was in prison at the time of the assassination plot, Shukra Raj Joshi was among those convicted for it. For this he was hanged in Teku, with a placard around his neck warning the public that they might meet his fate. There is now a memorial where he died, and a stand-in for the tree that he hanged from, growing at crooked angles on the bustling thoroughfare.

Two members of the Praja Parishad, Dharma Bhakta Mathema and Dasrath Chand, and a member of the Nepal Nagarik Adhikar Samiti, Ganga Lal Shrestha, were also put to death by the maharaja. The historian Rishikesh Shaha has written of their assassinations:

> Dharma Bhakta Mathema, who gave the King lessons in wrestling, was hanged from a tree on the night of 24-25 January 1941, on the road leading to the temple of Pashupatinath. Three nights later, Dasrath Chand and Ganga Lal [Shrestha] were shot to death on the bank of the Bishnumati River on the eastern outskirts of Kathmandu, near the temple of Shobhabhagvati. Their bodies, with bullet marks, were left tied to posts till 12:30 p.m. the next day.

These four men—familiarly called Shukra Raj, Ganga Lal, Dharma Bhakta and Dasrath Chand—we now held up as martyrs for democracy. Two other men—Tanka Prasad Acharya and Ram Hari Sharma—became 'living martyrs': They were sentenced to death, but because they were of the priestly Bahun caste, they could not, by the laws of sanaatan dharma, be killed without incurring great sin. Instead they were publicly disgraced by having their hair shaved off and being paraded through town on mules, before being thrown in jail.

Though these dissidents had allied with King Tribhuvan Bir Bikram Shah in the assassination plot, they were not all monarchists. Already, in the 1940s, there were muffled calls for republicanism in Nepal. Most visibly, the Raktapat Committee, an underground group whose name translates to 'The Bloodshed Committee', was spreading pamphlets that agitated for violence to establish a state free of monarchs and maharajas of any kind.

All this dissent was led by select members of the bourgeoisie, yet it garnered wide popular support. Yogmaya, who could be called Nepal's first woman poet, gives us some indication of how widespread anti-Rana sentiment was at the time. She was a Bahun-caste girl from the Arun valley in east Nepal who was married, and also widowed, while still a child. She then left home to remarry and have a child in nearby Darjeeling, India. Later she returned—with no husband or child to show for herself, and having discarded her caste—to set up a hermitage near her birthplace. There she railed against sanaatan dharma and Juddha Sumshere Jung Bahadur Rana's rule—the 'rule of evil'—in her politically charged poems and prayers:

> Going on pilgrimages to cleanse their sins,
> Tyrants and cheaters rush there to die.
> Earlier they plundered the belongings of the poor,
> Now they pay their expenses with that loot.

She is shown, in a portrait based on her followers' descriptions of her, with a shaven head. Criticizing the caste system, opposing taxes levied on the poor and arguing for the end of child marriage and for the rights of widows to remarry, she issued a moral challenge to the maharaja. Her demand was for 'dharma raj', a divine rule free of the power abuses of religion. In 1940 she and scores of her followers threatened to immolate themselves if the maharaja did not heed their call for dharma raj. Many of her followers were of the priestly Bahun caste; their deaths could shatter the maharaja's moral credibility. He dispatched army troops to arrest them, hoping to prevent their deaths. But when they were released, Yogmaya led sixty-nine of her followers to the fast-flowing waters of the Arun River, where they drowned themselves in protest.

Outside the kingdom, the Second World War exploded, and the maharaja offered additional troops to the British. This time, up to 2,00,000 Nepali men fought for the Allies. Once again they reached the far corners, serving in Iraq, Malaya, Tunisia, Egypt, Cyprus, Italy, Greece, Burma and Assam in India. They saw, alongside the brutality of war, the material, social and political progress of the larger world. Their own kingdom must have seemed to them to be stuck in a different, dark age.

Maharaja Juddha Sumshere Jung Bahadur Rana retired after the war, becoming the first maharaja to willingly give up his post, which too is progress: to resign instead of being overthrown. Some say that his nephews, the sons of Chandra Sumshere Jung Bahadur Rana, had a soothsayer convince him that he had only one year to live, during which time he would do well to devote himself to prayer. (For this or other reasons, a lasting rivalry sprang up between the inheritors of the Juddha and Chandra lines, a rivalry said to explain the queen's dislike of the crown prince's girlfriend, which resulted—so we are told—in the 2001 royal massacre.) Others say the maharaja felt guilty for having put so many dissidents to death, for having killed so many of the Bahun caste. Though as penance he had donated 1,000 cows and distributed gold worth his weight to the poor, he felt burdened by sin.

This maharaja had been roundly unpopular, but it is not that he had done nothing for the country. He extended telephone lines beyond Kathmandu, to the southern Tarai plains. He issued paper money, established the Nepal Bank and began provident funds and pension plans for government employees. He set up the Sundarijal power plant and extended the reach of electricity, which resulted in some progress: a jute mill, two match factories, a cotton mill, a plywood mill, a bobbin factory and rice mills in the southeastern districts of the country. He appointed a government publisher (who also acted, conveniently, as the official censor), allowed a few private schools to be opened, and set up a board to certify school-leaving certificates. During his reign a tuberculosis hospital was built in Tokha, on a hill north of Kathmandu. General hospitals were opened in Lalitpur and Makwanpur Districts, and veterinary doctors were stationed around the country. In 1942, an airplane landed in Nepal for the first time.

On balance, though, this had been all too little too late.

Scattered points of dissent began, in the mid-1940s, to coalesce under the newly forming political parties. Most of these parties were based across the border, in India. In Benares, a committee of the All-India Nepali National Congress came together in 1946 under, among others, Krishna Prasad Bhattarai. The same year, in Darjeeling, former Gurkha soldiers set up the All-India Gorkha Congress. Another, bigger Congress party, the Nepali National Congress, was formed in Calcutta in 1947 with the support of the Indian Congress party. Former Praja Parishad member Ganesh Man Singh—who had made a daring jailbreak from Kathmandu and gone into exile in Calcutta—and the historian Dilli Raman Regmi and the lawyer and writer B. P. Koirala (all democratic heroes of Nepal) were among those who founded this party, the precursor of today's Nepali Congress Party.

The Nepali National Congress elected as its first president the Praja Parishad's head and 'living martyr' Tanka Prasad Acharya, who was still in jail in Nepal. After a few leadership squabbles, party activists set to work, supporting Nepal's first labour strike at the jute mill in Biratnagar town, in the southern Tarai plains. The strike also enjoyed the support of other activists such as

Man Mohan Adhikari, a communist then living in exile in India.

Socialist and communist thinking was spreading rapidly in the country. But among all the political activists of the newly formed parties, the one who most fired the public's imagination was B. P. Koirala. BP: that is how Nepalis know him, by his initials. A legend, a myth, a figure who came to personify Nepal's struggle for democracy in all its courage and compromise.

BP was born into a well-to-do bourgeois family, one with a rebellious bent. His father had opened schools against the state's wishes, and had once, in protest, mailed the rags of a poor man to Maharaja Chandra Sumshere Jung Bahadur Rana. For such deeds he had been forced into exile, and his properties had been confiscated.

The father's ethics had passed on to his progeny. In Benares, from high school on, BP had been involved in India's independence movement, facing arrest several times. He had followed Gandhi's civil disobedience calls and been instrumental in organizing a strike in a mill in Bihar. In the 1930s he moved from his earlier communist politics towards socialism, but his activism remained undiminished—in 1942 he was arrested and sentenced to three years in prison for inciting India's Gurkha soldiers to disobey the British. By the time he came to Nepal in 1947, to help organize the jute mill strike in Biratnagar, he was mature in political vision. The striking labourers were demanding better working conditions, higher wages, health care and drinking water in residential areas. BP championed their cause so effectively that he was arrested and jailed for three months.

This happened during the rule of Padma Sumshere Jung Bahadur Rana—the eighth maharaja and the first of the third generation of Ranas. He had come to power in 1945 on a populist note, saying he wanted to serve the people, and he seemed genuinely liberal. Or maybe he was weak. He wept a lot.

For a Rana he was also poor, and his extended family looked down on him, even suggesting that he supported the political parties. This, because he had relaxed restrictions on King Tribhuvan Bir Bikram Shah's movements and had allowed him to go to Calcutta in 1946 for a health check-up. The king, already a heart patient at age forty, had used this opportunity to secretly meet with the Nepali National Congress. Shortly afterwards, the party, presided by BP's half-brother M. P. Koirala, had launched a civil disobedience campaign throughout Nepal.

Encouraged by this campaign, hundreds of students of the Sanskrit school in Kathmandu demonstrated, demanding better housing, higher wages for teachers and a modern curriculum. Dissent was spreading. Maharaja Padma Sumshere Jung Bahadur Rana wept. As a concession he promulgated the 1948 constitution, and though it protected the Rana family's right to inherit the prime minister's post throughout eternity, it was a constitution nonetheless, Nepal's first. It set up a bicameral legislature—with a national council and a council of courtiers—and a high court. It also made provisions for village, town and district councils.

The Nepali National Congress opposed this constitution; they would settle for nothing less than democracy. But the maharaja was beyond caring what they thought. He went to India, and after some last-minute dithering, resigned.

This ushered in the rule of Mohan Sumshere Jung Bahadur Rana, the last maharaja.

Around this time, in 1949, the Communist Party of Nepal formed in Calcutta, attesting to the hold of radical thought on the popular imagination of Nepalis. Though most of its leaders, like Man Mohan Adhikari and Pushpa Lal Shrestha, were of the bourgeoisie, they espoused revolutionary ideals. The party released its manifesto and had *The Communist Manifesto* translated into

Nepali—a century after its publication in German.

Maharaja Mohan Sumshere Jung Bahadur Rana tried to forge on. He established a National Economic Planning Commission, and signed the Peace and Friendship Treaty and the Trade and Commerce Treaty with newly independent India—treaties on the continued recruitment of Gurkhas to the Indian army and on trade limits, which are both still in effect today. To deal with the growing challenge to his rule, he banned the Nepali National Congress and had BP arrested, but the party continued to operate underground. Then some of the maharaja's own people, freethinking 'C'-class Ranas—Subarna Sumshere Jung Bahadur Rana and Mahabir Sumshere Jung Bahadur Rana—went into exile in Calcutta and formed another Congress party, the Nepali Democratic Congress. In response, the maharaja cracked down on an entirely different party, the Nepal Praja Panchayat party—only to have popular sentiment turn against him, for this other party sought simply to bring the 1948 constitution into practice, a moderate enough goal.

In 1949, BP—imprisoned in an old stable, in conditions that tested his health—began a hunger strike that lasted twenty-nine days, arousing wide public sympathy and winning his release. He immediately went into exile in India, where the Nepali National Congress joined hands with the Nepali Democratic Congress to establish the Nepali Congress Party (the party as it exists today). The party then launched on a violent-if-need-be struggle for democracy.

The Indian Prime Minister Jawaharlal Nehru, who had till then supported the Rana maharajas, crucially switched his support to the political activists at this time. This enabled King Tribhuvan Bir Bikram Shah to force an end to Rana rule, which he did in a dramatic, if not entirely heroic, fashion.

On 5 November 1950, the king, living under constant

surveillance at the Narayanhiti palace, requested the maharaja's permission to attend a picnic and hunting expedition. The maharaja—privately vexed with the king, wondering whether to replace him with his son—granted permission. It was a mere picnic, after all. Taking with him his three sons and his eldest grandson, Birendra Bir Bikram Shah (victim of the June 2001 massacre), the king headed out of the Narayanhiti palace grounds. But instead of proceeding into the wilds, he fled the motorcade to seek shelter in the Indian embassy nearby. This was, let us say, the Shah dynasty's turn at civil disobedience. After four days, Jawaharlal Nehru sent an Indian Air Force jet to fly the royal family to Delhi.

This was quite a slap in the face for the maharaja. Mohan Sumshere Jung Bahadur Rana took the king's remaining grandson, Gyanendra Bir Bikram Shah—today's king—and put him on the throne. (Pictures of the three-year-old king found wide circulation when Gyanendra became king again after the June 2001 massacre.) The legitimacy of the child-king was immediately contested. Leading the popular agitation, three hundred members of the Congress Mukti Sena, the militant wing of the Nepali Congress, launched armed attacks in the southern plains of the Tarai. Then the revolution spread to the hills: Palpa, Gorkha and Pokhara towns fell into rebel hands. With Nehru, too, continuing to recognize the exiled Tribhuvan Bir Bikram Shah as Nepal's rightful king, Maharaja Mohan Sumshere Jung Bahadur Rana eventually had to bow. Envoys went to Delhi to take part in negotiations with the exiled king and the Nepali Congress.

The Communist Party of Nepal, left out in the cold, disapproved of the three-way negotiations, but the Rana maharaja, the Shah king and the Nepali Congress went ahead despite this— all three camps were traditionally hostile towards the communists anyway. The compromise they reached gave the Ranas and the

Nepali Congress five seats each in a ten-person interim cabinet. This cabinet was meant to set up a constituent assembly, which would then promulgate a democratic constitution and hold elections for Nepal's first democratic government.

On 15 February 1951, after his three-month exile in Delhi, King Tribhuvan Bir Bikram Shah returned to Kathmandu to claim the throne as a constitutional monarch in a democratic system.

THE HAZE

What went wrong after that is anybody's guess. Not really. But that is how it feels, because most books on Nepal's history conclude with the happy ending: *And so democracy was won!* The reasons why the king took back absolute power ten years later are lost in a haze of speculation. The political parties were unprepared to govern, some say. Others say that the king, his family and courtiers undermined democracy, schemed for its downfall. With the Ranas out of the way, they had no further use for the Nepali Congress. Some also say that Nepal just wasn't ready for democracy. Their implication, of course, is that it still isn't.

The period from 1951 to 1960 saw nine short-lived governments. The former maharaja, Mohan Sumshere Jung Bahadur Rana, served as the prime minister of the first government, the Rana-Nepali-Congress interim government of 1951. But there was no love lost between the Ranas and the Nepali Congress politicians. BP, serving as the home minister, eyed with particular suspicion a newly formed conservative party called the Bir Gorkha Dal, which supported the Ranas. In an unfortunate misstep, he invoked the Public Security Ordinance to arrest this party's members, and riots erupted as followers of the Bir Gorkha Dal attacked BP's house. The Congress Mukti Sena retaliated violently. In the melee, the Nepali Congress leaders had to seek shelter in the Narayanhiti palace, allowing the king to play the role of their arbiter. Then—in a move that acknowledged the influence of India's ministry of external affairs upon the king himself—BP and Mohan Sumshere Jung Bahadur Rana went to Delhi for arbitration by Jawaharlal Nehru.

Upon returning to Nepal, the Ranas and the Nepali Congress continued to clash, even as an alliance of other parties began to protest the Public Security Ordinance. To end all this Rana-Congress feuding, the king set up an advisory committee consisting overwhelmingly of Nepali Congress and independent politicians. He apparently forgot to consult the prime minister before doing so, however. The Ranas and the Nepali Congress clashed over this; they clashed over the death of a young man in a student demonstration; they clashed till BP finally resigned, appealing to citizens to complete the democratic revolution. The interim government collapsed.

This ended Mohan Sumshere Jung Bahadur Rana's nine months as prime minister and the rule, extraordinary or ordinary, of the Rana clan.

The next government also lasted nine months. Because BP had stirred controversy by invoking the Public Security Ordinance, and because his half-brother M. P. Koirala was more comfortable with the king's pro-India bent, Tribhuvan Bir Bikram Shah appointed M. P. Koirala the prime minister this time.

M. P. Koirala had not come from nowhere; every bit as politically engaged as his brother, he had become president of the party when his brother was jailed, and he still held the post. (Altogether three Koirala brothers—BP, MP and GP—would serve as Nepali Congress prime ministers over the years.) But as soon as his half-brother became prime minister, BP challenged his legitimacy. The squabbling between the two brothers eventually caused the Nepali Congress to splinter into the Leftist Nepali Congress, the Nepali People's Congress and the Nepali National Congress, diminishing the party in the eyes of the public. But BP—a democratic socialist in the Nehruvian mould—was adamant. He saw his half-brother's appointment as evidence of royal meddling, and he would not cooperate.

Meanwhile, the demand for liberty and equality was growing. In the countryside, the poor were also taking to leftist ideology. The first labour union, as well as the first labour strike in the government, had already been organized; now, land uprisings were spreading from Dang and Dhangadi to the other far-western communities. Traditional social hierarchies, too, were toppling. The traditional ruling caste—the Chettri-caste Ranas and Shahs—were now sharing political power with the caste that controlled the political parties, the Bahuns. But the scores of long-ruled ethnic nationalities wished to be free of both Chettri- and Bahun-caste domination.

Their wish was expressed when, in 1952, the Raksha Dal, a contingent of the government's armed police, mutinied, capturing Singha Durbar, the airport, the Radio Nepal station, Nakkhu jail and several government offices. They had done so to release from prison two advocates of the independence of ethnic Rai and Limbu people—collectively called the Kirants—as well as K. I. Singh, a communist leader and anti-India nationalist. The Raksha Dal mutiny was suppressed by the end of the day, but by this time K. I. Singh had fled for Tibet. Prime Minister M. P. Koirala responded by banning the secessionist Kiranti organization, the All-Nepal Rastriya Mahasabha. For good measure he also banned the Communist Party of Nepal. Both bans would only inflame popular resentment.

Through this, the Koirala brothers kept squabbling. The first meeting of Parliament—consisting of members nominated by the king—adjourned when BP criticized the king's speech. The Parliament never met again. Within the Nepali Congress, BP eventually unseated his half-brother as the president, arguing that the same man should not be both prime minister and party president. Relations between the brothers grew so acrid that Jawaharlal Nehru urged them to make peace, and the Indian socialist leader Jayaprakash Narayan even took them to Poona to help them resolve their differences, but to no end.

BP eventually had M. P. Koirala suspended from the Nepali Congress, whereupon the latter formed his own party. Then he resigned from the prime minister's post. The king briefly appointed a Royal Councillor's Regime to govern the land, and then, on 15 June 1953, he reappointed M. P. Koirala as prime minister of the third 'democratic' government.

Nothing had come of the original plan to elect a constituent assembly to draft a new constitution. By default the country moved, instead, towards holding regular elections.

The first municipal elections took place in September 1953 in Kathmandu. Seventy-three candidates vied for the 56,000 votes for eighteen seats for ward councillor. It came as a massive surprise that the banned Communist Party of Nepal won six seats, rivalling the country's oldest party, the Praja Parishad. The Nepali Congress won only three seats. M. P. Koirala's party, the Rastriya Praja Parishad, managed two seats and the Gorkha Parishad one. Alarmed by the communists' popularity, the non-communist parties formed a league of democrats—but, typically, the league broke down amid spats.

King Tribhuvan Bir Bikram Shah was meanwhile becoming infirm (government documents later blamed the unruliness of democratic politics for weakening his heart). During his 1954 medical visits to India and France, he entrusted Prime Minister

M. P. Koirala with the task of setting up a broad-based government. M. P. Koirala promptly inducted into government members of his own party, of the Praja Parishad, and of two splinter Congress parties. He even inducted an independent. But he left out members of the Nepal Communist Party, still under ban, and also of BP's Nepali Congress.

BP led a series of protests. His party rallied against the curtailment of the Supreme Court's power, against the Koshi River Treaty with India and against Indian interference in Nepal's internal affairs. The ailing king, desperate to be done with such querulousness, set up an Advisory Assembly—the second such assembly, a make-do Parliament—composed of a more inclusive smattering of parties. But this turned out to be a cantankerous group. Meetings were unruly, with temper tantrums thrown all around. BP's Nepali Congress boycotted the assembly altogether, preferring to foment popular discontent from outside the government. In 1955 it launched a nationwide protest.

The king left with his family for heart surgery in Switzerland. Two months later he sent back Crown Prince Mahendra Bir Bikram Shah, and through a radio announcement informed the public that he had vested his powers in his son.

The crown prince was thirty-five at the time. He was a strong-willed man: He had once handed in abdication papers in order to marry a second wife (after his first wife's death) against his father's wishes. BP, then home minister, had refused the abdication papers and had patched up the quarrel between father and son.

The first thing the crown prince did was accept the resignation of Prime Minister M. P. Koirala. He promised to personally oversee several government offices, and in a public speech, he berated the political parties: It was a matter of shame, he said, that in the past four years the country had not mustered up four accomplishments to boast of.

He was not a man to brook muddling, Mahendra Bir Bikram Shah. He became the ninth Shah king when his father died in Switzerland on 13 March 1955. Two months later, instead of appointing another prime minister, he effected direct rule, appointing five advisers to guide him. This was 'democratic' government number four.

The political parties protested fiercely against the king's direct rule, but Mahendra Bir Bikram Shah proceeded unhindered. He sent delegates to the Bandung Conference; he passed a series of dictates on land reform, tillers' rights, interest rates and land taxes. To restore some glory to the Shah dynasty, he set conservative intellectuals on the task of re-imagining Nepal as one nation under a Hindu god-king, ethnically diverse and yet unified by a single language—the Nepali language. Suddenly Nepal was a proud nation of Gurkha warriors wielding khukuris, a country that had never ceded its independence to Britain or India. It boosted the new king's image that the country was granted United Nations membership in 1955 (it had been trying to get this for decades). The king established ties with China, and toured India. A year later, he appointed Tanka Prasad Acharya of the Praja Parishad as the prime minister—sidestepping other more popular political leaders—and set up a council of ministers from the same party.

There was so much to do. Government number five swung into action, opening the Nepal Rastriya Bank, stabilizing the exchange rate between the Indian and Nepali rupees, vesting the Supreme Court with independent rights and organizing government work into distinct sectors such as education, health, forestry, agriculture, engineering, administration, foreign affairs and royal palace affairs. Nepal joined the World Postal Union. The government lifted the ban on the Communist Party of Nepal. The national dairy was opened, as was the first diesel powerhouse. The government launched the first five-year plan, aimed at building infrastructure: roads, airports, transport and communication lines. The king himself travelled in high plebeian mode to Bhairahawa, Biratnagar, Butwal, Lumbini, Pokhara, Doti, Dhangadi, Dadeldhura, Baitadi and Dipayal to get in touch with his subjects.

But the political parties excluded from government kept naysaying, and even ministers of the favoured Praja Parishad were asking why the king was omnipotent in a purportedly democratic government. So Prime Minister Tanka Prasad Acharya outlawed all criticism of the king in print. When demonstrations broke out over food shortages, the prime minister denounced the people as hooligans. When the political parties demanded parliamentary elections, the prime minister declared that people preferred the direct rule of the king. The political parties reacted angrily to this. Tanka Prasad Acharya resigned. He had been in office a mere six months.

The next government, the sixth, had an even briefer tenure. The prime minister this time was, astonishingly, the communist leader who had been let out of jail in the Raksha Dal mutiny three years ago: K. I. Singh. His anti-India views found favour in Mahendra Bir Bikram Shah's court, which was staunchly nationalist, in contrast to his father's pro-India court. Still, why choose K. I. Singh when there were more obvious leaders around, like, for instance, BP? The Nepali Congress viewed the king with great mistrust, a mistrust that was quite mutual.

Not surprisingly, K. I. Singh could not garner any support from the other political parties. So he pressed on alone, till, four months on, he passed a rule that the Nepali language was to be the medium of instruction in all schools, and announced a delay in parliamentary elections. With these two acts he became so thoroughly unpopular that the king dismissed him and once again effected direct rule.

By now a variety of Congress parties had formed a democratic front against the king's rule. Though outside this front, the Communist Party of Nepal too was calling for parliamentary elections. (The original plan to elect a constituent assembly had been forgotten by now.) The king finally relented. In May 1958 he appointed the eighth 'democratic' government under a new prime minister, Subarna Sumshere Jung Bahadur Rana, asking him to carry out parliamentary elections. Meanwhile, the king also set a hand-picked commission consisting of two members of the Nepali Congress, one member of the Gorkha Parishad and a constitutional expert from Britain (which famously has no constitution) to draft a new constitution for the country.

The constitution that resulted was quasi-democratic. It provided for the basic bourgeois liberties—freedoms of speech, religion, political belief—and upheld the right to equality among citizens. It set up a system for bicameral representation with a council of ministers, an institutionalized administration system, an independent judiciary and an auditor general's office. Yet it also acknowledged the ultimate supremacy of the king, whom it placed above the law and to whom it gave the role of heading the army. Provisions were also made for the declaration of a state of emergency and for the king to take over should the government fail.

This 'democratic' constitution was promulgated in February 1959, as the parliamentary election got under way. Seven hundred and eighty-six candidates from eight political parties ran for 109 seats throughout the country in what was Nepal's first nationwide exercise of democracy. Voting lasted two months due to the difficulty of transporting ballot boxes to and from remote areas. This time it was the Communist Party of Nepal's turn to be surprised: Only four of its candidates won. Seventy-four of the winning candidates were from BP's Nepali Congress. The Nepal

National Gorkha Parishad had nineteen winning candidates. One woman alone was elected to Parliament. Roughly 30 per cent of those elected were of Chettri caste and 35 per cent of Bahun caste.

There was no longer any denying the Nepali Congress's right to govern. King Mahendra Bir Bikram Shah established government number nine, Nepal's first truly democratic government, in 1959. This time B. P. Koirala was the prime minister.

BP. Two years later he was jailed on King Mahendra Bir Bikram Shah's orders. His democratic socialism had angered the centuries. In a period of two years he raised new taxes; scrapped the age-old birta system of granting tax-exempt land to favoured families of the Ranas; and ended the system of rajautas, or 'minor kings', that granted the families of ancient kings the right to raise taxes and settle disputes in their former kingdoms. He nationalized the forests after some wrangling over compensation rates with the king's brothers, who were timber contractors; he enforced the use of Nepali currency; and he promoted industrialization.

All this harmed the interests of the traditional elite. But BP's government did what governments are supposed to do: It instituted administrative reform, opened schools, added a master's programme to the Tribhuvan University, built drinking-water taps and irrigation systems, started international flights, set up 15,000 phone lines and a network for radio communication, designated land for the landless and made provisions to house Tibetan refugees. The Indian Prime Minister Jawaharlal Nehru visited Nepal and the two countries signed an agreement on the Gandaki River. BP went to China and signed agreements on financial aid and the demarcation of the border. Nepal appointed a representative to the UN, and set up diplomatic relations with fourteen countries.

Yet, there was trouble. Over the previous decade the Nepali people had felt let down, for 'democracy'—or rather the long interregnum of attempted democracy—had delivered them little. Their disappointment was easily manipulated by the traditional elite, who vociferously opposed the eradication of tax-exempt lands and other age-old privileges. Confrontations were staged in eastern Nepal as high-caste Hindus lashed out against the increasingly assertive ethnic nationalities. In the far-western regions, conservatives were calling for a return to the rule of the kings who had predated Prithvi Narayan Shah. Orthodox Hindu leaders such as Yogi Narahari Nath were demanding to cede from the secularist central government, leading violent anti-democracy demonstrations in Gorkha District. Groups of landowning farmers were agitating against the parliamentary system, petitioning the king to take over and protect their landholdings. Similar unrest was taking place in Dang, Baglung and Nepalgunj: Conservative voices were being orchestrated into a call for a royal takeover.

The Nepali Congress had not foreseen this backlash. To make matters worse, shortsighted party members who had been denied minister posts were criticizing the government vocally, threatening to splinter the party. In the villages the richer landlords and moneylenders had joined the Nepali Congress, and they were harassing rival communist-sympathizers, creating disillusionment among the politically neutral masses. In Kathmandu, BP, unfortunately, was now the president of his party in addition to being the prime minister, exactly what he had once opposed his half-brother M. P. Koirala for being. The party itself was not democratic in its working style. The Koirala family was monopolizing power. And some party members, including Tulsi Giri and Biswabandhu Thapa, were covertly working for the king.

The other parties were in equal disarray. Because M. P. Koirala had previously banned them, and BP had not spoken against this, the Communist Party of Nepal often viewed the Nepali Congress as a bigger enemy than the king. It began agitating against the

ruling party's import of clarified vegetable butter, and the Nepal-
India treaty on the Gandaki River. The party's general secretary,
Keshar Jung Rayamajhi (who was serving as the chairperson of
the Royal State Council at the time of the 2001 royal massacre),
was also secretly reporting to the king.

Emboldened by the information passed on by his plants in
the political parties, and confident of his strong standing, King
Mahendra Bir Bikram Shah invoked the powers vested in him
by the 1959 constitution to effect a coup, now called the 'royal
coup'. He dissolved BP's government on 15 December 1960,
explaining in a radio address that he had been forced to do so to
stop corruption. Army troops arrested BP at an open-air meeting
at Tundikhel in the heart of Kathmandu. Over ninety people,
mostly members of the Nepali Congress, were jailed within a
week. A month later the king had banned all political parties in
order to set up the Panchayat government. BP was to remain in
jail for the next eight years.

THE MONARCH TAKES A STAB AT DEMOCRACY

The Narayanhiti royal palace where the Shah kings live today was
built in the late 1960s by Pock and Chatterjee, an architecture
firm based in Calcutta. It was built in a self-consciously 'Nepali'
style, reflecting King Mahendra Bir Bikram Shah's nationalism.
Eschewing the gilded excesses of the Rana era, it adopts a
common touch. Its plain brick facade signals the era's populism,
and acknowledges that the masses matter, that equality must be
alluded to symbolically, even by a king, for it is demanded by
the times: I am of you; I am like you; I represent you. But
the building does not give up Rana-era marble or Malla-era
woodwork, for it is a palace, after all. While its glass front alludes
to scientific-materialist twentieth-century progress, its pagoda roof

hearkens to kingdoms past, kingdoms in which palaces are not just palaces, but also shrines enjoying divine sanction.

In front of the palace is a wide avenue lined with shops, boutiques, travel agencies, banks, restaurants and hotels. Urban sophisticates—who sometimes find the tourist district a bit downmarket—flock here for lunch, sampling cheeseburgers, soba, daal makhni and pizzas. The boutiques boast everything from embroidered chiffon saris to Nike shorts, and tourism-industry T-shirts with five hairy beasts: yak yak yak yak yak. Everything from Shiatsu massages to haute couture to pricey antiques can be found here.

Past the commercial stretch stands a statue of King Mahendra Bir Bikram Shah, in full regalia. This statue is carefully guarded nowadays by armed policemen. Demonstrations—other than those staged by Hindu groups—are not allowed anywhere near it. Democrats and Maoists alike would be likely to target this statue. In 1990, during the People's Movement to restore democracy, protestors were shot down for climbing the statue to deck it with a garland of shoes. Pictures of this time show men exuberantly clambering atop the statue minutes before they were cut down by bullets. If one was to believe, as King Mahendra Bir Bikram Shah had claimed, that the Panchayat system was indeed a democracy— only of a unique and indigenous kind—then these men had died for no reason at all.

What was the Panchayat system? Put this question to Nepalis today and we will each offer our own answers. People are divided as to whether Mahendra Bir Bikram Shah's royal coup was a self-serving act on the part of a dictator or whether it was justified on grounds of national interest. Panchayat apologists will say that the political parties were forever bickering. The endless stirrings and uprisings of the people would have led to disintegration, inviting a takeover by India (this is what many Nepalis say even now: Only the king can unite us against big brother India). And anyway, they argue, Panchayat *was* a democracy, a 'one-party democracy' of the style of communist countries, except that the single party in power was not communist but monarchist. This was no one-size-fits-all Western parliamentary democracy, but a unique 'guided' variety, because really, how could parliamentary democracy work in a country like ours? Poor people need food and shelter and security; we need development, not freedom.

Democrats will argue that Panchayat was a regression to kingdoms past. It re-established medieval courts rife with intrigue; it stifled fledgling civil liberties and aborted nascent civil institutions. Mahendra Bir Bikram Shah used the Panchayat to turn Nepali citizens back into subjects. It made the country languish and made us all lose years.

The Panchayat system was instituted almost two years after the royal coup, in 1962, with a new constitution. Hoping to one-up the political parties by being more democratic than they, the king had the new constitution set up over 3,000 village assemblies, called village panchayats (or town panchayats in urban areas). This remains the blueprint for the structure of government today. Village panchayats elected members to seventy-five district-level panchayats. These district panchayats in turn elected members to fourteen zonal councils. From the members of these zonal councils, ninety were elected to the national-level 125-seat Parliament, called the National Panchayat. In addition, there were also 'class organizations' at the district and national levels—consisting of a women's organization, a youth organization, a peasants' organization, a workers' organization, an ex-servicemen's organization and a graduates' organization—and they elected nineteen members to the National Panchayat. The king directly appointed sixteen additional members to it, including the prime minister. And he retained absolute power—not least over the Royal Nepal Army. Despite this, the Panchayat system was the most inclusive structure of government that Nepal had had till then.

Mahendra Bir Bikram Shah was the only smart king after Prithvi Narayan Shah; whether or not they agree with his politics, people will grant him that. Foiling an assassination attempt and simmering opposition, he enlisted the help of newly educated 'technocrats'—officials with specialized knowledge—to launch a project of national development. For development, not democracy, was the king's line; development was his excuse for doing away with democracy.

Foreign aid, which had just begun as an industry around the world, supported the king's vision. Suddenly the government's entire focus turned to the development of small farmers, the development of forest resources, the development of cooperatives and development through industrialization. Banking and foreign exchange would develop Nepal. Tourism would develop Nepal (members of the royal family were among the first to open hotels and casinos). Big dams and hydroelectricity would develop us, for the rivers were white gold.

The logic for all this development work was paternalistic. In a country of subjects, an ethos of charity prevailed: The government must serve the poor. Much money was spent on building roads and transportation systems. There were plans to open health posts and build schools. Primary health care and family planning programmes were launched.

Not least of what the king wanted to develop was a national identity. One of the most enduring legacies of this period was the wilful re-imagining of a common Nepali identity. Conservative intellectuals set to writing histories vilifying the Ranas—the former maharajas-cum-prime ministers—and glorifying the

Shah dynasty. Prithvi Narayan Shah's description of the country as 'a garden of four castes and thirty-six ethnicities' filled the government-issue textbooks, though it grossly misrepresented the country's diversity. The king opened the Royal Nepal Academy, inviting ethnic Nepali singers and writers from Darjeeling, Sikkim and Assam in India to infuse the country with modern forms that were nonetheless very Nepali. A Nepali-language literary canon was invented, with the nineteenth-century Khas-language poet Bhanubhakta Acharya heralded—falsely—as the country's 'first poet'. The king himself wrote songs under the pseudonym M. B. B. Shah, and these songs were broadcast ad nauseum over Radio Nepal. (Meanwhile, BP's novels, some of which rank among the best of Nepali literature, were banned.) The king also encouraged games and sports to engender national unity.

The 1967 Gaun Farka Rastriya Abhiyan, or the 'Return to the Village National Campaign', enforced a comprehensive indoctrination of Panchayat philosophy. The king had by then co-opted most of the agendas of the banned political parties. He had revised the Muluki Ain or Law of the Country and abolished the caste system, and had, in a land reform act, superseded BP's earlier land reform measures.

He was intelligent, Mahendra Bir Bikram Shah. He was stylish as well. He wore sunglasses at night (to hide his crossed eyes, some sniggered). His Panchayat courtiers tried to curry favour by mimicking him, absurdly wearing sunglasses at evening soirées.

THE STATE OF SCHIZOPHRENIA

By the time King Mahendra Bir Bikram Shah died in 1972, and his son, the tenth Shah king, Birendra Bir Bikram Shah—the king killed in the June 2001 massacre—came to the throne, a chasm had opened between the official and underground realities of Nepal.

The political parties were all banned. At the start of the '70s, BP had been let out of jail, and he had gone to live in India, from where he was heading an exile movement to restore democracy. The country's youth, especially in the politically charged college campuses, were itching for change. In August 1972, under BP's leadership, students at the Tribhuvan University launched a hunger strike, and a hundred armed sympathizers of the Nepali Congress killed a policeman in the eastern Tarai plains. The communist movement too was gaining appeal among the youth. One faction of the endlessly splintering Communist Party of Nepal, led by the brothers R. K. and C. P. Mainali, launched a violent campaign in 1972, killing a family of landlords in the eastern Tarai before retracting from the policy of violence.

It was an insubordinate time. In 1973 Durga Subedi and other Nepali Congress activists hijacked a Royal Nepal Airlines Corporation plane and made off with 30 million Indian rupees to finance their democracy struggle. Other armed attacks led by the Nepali Congress continued, and an assassination attempt took place against the king in 1974. Meanwhile, the communist movement—now divided between the 'Peking' and 'Russia' schools—gave birth to a new party called the Communist Party of Nepal (Fourth Convention), which soon eclipsed the old Communist Party of Nepal.

The Panchayat government did not, for its part, lack for supporters. Sikkim's annexation by India in 1974 (aided by the country's democratically elected Parliament, which voted to hand over its sovereignty) greatly helped to boost the power of the monarchists in Nepal. They now told the nation, over and over: *If Mahendra Bir Bikram Shah hadn't rescued us from the political parties, they would have handed the country to India.*

The new king was himself affable. He was not, like his father, shrewd. He had studied at Eton and audited classes at Harvard and

Tokyo University, but he came off as a well-meaning simpleton, a bit like a placid pot head. In contrast to his wife, née Rana, he dressed humbly, and sometimes even wore old, patched clothes. His easy ways did endear him to the public, but his politics could be bafflingly inconstant.

In response to all the opposition to the Panchayat system, the king appointed a Reform Commission in 1975, but instead of liberalizing the Panchayat system, the reforms revived the Return to the Village National Campaign, by now despised as an instrument of Panchayat indoctrination. The reforms also handed the king the power to monitor government elections. Had the king really intended these mock reforms? Or was he being manipulated by hardliners? One growing theory was that a clique within the palace—led by the king's brothers, Gyanendra and Dhirendra Bir Bikram Shah, and Queen Aishwarya Rajyalaksmi Shah—was checking the king's liberal inclinations. Dubbed the 'bhoomigat giroha', or the 'underground gang', this hard-line clique was so shadowy an entity that it may not even have existed. But most people believed it did. Was it steering the king to the right? It was hard for the public to say.

In late 1976 B. P. Koirala and fellow Nepali Congress leader Ganesh Man Singh decided to return to Nepal to continue their agitation from their homeland. They were arrested upon arrival. Had the king really intended to do this? No one could tell.

Little of the political dissent of the Panchayat era was apparent on the surface. To the world, Nepal looked like an idyll. Cat Stevens was famously singing about Kathmandu, tourists were flocking to the low-budget guest houses and hash dens of Freak Street, and starry-eyed dharma seekers were gathering around their chosen gurus at the temples and monasteries. The Nepal in which the banned political parties were trying to wrest power out of the king's hands remained invisible to the untrained eye, to all those who did not know how to look for them.

It wasn't just foreign visitors who misread the country. The myths of the Panchayat era had so confounded the Nepali bourgeoisie that they, too, could not see the truth clearly any more. I, for one, growing up in a stock bourgeois family in Kathmandu, lacked the tools to decipher the signs of dissent simmering not far below the surface. I heard about BP, though who exactly he was and why everyone was in awe of him I did not know. When I heard about the violence of the communists, who had been inspired by communists in Naxalbari, India, I foolishly inferred that Naxal, a neighbourhood in Kathmandu, was somehow dangerous to visit. I never heard of the Nepal Communist Party (Fourth Convention) in its heyday. I did hear—at the Jesuit convent school that I attended—that the communists would behead me and my classmates because that was what they did to children who had been privileged enough to go to school, especially a private one. All this spotty information confused me very much.

This was not entirely my fault: BP was eventually stricken with cancer, and sent twice by the king to the United States for treatment, though BP was—wasn't he?—against the king. In 1978, BP was acquitted of treason charges in a proceeding that was—wasn't it?—more or less a mock trial. When people talked about all this (or whispered about it, as they tended to), I felt like I was hearing secrets that no one must know about, but that, for some reason, everyone did know about.

In this closed atmosphere, Kathmandu grew schizophrenic. The old and the new, the agrarian and the urban, the low-tech and the high-tech, the local and the global began to press together at jagged angles. Yet, though everyone lived in great proximity to each other and knew something about everyone else, nobody could stand back and see the whole picture, nobody could ascertain the truth. All our facts were partial, and so our judgements were suspect. What convictions we held, we held tentatively. We could not fully trust ourselves.

Neither could we trust each other. The Kathmandu of the 1970s was teeming with alleged intelligence agents, or people reputed to be such: 'CIDs', they were called, or Central Intelligence Department employees. They were said to inform on dissidents, who could suffer repression, including police harassment, arbitrary arrest, detention without trial, mental and physical torture and disappearance. Most prisoners in Nepal, even today, do not have access to lawyers. Torture is still the norm in custody. In Panchayat times, it was a matter of course for the police to lash detainees with wet stinging nettles (the sting being more potent when wet); to cake them in sugar and release red ants on them; to make them inhale burned chillies; to constrain them in wooden leg stocks; to beat them with heated bamboo or plastic pipes; to beat or burn the soles of their feet; to give them electric shocks; and to make them squat in a demeaning, awkward position known, by all schoolchildren punished in like manner, as the 'chicken' position. This was in addition to the more common methods that the police used: beating, raping, threatening, strangling, near-drowning, ripping out nails or pushing pins under them, forcing detainees to perform impossible physical tasks, or hanging them upside down, subjecting them to sodomy.

And so we instinctively lowered our voices when we spoke of the government, our eyes scanned the doors and windows, and we resorted to euphemisms and codes. So unsafe did people feel about expressing dissent, we developed layers and layers of personae, revealing only those layers that the situation called for. Our beliefs seemed to shift and alter and mutate as we perfected the art of dissembling, because we ourselves were not certain of anything.

What we lost was the habit of seeking out the truth. The bourgeoisie of Kathmandu mingled with the lesser royals and high-society Ranas and the courtiers—ministers, high-level bureaucrats and middling officers—all equally uncertain as to what, in our society, was real. It was only the political activists—and the dissident left/liberal intellectuals who supported them—who saw things somewhat clearly. They lived, after all, on the dark side of the state. They could not be fooled by its surface idyll.

A boom in the population had, by now, turned Nepal into a demographically very young country, with half the population below the age of twenty. In the end the youth would force a change. By the late 1970s, the political parties had set up underground student unions in Tribhuvan University's campuses throughout the country, and their student activists were creating a groundswell of pro-democracy sentiment. To check them, the government set up a student union of its own, the Rastriya Swatantra Bidyarthi Mandal, many of whose most thuggish members, known derisively as 'mandalays', were on the dole of the government's National Sports Council.

The mandalays began to clash with student activists demanding freer access to higher education. In 1979, Zulfikar Ali Bhutto's hanging in Pakistan sparked an all-out student protest. Activists of the Nepali Congress and the 'Moscow' and 'Peking' communist factions massed before the embassy of Pakistan to protest the hanging, only to suffer brutal retaliation by the mandalays and the police. This retaliation spurred nationwide demonstrations. In the end the king conceded greater access to higher education.

The 'Peking' faction of the communists held out, though, for reforms to the entire Panchayat system. Riots erupted in Kathmandu, and student activists burned the office of the government-owned *Gorkhapatra* newspaper and set cars on fire outside the office of the Royal Nepal Airlines Corporation. Schools and campuses all over the country were forced shut by a series of strikes. Public revolt was the most widespread it had been since the 1950s.

King Birendra Bir Bikram Shah could have chosen to suppress them. He bowed, instead, to the students' demands, announcing on 24 May 1979 that the government would hold a referendum, the first and only in Nepal. The people could vote either to retain the Panchayat system or to opt for multiparty democracy.

This announcement was greeted with vast elation. The bourgeoisie thought: Our king is benevolent after all! But immediately afterwards, the king began to campaign in favour of Panchayat by making populist gestures that promised more than they would deliver. He started by scrapping the unpopular Return to the Village National Campaign, and appointing reformist Surya Bahadur Thapa as prime minister.

Surya Bahadur Thapa is credited with—or blamed for— defeating multiparty democracy in the referendum. His government announced that should the Panchayat system win, the king's absolute power would be curtailed. The referendum date was set for May 1980: A yellow box on the ballot paper would stand for Panchayat and a blue box would stand for multiparty democracy. 'The colour of the sky is blue, the colour of perspiration is blue,' a dissident song of the day went; the government promptly banned it. BP, who was ailing, was forbidden from leaving Kathmandu as the referendum date neared. Barely a month before voting, the king declared an amnesty for all political prisoners.

Unlike the government, the banned political parties enjoyed no state resources with which to campaign. They had to conduct their campaigns underground, and in a sketchy, disorganized manner. It did not help that the parties were also all hopelessly divided; the old squabbles continued even as ever new ones kept erupting. Within the Nepali Congress, BP had by now become so moderate as to seem morally compromised, and was being challenged by the fiery leader Ganesh Man Singh. The ever-splintering communist movement, meanwhile, had given rise to the new Nepal Communist Party (Marxist-Leninist), which was now overtaking the Nepal Communist Party (Fourth Convention). Despite this, the political parties looked poised to win.

Yet in May 1980, the Nepali people voted by 54 per cent for the new, improved Panchayat. Though the elections were largely held to be rigged, BP accepted the result, further tarnishing his image as being compromise-minded. Ganesh Man Singh and other Nepali Congress and communist leaders did not accept the result. But the result stood.

After the referendum the king's powers were slightly curtailed. He no longer appointed the prime minister; instead, the prime minister was elected by the National Panchayat, whose members themselves were elected directly from their constituencies for the first time (instead of passing through the village–district–regional tiers). The National Panchayat was also made accountable to the prime minister, and not just to the king. However, ultimate power was still granted to the king, and the newly formed Panchayat Niti Tatha Janchbujh Samiti, or 'Panchayat Policy and Evaluation Committee', gave the monarch arbitrary power to investigate anyone he wanted.

A deep gloom crept over the bourgeoisie. Why was the king always so inconstant? Had he come under the sway of the palace's 'underground gang'? In the public imagination, the underground gang became responsible for almost everything that was going wrong with the country.

For much was going wrong. The referendum had brought to light the political agitation that lay hidden beneath the country's surface. In 1981, in the elections that made Surya Bahadur Thapa the first elected prime minister of the Panchayat era, the underground political parties also fielded independent candidates, with the hope of infiltrating the National Panchayat. But the palace, too, fielded royalist candidates. The resulting National Panchayat was rife with hostility between the independents and the royalists.

The political parties' policy of infiltrating the government was not without its critics. After BP died of cancer in 1982, the Nepali Congress leadership passed on to Ganesh Man Singh, K. P. Bhattarai and G. P. Koirala, all of whom preferred to oppose the Panchayat from outside. The communist parties, too, argued bitterly over whether to oppose the Panchayat from within or from outside.

Addled by the split within the palace (with its liberal king and the hard-line underground gang), the split in the National Panchayat (with its independents and royalists), and the splits in the political parties (with their pro- and anti-infiltration policies), the bourgeoisie found it impossible to know who was doing what and why and to what end.

In 1985, bombs exploded at the gates of the Narayanhiti palace, at Singha Durbar and in Hotel de l'Annapurna, which was owned by the king's sister. Some said that the Nepali Congress was behind the bombings; others credited one of the smaller communist parties, the Janabadi Morcha. The Janabadi Morcha leader Ramraja Prasad Singh even claimed responsibility for the bombing, but then rumours spread that he had been paid to confess: The palace's hard-line underground gang wanted to deny the Nepali Congress, who had really been behind the bombings, any credit for it. A host of conspiracy theories burgeoned after a colleague of Ramraja Prasad Singh was murdered only days after publicly stating that he didn't believe that his colleague had been behind the bombing. Ramraja Prasad Singh was himself meted a death sentence, but later granted amnesty. So, what were the 1985 bombings about? Ask your average Kathmandu bourgeoisie today. You will receive a variety of answers.

The iconoclastic poet Bhupi Sherchan has written:

> These deities digging up dirt in the middle of the streets
> these people who understand yet remain dumb
> this earthquake-stricken shrine and
> these jagged temple roofs
> these lords who stand as statues at the intersections:
> when I see all this
> always here always like this always the same
> —my history of windstorms seems wrong to me.

Every event of the mid-1980s came with endless interpretations, explanations and theories, but with few certainties.

THE POLITICAL ACTIVISTS RESCUE
THE BOURGEOISIE FROM ABSOLUTE MONARCHY

Through the 1980s the Kathmandu bourgeoisie grew in numbers, but they had few options for financial betterment. The private sector operated under tight restrictions, with the king's relatives owning shares in the country's most lucrative industries and businesses. Queen Aishwarya Rajyalaksmi Shah headed the Social Services National Coordination Council, which controlled all foreign funds that came to non-government organizations. The king's brothers headed semi-government trusts and the king's sisters controlled much charity work.

Sixty per cent of the national budget came from foreign grants and loans. (The figure is just as high today.) The most able and well connected of the graduates in the workforce joined non-government organizations, coining slogans that could attract foreign funds. One after another slogan was bandied about on women's rights, children's rights, family planning, awareness-building, irrigation, adult literacy, electrification, small-loan schemes, immunization, legal education, toilet construction. (The catchphrases of today are 'social inclusion' and 'conflict resolution'.) The international donors heard what they wanted to hear, and paid up.

But even combined, the government, business and non-government sectors could not offer adequate employment, and so the Panchayat system became increasingly despised. Its own apologists were sparring with each other by now. Around the Panchayat's twenty-fifth anniversary in 1986, the National Panchayat was split between Surya Bahadur Thapa's and Lokendra Bahadur Chand's factions. Dispirited officials were giving themselves over to corruption as one after another scandal erupted in the government.

Television came to Kathmandu in 1985, and the brick-and-concrete homes of the valley erected antennae on their roofs to show their neighbours that they had a TV set (even when they did not). Nepal Television's programming was crude, but its overall effect was to connect the bourgeoisie to the larger world, or at least to a sense of the larger world. Kathmandu's streets emptied during evening transmission hours as families, and sometimes entire neighbourhoods, gathered around to watch the Hindi tele-serial *Mahabharata*. How to wade through the ethical quagmires of a kingdom gone wrong? The convoluted epic fired the Hindu imagination.

Afterwards, on the news, the king's activities hogged the headlines, even when all he had done that day was to, say, inaugurate a public tap. The international news came last, as though an afterthought. This was when the two Germanies were nearing unification and perestroika was breaking up the Soviet Union. The TV-addicted middle class could not help but be rankled by the meagreness of Nepal's achievements. Was it really worthy for the king to inaugurate an agriculture fair? Was he truly unaware of the corruption in the government, of the misuse of privilege by his family? Weren't there more pressing things for him to do?

Unable to hate the king—for he was so nice—the bourgeoisie began to hate the palace's underground gang. The journalist Padam Thakurathi, who had been writing on drug trafficking and idol smuggling by members of the underground gang, was shot at his home by an intruder. The king's younger brother Prince Dhirendra Bir Bikram Shah's ADC and others, including a member of the National Panchayat, were convicted for the shooting, but—in a country where truth had been elusive—people continued to believe what they wanted to believe: The underground gang had shot the journalist.

Despite their considerable dislike of the Panchayat system, the bourgeoisie could not quite embrace the banned political parties, however. We had been taught to fear them; Panchayat-time nationalism fed on fear-mongering: *If the Nepali Congress comes to power, it will hand the country to India! If the communists come to power they'll kill us all!* Besides, were we poor, uneducated Nepalis ready for democracy?

So, instead of looking for political solutions, we became obsessed with royalty-watching, reading every sign given off by members of the royal family for clues about our future: What had the king done today? What had he said? What did it all mean? Surely good would prevail over evil? Just look at the *Mahabharata*—politics was all about tactics. The king was good but weak; he was being out-manoeuvred by the evil underground gang.

But how long can one tolerate stagnation? The bourgeoisie got distinctly frustrated when the king launched a campaign to have Nepal recognized internationally as a 'Zone of Peace'. Panchayat apologists spewed out much gobbledygook to explain what a Zone of Peace was. It was, we were told in heated nationalistic tones, the king's attempt to free Nepal of India's influence: If we were recognized by the world as a Zone of Peace, then India would be less likely to take over. But to suspicious ears it sounded as though the king hoped to quell internal dissent by obliging his subjects to be peaceable. Siddhartha Gautam's birthplace Lumbini suddenly became big now: The Buddha was one of us. Nepal was one of the non-aligned nations. We believed in disarmament. We stood for peace and harmony. We were the mythical Shangri-La. Who couldn't love us? It was endlessly camp to have our king promote us as a poor but happy mountain people. We rolled our eyes in disbelief.

By the end of the 1980s the banned political parties had infiltrated the National Panchayat enough to destabilize the system from within. Outside the government, the communist movement had birthed an array of small, splittist communist parties of Nepal— including two called Masal and Mashal, one of which was to later launch the present Maoist insurgency. The largest communist party at the time was the Communist Party of Nepal (Marxist-Leninist). The Nepali Congress, for its part, was beset by personality clashes among its leaders. Yet more and more ordinary Nepalis were pinning their hopes to their ideal of democracy.

The vernacular newspapers, allied to one or another political party, became increasingly emboldened to speak against the government, at times even criticizing the palace's underground gang and other members of the royal family. The editors of *Saptahik Bimarsha* faced arrest, and other papers were often raided and closed down, or their editors and reporters harassed. But they were not deterred. Doctors, lawyers, business people, writers and poets formed their own pressure groups in a loose federation of the like-minded. The Human Rights Organization of Nepal, set up under the leadership of the historian Rishikesh Shaha, was galvanizing public opinion against government excesses.

Hollowed of moral legitimacy, the Panchayat system stood on its shaky legs anyhow, withstanding, one after another. mismanagement, abuse and corruption scandals. What finally toppled it was a blockade by Rajiv Gandhi's government in India. Weeks before the trade and transit treaties between India and Nepal came up for renewal in 1988, India began to demand that they be lumped into one and renegotiated. The Nepali government refused to comply. The Indian government retaliated by imposing an embargo, closing all but two transit points, subjecting the Nepali people to severe fuel rations and shortages of oil, food, construction materials and other imports.

Hoping to spark nationalistic anti-India fervour, the king imposed austerity measures. No such fervour was sparked among the bourgeoisie, suddenly forced to queue up for rations. Instead, our moribund royalty-watching intensified: Would the very nice king please stop subjecting us to hardship? Or would the palace's underground gang now prevail, and take control of our lives? Queen Aishwarya Rajyalaksmi Shah, supposedly a member of this gang, was often shown on the evening news receiving funds from international donors. The sight of her holding purses of cash while the rest of the country was expected to endure hardship angered the bourgeoisie and made her the object of public derision. She was said to be an unloving mother, a shrill, castrating wife, a meddler, a manipulative shrew. It did not help that she decided, in the late 1980s, to start wearing her sari backward, in a throwback to the Victorian style of the Rana era.

As for the alleged perpetrator of the June 2001 royal massacre, Crown Prince Dipendra Bir Bikram Shah, his every gesture was now scrutinized for signs of the future. The crown prince had been cute as a boy, with his mother's large eyes accentuated by a red teeka on his forehead. He would make a reasonable king. Or would he? The first clear sense that he was not perfect came when, as a student at Eton, he had disgraced himself by being found drunk in a gutter. Brought back by his family to Nepal, he scored top marks in college—much to the annoyance of other top students. Over the years he had gained weight, losing his looks. Some said that he was mentally retarded, and a mama's boy; others said he was brilliant, and even-keeled in temperament, like his father. He was extremely pampered, people said. No, he was raised strictly—his mother even beat him. He had been very civic-minded in his school days. No, he used to run away to smoke pot with his uncle, the king's youngest brother. He was sweet. No, he was arrogant. He had a steady girlfriend whom he loved dearly but whom his mother wouldn't let him marry. No, he was a philanderer, a playboy...

It takes less than twenty minutes to complete an early-morning walk around the outer wall of the Narayanhiti palace, yet nobody knew much about the crown prince, our future king, growing up there. In the annual family photograph that the Royal Palace Secretariat released, he, his sister, Princess Shruti, and his brother, Prince Nirajan, always looked gangly and graceless. Dipendra Bir Bikram Shah would never be the king of Nepal, fatalists said. Birendra Bir Bikram Shah was slated by the stars to be the last Shah king.

After the blockade by India, the underground political parties finally came together, rescuing the bourgeoisie from our endless fretting about the present and future kings. Overcoming, for a while, their abiding fondness for 'splittism', seven communist parties formed a coalition called the United Left Front. The ULF then joined hands with the Nepali Congress in an alliance of the 'progressives' and 'democrats'.

The People's Movement to reinstate democracy began in the winter of 1989. At first the entire enterprise appeared very unlikely. But as the leaders of the political parties were arrested, younger activists kept the movement alive, and Kathmandu and other urban centres of Nepal broke out in riots and demonstrations. Soon this became the most popular political movement Nepal had ever witnessed. For the first time, the king became subject to public ridicule. Chants of 'Biré, scoundrel, leave the country' were hurled at him, while the queen was taunted, in cartoons sketched on public walls, as a money-grubber and, in a streak of Hindu misogyny, a whore. Members of the palace's underground gang were hunted off the streets, their houses burned and their windows smashed, and the infamous mandalays became targets of violence.

When the police cracked down, their brutality crackled on the crude walkie-talkies that they used to communicate with their superiors, which could be intercepted by FM radios. Thousands of arrests took place, and between sixty to hundred people were killed in unprecedented violence by the state. The Kathmandu bourgeoisie followed every riot, every crackdown, every arrest and every death on FM radio, becoming more and more sympathetic to the political activists.

The People's Movement sometimes quietened and sometimes gathered fury. When the left/liberal intelligentsia—doctors, lawyers, writers and artists—also joined in, the Kathmandu bourgeoisie was finally emboldened to support it fully. The world in 1989 was being swept by a wave of democracy. We too were ready, at last.

For some months King Birendra Bir Bikram Shah stubbornly refused to give in. But then, on 9 April 1990, in a move that would forever fix his image as a likeable king, he reached a settlement with the Nepali Congress and the United Left Front, and removed the ban on political parties. Surpassing all expectations, he also conceded to their demand for parliamentary democracy: A new constitution would be drafted, he announced. All Kathmandu lit up in elation after this announcement was broadcast on Nepal Television.

Democracy. Again. Parliamentary democracy. At last. This time it would be for real. A heady optimism overtook us all.

In the Nepali language, there are five forms of address, five ways to say 'you'. The term 'sarkar' was reserved for the kings, who addressed their subjects not by the next term down, 'hajoor', or even the next one down, 'tapain', but by the second-to-last term of address, 'timi' ('timi' is also reserved for adults addressing children). When the Nepali Congress leader Ganesh Man Singh asked the king to no longer address people in the 'timi' form, but to use the respectful form 'tapain', something palpably altered within all Nepalis. We had become citizens. Something transformed in our country when the communist leaders simply joined their hands in namaste without bowing before the king as all the politicians of the Panchayat era did. We got a sense of what it meant to be sovereign.

It felt as though a spring wind were sweeping down to blow away the haze that had for so long obscured our view of ourselves. It felt as though we could look around and finally see the truth.

THE
POSTMODERN
DEMOCRACY

THE PERILS OF BAD POLITICS

A statue of Prithvi Narayan Shah now stands outside the Singha Durbar's main gate, with his index finger raised to say: One country. Parliament house, in the palace behind him, was meant to be the seat of democracy. It replaced the National Panchayat under the 1990 constitution. But another spot nearby turned out to be a greater hotbed of democratic activity: Due west from the Singha Durbar is a circle shaded by trees, home to the Bhadrakali temple. At the temple's foot is a small, unassuming fenced-off park where, after 1990, protestors gathered by the hundreds, even thousands, to stage sit-ins, strikes, rallies and demonstrations. Groups championing the rights of workers, Dalits, women, the landless, bonded labourers and ethnic nationalities gathered here regularly, demanding the liberty and equality that they thought they had won in 1990, but that, as it turned out, they had not.

In 1990 more than 40 per cent of Nepalis were living below the poverty level, on an income of less than 4,400 rupees a year. There was hardly any private sector to speak of. The law did not treat women as men's equals. Systematic discrimination against the 'low' Dalit castes and the ethnic nationalities forced millions of Nepalis to lead desperate lives, or to leave the country to find work abroad, in India or further afield, in Korea and the Gulf. Bonded labour, though illegal, was still practised, and some of the democratic political leaders themselves kept indentured labourers to work their fields. What professional groups did exist lacked functional unions. The very concept of universal health care was alien; education standards in the schools were dismal; and services like drinking water, roads and electricity were unavailable to the majority. The Nepali Congress and the reconfigured Communist Party of Nepal (Unified Marxist Leninist) were charged with the near-impossible task of meeting many long overdue demands.

Unsurprisingly, the generally Bahun-caste, bourgeois-class, by now ageing, sometimes crusty and old-fashioned, patriarchal Hindu male leaders of these parties were not up to the job. They had, after all, spent their lives as political activists; they had little experience in governance.

Their failures began to show even as the new constitution was being drafted. Unable to think beyond the national myths of the Panchayat era, they defined Nepal as a Hindu kingdom (rather than as a secular one, as demanded by the ethnic nationalities), and they granted the king powers beyond those of a strictly ceremonial constitutional monarch. Most problematically, they allowed the king informal sway over the Royal Nepal Army by placing it under a Defence Council so weak as to be completely ineffectual. Through Article 127, the constitution also granted the king full discretionary powers in case of a constitutional crisis (this clause resembled the one that the king's father had invoked to effect his 1960 royal coup).

What resulted was a democracy that looked like a democracy, but that functioned as an elite class and caste cartel, a democracy lacking democracy, a postmodern democracy. All ethical issues were conceded to power struggles and realpolitik.

Most people had of course expected some turbulence. But they were shocked by the hurricane-speed of moral compromise.

Krishna Prasad Bhattarai of the Nepali Congress served as the prime minister of the first interim government, which oversaw the drafting of the constitution. He also established the Mallik Commission to identify those responsible for the excesses against the People's Movement, and recommend action against them.

In the first parliamentary elections of 1991, the Nepali Congress won with a majority of votes. But when G. P. Koirala became the prime minister, he buried the Mallik Commission's report, effectively extending protection to Panchayat-era hardliners. He had discovered, apparently, that the Nepali Congress could not survive without the patronage of these politicians, who still held sway in the rural areas and in Kathmandu's inner circles. The CPN (UML) had also come to the same conclusion. By the end of a year, both parties had welcomed as members several Panchayat politicians, often allowing them to outrank long-time party cadres.

The small but ambitious business community—under a suddenly liberalized economy—wasted no time to buy influence. Whispers of corruption started up, and grew louder as government members accepted 'ideologically driven' bribes to stock their parties' coffers. Then some ministers began to trade favours for personal gain, and members of Parliament and district officials began to hobnob, very visibly, with contractors and commission agents...

The competitive structure of parliamentary democracy, pitting party against party, helped anti-democratic interests to position themselves influentially. G. P. Koirala greatly mistrusted the CPN (UML); he viewed communists as a greater political threat than the royalists. When the CPN (UML) swept the first local elections for the Village Development Committees (or VDCs, the renamed Village Panchayats), G. P. Koirala skipped them and decentralized power to the District Development Committees (or DDCs, the renamed District Panchayats), the majority of which were in his party's hands. Under his leadership, the party was particularly pragmatic. The Panchayat-era politicians who had joined the Nepali Congress after 1990 were locally dubbed the 'chaite kangress', or the 'late-season Congress'. With the zeal of new converts, they began to harass their left-leaning 'enemies' by withholding development projects in CPN (UML) strongholds and allocating budgets only to Nepali Congress voters. International aid and national non–government organizations were also lobbied, pressured or hounded by G. P. Koirala's government into working in ways that were politically expedient for the Nepali Congress.

This ended the left/liberal unity of the People's Movement. As the political parties fell out, the country's intellectuals also broke into flanks of 'democrats' and 'progressives' which criticized their political opposition vociferously, while defending their own parties, no matter how questionable their behaviour.

More shocking were the personal rivalries among the leaders of each party. The Nepali Congress's 'chaite kangress' soon shifted from harassing leftists to harassing members of their own party, those who sided with Krishna Prasad Bhattarai against G. P. Koirala. The party's third leader, Ganesh Man Singh, was criticizing G. P. Koirala vocally, accusing his family of monopolizing power. Koirala loyalists in turn accused him of wanting key positions for his wife (who had headed the first women's rights organization in the country) and his son (an established politician). Taking strength from this fallout, Krishna Prasad Bhattarai set up a 'rebel' faction within the party. The three septuagenarians, who had dedicated their lives to bringing democracy to Nepal, were now feuding openly.

All this bad politics bewildered people. Apologist 'democrat' and 'progressive' intellectuals could not, in their lectures or talks or copious, jargon-filled articles, explain why personal rivalries mattered. Royalists, meanwhile, were already gloating: The political parties were acting like a coalition of fools.

This foolishness peaked when the Nepali Congress's 'rebel' faction threatened a no–confidence motion against G. P. Koirala. G. P. Koirala fought back by unilaterally dissolving Parliament and calling for snap elections, confident that his faction of the party would come back victorious, having routed the rebel faction.

He was wrong. The November 1994 elections saw considerably more vote buying, ballot stuffing, booth capturing, intimidation and rigging than the first parliamentary election, by all the major parties. When the votes were counted, the CPN (UML) came out as the largest party, though it did not win enough seats to form a majority government. A chaotic era of minority and coalition governments began.

Man Mohan Adhikari became the prime minister in November 1994, the first communist prime minister in the world to win a democratic election. He was heading a minority government. But his party was in as much disarray as the Nepali Congress. Its charismatic General Secretary Madan Bhandari had been steering the party away from communism towards more democratic leftist politics when he died in December 1993, in a car crash that had left everyone whispering of political assassination. (G. P. Koirala's government had written off the crash as an accident, but many thought that Madan Bhandari had been killed for being, in the communists' words, a 'capitalist roader'. The car driver, who survived the crash, later joined the Nepali Congress, and a decade later was murdered in mysterious circumstances.) At Madan Bhandari's death, the CPN (UML) was caught in suspension as an awkward communist-but-market-friendly party, a socialist-or-even-liberal-in-ideology party that, however, could not risk losing its grassroots supporters by eschewing red politics altogether. The party's neo-Marxist reformism was clashing against its own Marxist-Leninist (and even Stalinist and Maoist) past.

Man Mohan Adhikari tried to reconcile these reformist and revolutionary urges. In its nine months in power, his minority government made one irreversible change to Nepal's governance: It instituted the quaintly named 'Aafno Gaun Afai Banau'—'Let's

Develop Our Villages Ourselves'—programme, which gave Village
Development Committees funds, for the first time, to oversee
grassroots governance. The communist-held VDCs could now
show up the Nepali Congress-held DDCs by constructing roads,
bridges and telephones for themselves. In another more obviously
populist move, the CPN (UML) also allocated Rs 100 per month
stipends to the elderly, hoping to counter the popular myth that the
communists killed anyone who was economically unproductive.

The CPN (UML)'s growing popularity alarmed the Nepali
Congress, while its reformist/revolutionary waffling infuriated the
smaller parties to the extreme left. Most people, however, were
more worried by how flagrant corruption had become by now.
Communist members of Parliament were beginning to build houses
in Kathmandu, vote themselves plush perks and benefits, and ride
around in distinctly un-communist Prados and Pajeros. They were
seen to have sold out on their promise of equality for all.

The CPN (UML) government collapsed in September 1994
when the Nepali Congress tabled a motion of no-confidence.
It is expedient to number the governments that followed, for
there were many (including the interim government, there had
already been three):

The prime minister of government number four, established
in September 1995, was a fifty-something leader of the Nepali
Congress's 'rebel' faction, Sher Bahadur Deuba. He was heading
a coalition of the Nepali Congress, the Rastriya Prajatantra Party
(RPP) and the Nepal Sadbhavana Party (NSP). But like the
Nepali Congress, the smaller parties of this coalition were self-
destructing for what seemed to the public like petty reasons. The
conservative RPP, formed after 1990 by Panchayat-era politicians,
split into two, one headed by Surya Bahadur Thapa and the
other by Lokendra Bahadur Chand, old rivals. The two resulting
parties were absurdly named RPP (Thapa) and RPP (Chand).

Their platforms were identical, and some members even floated back and forth between them.

In March 1997, RPP (Chand) broke off the coalition with the Nepali Congress, and joined forces with the CPN (UML) and the NSP to form the fifth government. Lokendra Bahadur Chand was the prime minister this time. This was a shock all around, for Lokendra Bahadur Chand had been the last prime minister of the Panchayat era. Nobody had thought, seven years ago, that he'd ever be in politics again, much less become prime minister so soon. The Panchayat-era elite had finagled their way to the centre of democratic politics.

The CPN (UML) lost much of its moral credibility by allying with Lokendra Bahadur Chand. Eventually, unable to reconcile its reformist and revolutionary factions, that party too split into two. The two resulting parties were called the CPN (UML) and the CPN (ML). Upholding the long-standing communist tradition of bickering with other leftists more than with the centrists or right-wingers, they hurled much vitriol at each other: The CPN (UML) accused the CPN (ML) of being splittist royalist saboteurs—like the 'Russian' faction of yore, which had abetted the 1960 royal coup. The CPN (ML) in turn accused the CPN (UML) of being capitalist roaders.

The ungainly RPP (Chand)-CPN (UML)-NSP coalition lasted seven months. After this, in an equally ungainly coalition, the Nepali Congress allied with the other RPP, the RPP (Thapa), as well as the NSP. In October 1997 Surya Bahadur Thapa, the man who had presided over the dubious referendum that saved the Panchayat system in 1980, became the prime minister of government number six. Again, the ideological bankruptcy of this coalition was shocking. The parties that had brought democracy to Nepal were now willing to compromise all in exchange for a short stint in power.

Corruption, meanwhile, was continuing briskly. With each new government, a new set of politicians got their turn at building houses, buying cars, opening businesses, starting up NGOs, junketeering, hobnobbing, schmoozing and carousing, and generally indulging their newfound wealth. And while the intellectuals allied to the parties could explain that democracy was difficult, and that the only solution to democracy was more democracy, they could not explain why people who had once given up all for democracy were now so bent on quick, mindless profiteering.

Eventually, G. P. Koirala rallied back within his own party, suppressing—for a while—the criticisms of the 'rebel' faction. With the backing of the CPN (ML), he came back as the prime minister of the seventh government in April 1998.

Eight months later, when this coalition broke down, he came back again as prime minister (for the third time) of the eighth government, this time forming an alliance with the CPN (UML).

Despite all this, Kathmandu was, after a fashion, booming. The free market system had led to a mushrooming of retail shops, media houses, hotels and restaurants, private schools and colleges, law firms, nursing homes, engineering companies, banks and financing companies. Tourism was flourishing. The non-government sector had also grown dramatically with the steady influx of international aid. Crop after crop of educated professionals either went into business or sought high-paying jobs in a bewildering number of non-government organizations. Those who could not find jobs in Nepal were going abroad; remittances from Nepali labourers and migrants in foreign countries were now rivalling the national development budget.

All this would not transform the country, of course. After all, schooling had begun only fifty-odd years ago in Nepal. Even now, only 8 million of the country's 23 million citizens were functionally literate. The professionals and intellectuals numbered a couple of million, scattered all over the country. Of these, only a handful were engaged in working for the greater good. In the legal field, for example, though the Tribhuvan University's law campus churned out batch after batch of lawyers, there were no more than three or four senior advocates with the capacity— and inclination—to address legal and constitutional quandaries or human rights issues. Similarly, a depressingly small number of women's rights activists made any significant contribution outside of seminars and street demonstrations. In the social sciences, academics were entangled in high, analytical-sounding language, and were unable to cut through to explain how to fix the messy party politics. There were hardly any historians digging through the ruins of the past. Our literary writers—mostly male, of Bahun caste, and stamped by Hindu mores—found little to say for the poor and excluded. Our economists were not offering useful insight. Only a few of the increasing numbers of journalists were upholding high standards.

Nevertheless, in Kathmandu there was a boom—a modest boom, all things considered, yet the greatest one that Nepal had seen.

Meanwhile, over 9 million Nepalis were living on earnings of less than a dollar a day, and growing increasingly frustrated. But we in Kathmandu were too busy bettering ourselves to do much for them. As the political parties wrangled for power, we of the bourgeoisie built our fenced-off houses, postmodern pastiche extravaganzas of concrete. We applied for better and better jobs, bought marvellous gadgets that were newly available in the supermarkets, enjoyed ourselves at parties and gatherings and hoarded our good fortunes. And out of liberal guilt we voiced occasional despair that the government wasn't doing anything for the people.

The people? You know, the poor people.

On 16 February 1996, the Communist Party of Nepal (Maoist)—a party about which little was known—launched what it called a 'People's War' by attacking banks in Gorkha District and burning the land deeds that villagers had placed as collateral against loans. The same day, they attacked police posts in Rolpa and Rukum Districts in the west, and set off a bomb at a soft-drinks bottling plant in Kathmandu. They also attacked a liquor manufacturer in Gorkha and looted the house of a 'feudal usurper' in Kavre District.

Though we in Kathmandu did not take this 'war' seriously, we understood, instinctively, why it had begun. The People's Movement of 1990 had spread enlightenment aspirations throughout Nepal. But because political parties were so occupied with their own power struggles, the majority of people had received very little from democracy. One example: In a study conducted in 2000 by the Forum for Women, Law and Development, 90 per cent of those interviewed said they supported equal rights for men and women. Yet, despite the best efforts of women's activists, all the parties in Parliament actively delayed a bill for women's rights. Ministers, bureaucrats and Supreme Court justices instead sounded shrill warnings that women's inheritance rights or abortion rights or divorce and alimony rights would damage the structure of Nepali society, and did everything possible to nix the bill. It was passed only after a nationwide discussion on it showed people to be overwhelmingly in its favour.

Whether it was in relation to women's rights or the rights of ethnic nationalities or the rights of Dalits—or any variety of social movements that were gathering force—the government made only late, hollow gestures. Those in power would do something for people, and that too half-heartedly, only if they formed unions, staged protests, went on strike, took to the streets. Even after the Maoist insurgency began, this remained the case.

It was only after bonded labourers staged a mass movement in the far-west, risking their families' futures, that the government declared them free of slavery. When the Dalits of the Chamar community in the eastern Tarai rose up against caste oppression, some members of the political parties at first opposed them. The lesson that people learned was that if they wanted anything from the government, they would have to get militant, because the leaders of the political parties would not listen to anyone who asked for anything nicely.

The Maoists seemed, at first, like a ragtag army that sprang out of nowhere. In fact, they—and the entire communist movement in Nepal—had a long if extremely convoluted past, which had come to light only very slowly after 1990.

The political activism of the 1940s had inspired peasants' land uprisings in the rural areas in the 1950s and after. Rukum and Rolpa Districts had long been communist strongholds, and areas of simmering ethnic Kham Magar dissent. It should surprise no one that communist ideology should have such quick appeal to those who had long been exploited, and who were seeking redress. It helped that the Soviet Union and the Republic of China were, from the 1950s on, supplying low-cost revolutionary propaganda to Nepal. Closer home, the left in India was stirring for revolution. The communists also took advantage of the fact that Nepal was off in a corner of the world, and even Pol Pot could be made to sound credible here (sometimes it seems as though we cannot fathom totalitarianism even today—most of our communist parties still revere Stalin). By the 1970s, then, there was a plethora of small, fractious communist parties working for the overthrow of the Panchayat system.

In the 1980s, as the CPN (Fourth Convention) went into decline, it spawned the CPN (Masal), which, in 1984, split into two parties, most confusingly named the CPN (Masal) and the

CPN (Mashal). The latter party was headed by Pushpa Kamal Dahal (known popularly as Prachanda), and had, as a prominent member, an India-educated PhD, Baburam Bhattarai. Prachanda, who was underground for much of his political life, was shown as a stocky, bearded man in the one photograph that the public had ever seen of him. Baburam Bhattarai, who had emerged occasionally from the underground, was known as a small, bookish man, very much the stereotype of a Bahun-caste intellectual, an erudite man good at spinning words.

Both the CPN (Masal) and the CPN (Mashal) remained outside the United People's Front during the 1990 People's Movement, joining in only for some of the more violent, and more decisive, demonstrations towards the end. After 1990, both parties had remained underground, eventually combining with the declining CPN (Fourth Convention) to form a new party named the CPN (Unity Centre). Prachanda served as the general secretary of this new party.

Though the central committee of the CPN (Unity Centre) remained underground, it floated an above-ground political wing called the United People's Front. In the second parliamentary elections in 1991, the United People's Front won nine seats, making it the country's third biggest party. Its strongest showings were in the western hills of Rolpa and Rukum Districts. Partly, this was a reaction against the Nepali Congress. Because of their communist leanings, the Rolpa- and Rukum-based supporters of the United People's Front had been subjected to mass harassment, arrest and torture by the police during G. P. Koirala's first tenure as prime minister. This had only heightened their antipathy to 'bourgeois' parliamentary democracy.

Like most other parties in Nepal, the CPN (Unity Centre) eventually split. By 1994, there were two underground factions of the party (both with the same name), and both had their own above-ground United People's Fronts. When Prachanda's faction of the party failed to secure recognition from the Election Commission for the 1994 snap elections, its above-ground United People's Front (led by Baburam Bhattarai) boycotted the elections. The faction of the party that did run for elections fared badly in the polls, and went into decline.

In 1995, Prachanda's CPN (Unity Centre) and Baburam Bhattarai's United People's Front renamed themselves the Communist Party of Nepal (Maoist), and decided to take up arms, articulating a strategy for a 'People's War' against the monarchy and 'bourgeois' parliamentary democracy. The Maoists handed the prime minister—then Sher Bahadur Deuba—a list of forty demands, and set a deadline for the government to respond.

From Kathmandu it all sounded so fey, the prospect of a Maoist insurgency. The Maoists launched their 'People's War' just before the deadline expired. But Kathmandu was not much bothered.

In the following weeks and months, stray reports filtered in that the Maoists had hacked off the hands of Nepali Congress supporters in Rolpa District, or that a few policemen had been killed. The government retaliated, putting into effect the Nepal Police's Operation Romeo, which unleashed a wave of terror against the villagers of Rolpa and Rukum Districts. Thousands of people were displaced from their homes as the police raided villages and arrested suspected Maoists, detaining them illegally and subjecting them to torture.

This should have outraged Kathmandu's civil society, but it did not, because we were all too busy with our lives. And were the Maoists for real? Who was this Prachanda anyway? Who had ever seen him? How far could he get, peddling discredited revolutions to villagers?

We in Kathmandu could not grasp the sheer appeal of Maoist ideology in the poverty-stricken countryside. Those joining the

Maoist insurgency were often young men—and many women—of little or no education, enjoying power for the first time through firearms. They 'liberated' the poor by forgiving loans, scrapping deeds and promising 'land to the tiller'. Setting up 'people's courts', they executed rough justice, killing or 'disciplining' their 'class enemies'—often members of the Nepali Congress. With Red Guard zeal, they banned liquor and punished those who played cards or beat their wives. They bombed government buildings and scared off non-government organizations and their profiteering contractors, and began to set up their own 'people's governments' in areas under their control.

Unwilling to take this seriously, Kathmandu gave in to easy speculation. Prachanda, word had it, did not actually exist. Baburam Bhattarai's education at the Jawaharlal Nehru University in Delhi had been sponsored by King Mahendra Bir Bikram Shah. The Maoists were secretly working in tandem with the palace. They would destroy the peace, and the king would find an excuse to effect a royal coup. Yes. This was nothing less than a royalist conspiracy to hobble parliamentary democracy.

Addled by such speculation, the bourgeoisie was unable to respond in any meaningful way when in 1998 G. P. Koirala, as the prime minister of government number eight, ordered the Nepal Police to crack down even more brutally against the Maoists in an operation named Kilo Sierra 2. Entire villages were razed to cinders in this operation, and, again, hundreds of villagers were subjected to arrest and torture. Yet only a handful of intellectuals in Kathmandu criticized G. P. Koirala for using the police as an armed wing of the Nepali Congress.

Kilo Sierra 2, effected in eighteen districts throughout the country, further inflamed mass sympathy for Maoism. As both the Maoists and the state stepped up their violence, more and more people were shot, hacked to death, kidnapped. Hundreds simply 'disappeared'. By the turn of the millennium, over 2,000, mostly poor, rural Nepalis had lost their lives to the increasingly bloody insurgency and counter-insurgency.

Through all this, the political parties would not stop wrangling for power.

Due in large part to the CPN (ML)'s decision to splinter off from the CPN (UML), the Nepali Congress came back to a majority in the 1999 general elections. At first it looked as though the party would use its mandate responsibly. G. P. Koirala even conceded the coveted prime minister's post to his party's 'rebel' faction: Krishna Prasad Bhattarai headed the ninth government.

But in no time G. P. Koirala decided that he must be the prime minister again. His loyalists spread gossip about K. P. Bhattarai's decrepitude and inability to control his cabinet's corruption. G. P. Koirala faced similar charges from his rival's loyalists. G. P. Koirala vs K. P. Bhattarai: In the newspapers, street-corner discussions and tea-shop exchanges, it was always GP and KP, GP and KP at each other's throats. G. P. Koirala loyalists went so far as to make lurid suggestions about their rival's buxom caretaker. Under immense pressure, Bhattarai finally stepped down in March 2000, and Koirala once again became prime minister (for the fourth time), heading government number ten.

Within days, his party's 'rebel' faction began pressing him to resign...

In Kathmandu, 'civil society' became the fog-bound place where we of the bourgeoisie met to voice our creeping anxieties on the perils of bad politics. A few royalist intellectuals began the old refrain: Had we really been ready for democracy? Some democrat and progressive intellectuals began to chime in as well. After all, even the political parties hadn't been agitating for *full* democracy in 1990; it would have been enough for King Birendra

Bir Bikram Shah to have lifted the ban on them; that would have been democracy enough. Hadn't the incompetence of the political parties warranted the royal coup in 1960? Perhaps we Nepalis did need an all-powerful king after all.

THE DIARY OF A BAFFLED BOURGEOIS

There came a time, at last, when it was no longer tenable for the Kathmandu bourgeois to deny the reality that democracy was failing. For me this came about eight months before the June 2001 massacre at the royal palace. It occurred to me that I did not like my ignorance about what was happening outside Kathmandu. I, a writer, a bourgeois with aspirations to being an intellectual, was perpetually lost, living in a mist of anxiety that would not clear. I was unhappy, and I was unhappy about being unhappy, for I knew that in the scheme of things I was immensely fortunate, and so should be happy.

Yet I found that every public disaster had the power to hollow me out. I was like a bad-politics junkie, and it felt as though bad politics were ruining my life. I kept up with what was happening in the country as much as any person, but watching the television news or reading the papers or listening to the radio left me feeling defeated—personally, intimately, as though tragedy had struck me or someone I loved.

There was no objective reason for this despair, because my own personal and professional life was quiet. I kept my contract with society. Like any proper bourgeois citizen I worked, I paid taxes, I contributed to causes that I believed in, I fulfilled my family duties, I communed with friends. I roughly functioned as I was supposed to. But for reasons I could not understand, my days were getting arduous. I kept seeing signs of calamity. Something bad would happen. I was not prepared for it.

My dread manifested itself as emotional malaise, a lagging in the heart. I would wake up, and before starting my work I would read the newspapers and feel fatigued before my day. I would scan some headline—the government-owned Royal Nepal Airlines Corporation (RNAC) had decided to lease a B-767 jet from Lauda Air. The mind is relentless—it fixates on details, it charts out scenarios, it mulls over implications. In leasing the Lauda Air jet, the RNAC was ignoring a directive by the Parliament's Public Accounts Committee. To lease the jet, the RNAC would have to offer a bank guarantee worth over a million US dollars, and an advance of one month's rent. Could the country afford this?

Why should that matter so much to me?

You're using everything as an excuse to be miserable, I would chide myself. But then I would pick up the papers and read something else, and my reason would dissipate. I began to believe, irrationally, that if something good happened in government all my troubles would go: If I could be sure that the country would not fall apart, I could get on with my life. I even thought: Maybe if G. P. Koirala resigns as prime minister I can be happy again. I knew this was ridiculous. But since 1990 G. P. Koirala had been prime minister four times, and the country had spent his leadership years in despair.

Didn't he know that the royalists were counting on democracy to fail? Conservatives said, 'You call the Congress a party of democrats? It's the private den of the Koirala clan!' I was never an ardent supporter of the Congress, but like most Nepalis, I had expected much from the party. But it, like the UML, had proved wanting. Not only that, the future of the political parties also looked bleak. Not having studied at the local college campuses, I had no feeling for the Congress or UML student unions, and thought the politicization of students a bad thing: Young people should study. Yet it was true that the students had forced the referendum of 1980. Without student activism in 1990, there would have been no democracy. But today's student activists seemed to act robotically on their party leaders' orders, flooding the streets for every last power struggle, but never pressuring them to take seriously the scores of honest issues that meanwhile lay ignored.

Amid the pell-mell of the days, I sometimes found it so hard to keep my mood up that I wondered if I should get a pill that would make me cheerful. Sometimes on my errands I passed the house of a psychiatrist. I did not know him well, but exchanged greetings with his wife and children when we met on the street. The doctor was successful—he drove a car—and appeared amiable and informal. He met patients at a clinic in his house. I wondered if I should go there. His patients, coming out of his gates, were skeletal teenage girls with their families or husbands, or elderly men and women being led by the hand, or couples glancing nervously around as they got on their motorcycles. They looked like people with genuine problems. What was my business among them?

I decided instead to take up meditation, and was lucky to find a teacher who moved through Tibetan Buddhist rituals lightly, instructing students on techniques to control the mind. I read doggedly cheerful self-help books that had become available of late in Kathmandu's bookshops. I also joined a gym where all the machines functioned, and hot water was available even in winter (when Kathmandu's houses were all dry) and I began to feel that maybe I would be all right.

The problem was, my happiness tended to last only as long as I was meditating or on the treadmill. When I went back to my room and began to write a story, the anxiety would return. Perhaps this was the problem—writing was so interior; I was stuck inside myself, being of no use to society. I spent too many hours alone, uselessly, before a computer in a room that got no sun.

When I did go out on work or errands, I would see the middle-class youth of Kathmandu all looking strangely ebullient, as though they did not know that their country was in crisis. Young women were baring belly buttons and enhancing their height with platform shoes; young men styled their hair and wore body-hugging T-shirts. I was glad that they were not despairing, and wondered if I could be like them—not indifferent to the problems around me, but able to be blithe, nevertheless, on a day-to-day basis.

It was, I knew, pathetic to be disabled the way I was. I was not, myself, politically engaged. I had watched the People's Movement from the side, and to be honest would not die if democracy were to fail: People do live in dictatorships of all kinds—perhaps they do not live fully, but they do live. And if, say, the king were to effect a royal coup, would I go to jail to bring back democracy, spend five, seven, ten, even eighteen years for this cause? Probably not. I felt passionately that the past decade had fostered many important, positive changes, but I couldn't always say what these were.

And sometimes positive things felt negative. For instance, groups were forming everywhere to organize their interests. Strikes had become increasingly common. In December 2000, hotel employees started demanding a mandatory 10 per cent service charge. Hotel owners refused them, and the government was slow in helping to negotiate a deal, and so all of Kathmandu's hotels closed on 11 December, forcing tourists to move into tents, private houses and makeshift accommodations. Cancellations poured in as a result, and many trekking companies went under.

My work slowed down as the rest of Kathmandu slowed

down. I wrote for hours every day, yet I always felt that I was falling behind or forgetting something important. It took a lot just to start writing after reading the morning papers. Maybe reading newspapers was the problem. They disturbed me. On 22 December, the Parliament's Public Accounts Committee summoned G. P. Koirala as part of its investigation into possible corruption in the Lauda Air jet lease, and I was wearied just to read the prime minister taking a high moral tone in response.

It felt like trouble was coming from every direction. On the day after Christmas, in the year 2000, violence erupted in Kathmandu. Bollywood actor Hrithik Roshan had apparently said something derogatory about Nepal. Students affiliated with the left parties were marching to the Indian embassy with a letter of protest when, inexplicably, riots broke out, at the end of which four people were killed and 180 injured. It was bizarre. Who cared what an Indian actor thought of us? Not anyone I knew. Yet, when I went out that afternoon, the streets were littered with stones and rubber tyres burned at the junctions, befouling the air. Similar riots took place around the country. By day's end, the government had blocked transmission of Indian TV channels. The Nepal Motion Picture Association and the Film Artists Association of Nepal had condemned Hrithik Roshan. The Gopi Krishna cinema hall declared that it would never screen his movies. Scores of irate press releases flooded the newspaper offices.

When the situation calmed, reports eventually emerged that the monarchist coterie of the king's youngest brother, Dhirendra Shah, had incited much of the rioting, alongside the Maoists.

So it wasn't just negative thinking. Malevolent forces were indeed coalescing against democracy, and the people—caught up in their small lives—would be left watching as their rights vanished one by one. After the Hrithik Roshan riots, I no longer wanted to live in Nepal. There were more riots the next day, and people of Indian origin were attacked. Walking on the streets, I became very conscious of looking like a hill Nepali; I suddenly loathed my mainstream features. Five hundred demonstrators and eighty police were injured by day's end. A Nepali actor, who had once offered to shoot the prime minister if he got orders from Dhirendra Shah, was one of the rioters arrested. The government announced a ban on all Hrithik Roshan movies. Hrithik Roshan, for his part, denied that he had said anything bad about Nepal— and protested that in fact he loved his Nepali servants. Scores of press releases were issued against him that day as well.

The riots stopped after it was verified, the next day, that Hrithik Roshan really hadn't said anything against Nepalis. So what had these riots been about? Nobody knew.

It was like that. We never knew where to look for trouble, and once we sighted signs, we never knew how to interpret them. We wanted to see all the bright, good things that democracy had brought us, but in Kathmandu the party leaders were forever bickering. Was this just a part of democratic culture, and was it right? On 28 December, fifty-six of the Congress party's 113 members of Parliament started an inter-party no-confidence motion against G. P. Koirala. The motion was led by the Congress's 'rebel' faction head, Krishna Prasad Bhattarai. G. P. Koirala survived the motion, but only by making party members vote in an open ballot, without secrecy. Was this right?

The opposition parties were no better. Nine leftist parties, not including the UML, called for a two-day nationwide general strike. Was *this* democratic culture? General strikes, or bandhs, had become common by now. This one took place on 1 and 2 January 2001—that was how we in Kathmandu started the new year, with no traffic on the streets and most shops and businesses closed. The tourism industry was hit hard by cancellations. Businesses were all beginning to flounder.

One day I thought: It is not fair to say that I blame bad politics for my unhappiness; my happiness actually *is* derailed by bad politics. I was keeping up with my meditation and exercise. I had even decided to take seriously to gardening, to tend to flowers. I also longed to visit my teacher at his monastery atop a hill on the outskirts of Kathmandu where the winds carried the fragrance of wild grasses and sunshine. Then suddenly it would all seem pointless: Any effort to make a life here would prove futile; the country was heading for all-out war.

In mid January, G. P. Koirala won the informal approval of the king to create an Armed Police Force to fight the Maoists. He said the Nepal Police had not been armed adequately, nor trained enough, to lead the counter-insurgency. Even so, their brutality during the Romeo and Kilo Sierra 2 operations had turned vast swathes of the countryside against 'bourgeois' parliamentary democracy. Wouldn't a more lethal police body just spawn more antagonism? G. P. Koirala thought not. He also hoped that by creating an Armed Police Force he could avoid deploying the Royal Nepal Army, whose first loyalties—many felt—were to the king and only then to the country. If the army got involved, democracy would be lost.

It wasn't just I who was controlled by public events; many of my friends, too, were in the same state. We were always looking for signs. Signs that our own lives—our nice, orderly lives—might eventually be compromised by all this trouble.

Around mid January, the Maoists issued the 'Prachanda Path'— their guiding principles. Prachanda—who many still believed did not even exist—was now said to be heading the CPN (Maoist). Surely this couldn't bode well. Some friends called, their voices thin with panic. I knew we shouldn't be so fraught, but the world was going badly, and I felt we had to keep watch.

On 5 February, opposition parties demanded G. P. Koirala's

resignation over the Lauda Air lease scandal, and over the government's inability to curb Maoist violence. Undeterred, G. P. Koirala formed a thirty-seven-member cabinet two days later. Five people had just died in a Maoist attack in Surkhet, west Nepal, in an ambush on the Chief Justice's convoy. The Chief Justice had survived only by chance. Immediately upon the formation of G. P. Koirala's cabinet, three people were reported killed in a clash between the police and the Maoists. Barely a week later, the Maoists exploded a bomb in Achham, west Nepal, killing two children and injuring eleven adults.

Life in Kathmandu was also growing chaotic. The Federation of Nepalese Transport Entrepreneurs organized a two-day strike of public buses and microbuses in response to student demands for a 50 per cent discount on fares, and a recent ban on vehicles more than twenty years old. The streets swarmed with people walking to work.

The day after the strike, 12 February, was the first day of the nineteenth session of Parliament, the winter 'working' session in which bills got passed. There was always a buzz at the start of these sessions. They were what the 1990 People's Movement had been for, after all. Thirteen bills were pending from previous parliamentary sessions, and two new bills were to be introduced. One was a bill granting women limited rights to inheritance and abortion, and the other a bill to govern political parties. The women's rights bill, in particular, was immensely urgent. It had finally been tabled after years of delay, and though it granted only limited rights to women (women could inherit parental property but had to return it to their families upon marriage; only married women could obtain abortions, that too with the consent of their husbands), these limited rights were great improvements on the current laws.

But the session was to end without a single full day of

work. On the first day, as the Speaker of the House Taranath Ranabhat struck the gavel, opening the session, a UML member of Parliament took the floor and launched a tirade against G. P. Koirala. Another UML MP called for a boycott of Parliament. After two and a half hours of debate, all of the UML MPs marched out of the House, followed by those of all the other opposition parties, almost half the total strength of Parliament.

On the winter session's second day, as soon as the Speaker opened the meeting, MPs from every opposition party except for the Nepal Sadbhavana Party circled the rostrum, chanting slogans against Prime Minister G. P. Koirala. The chanting lasted six minutes, after which the Speaker adjourned the meeting.

The following day the same thing happened. Members of Parliament even exchanged fisticuffs.

The boycott of Parliament continued for days. Wasn't the UML discrediting democracy? Weren't all the parties doing so? On 16 February, G. P. Koirala met with the opposition parties in an effort to negotiate a way past the stalemate, but they continued to demand that he resign, and this he would not do. Three days later, a brawl erupted in Parliament as the minister for culture, tourism and civil aviation tried to present a government defence of the Lauda Air jet lease. As he headed to the rostrum, a UML member of Parliament pulled him back. The two exchanged blows, then others joined in the fracas, and the meeting was adjourned.

The dysfunction of Parliament was making the Maoists look justified in criticizing 'bourgeois' parliamentary democracy. The political parties were behaving irresponsibly. And the bourgeoisie was beginning to want to be saved by the king... An old pattern was repeating itself.

King-watching became an obsession all over again. On 26 February, King Birendra went on a state visit to China, and while members of Parliament wrangled, the media focused, with much adulation, on this visit. Would the king please step in to save the country? That was the undertone of the press coverage.

There were also reports at this time that the Royal Nepal Airlines Corporation had suffered a loss of 80 million rupees during the month and a half of Lauda Air service.

And then it was March. The weather got balmy, the sky seemed to lift, and all of Kathmandu was swept by winds and breezes. In between my writing hours, I remembered to take time to appreciate the small beauties of the world: How pretty, the gentians, pinks, toadflax, daisies and asters in the garden of my family home. I met friends more often, and I even, now and then, had fun. I scoured bookstores and tried to find international magazines to read so that I could gain a larger picture of the world. But the newspapers were hard to put down.

The parliamentary session of 1 March lasted for less than five minutes. There was a two-minute session four days later.

There were more sinister signs. In a single day, thirty-four Nepalis, mostly children, died of measles in Kalikot District. On the same day, the army was posted to the major custom points along the Indian and Chinese borders to check cross-border smuggling. According to the Federation of Nepalese Chambers of Commerce and Industry, goods worth 10 billion rupees were smuggled through the Indian border every year, and one billion rupees worth of goods through the Chinese border. The police and the government's revenue administration had been unable to check smuggling, and so the army had been called in to take over civilian duties.

Hotel employees were threatening another strike, again demanding a 10 per cent service charge. Unable to negotiate a deal with them, the government declared the hotel industry an essential service, banning its employees from going on strike.

As the days progressed the news got more and more disheartening. On 11 March, cadres of the UML and the CPN (Maoist) held joint mass rallies in Liwang, the capital of Rolpa District and the heartland of the Maoist insurgency. Had the mainstream left lost its cadres to the Maoists? Or were they two faces of the same coin? Twenty-four children died of an epidemic in Humla District on the same day. A report came out saying that there were 77,000 child labourers in Nepal. The editor of the Maoist-affiliated newspaper *Janaadesh* was released from jail after a two-year incarceration, only to be arrested again. The lease of the Lauda Air jet was still under investigation by the Public Accounts Committee.

If things got bad enough, a strongman would step up, asking us to trade in our freedom for his efficiency. That was how democracy usually ended. King Birendra would effect a royal coup. Suddenly, everyone was saying he would take over. Many were saying he should.

Some people, of course, were able to see what they wanted to see and ignore what they didn't want to see, the way tourists who come to Nepal look at terraced fields and see their beauty but remain blind to the hard labour they extract from tillers. Some of my friends felt confident that democracy could not be defeated. The king just couldn't take over: democracy was too deeply rooted by now. Others just didn't care one way or the other. Some laughed as they heard that the Maoist leader of area no. 2, cell no. 10 of Kalikot District had ordered villagers to support the insurgency by killing dogs, because their barking alerted security forces to the Maoists' movement. 'Anyone who defies this appeal will be severely punished by the people's government according to the people's decision,' the Maoist newspaper reported.

April was a harrowing month, crowded with vague, unfocused

anxieties. I slept heavily, and my dreaming was dense.

On 2 April, more than five hundred Maoists armed with rifles, bombs and grenades attacked two police outposts in Rukum and Dolakha Districts, killing thirty-five policemen and abducting twenty-four more. Seven Maoists were also killed in battle. This was the single bloodiest incident since the insurgency started. In Kathmandu, bombs went off at the houses of a Congress member of Parliament and a former inspector general of police. The next day, Maoists looted arms and cash in several places.

The day after, Congress leaders ended Parliament's winter session. Not a single bill had been tabled; not a single full discussion had taken place. The final meeting of the session lasted two minutes. Though they had done nothing during the session, the members of Parliament were paid 6.2 million rupees, plus allowance and transport fares. This was the last session of Parliament the country was to have.

At about this time, a conspiracy theory that the palace was working in tandem with the Maoists gained ground. The 4 April newspaper reports had it that Maoist leaders Prachanda and Baburam Bhattarai had met a royalist member of the Upper House, Ramesh Nath Pandey. Why was the palace meeting the Maoists? Was the palace's shadowy 'underground gang' supporting the insurgency to eventually justify a royal coup in the name of counter-insurgency?

Yet if the royalists and the Maoists were succeeding in squeezing out democracy, it was because the party leaders were doing their bit to discredit themselves. On 4 April, again, the student wing of the splintered-off communist party, ML, called for a chakka jam, a shutdown of traffic. Two days later the same student group effected a nationwide general strike, and all schools, industries and businesses were forced shut. Meanwhile, a wave of panic was sweeping over the bourgeoisie: The Maoists were winning! On 8 April newspapers reported eighty people dead in the past six days of the insurgency and counter-insurgency. The police had started deserting their remote posts. On 9, 10 and 11 April, the Maoists held elections for the representatives of each of Rolpa District's fifty-one Village Development Committees, which they had renamed 'Village People's Committees'. They planned to form republican governments in their strongholds.

G. P. Koirala was bent on suppressing the Maoists by force. On 12 April, the king re-promulgated the Armed Police Force Ordinance. Three days later, the Maoists looted 9 million rupees from a Jhapa District bank. The UML and the other left parties, meanwhile, continued trying to unseat the prime minister. At 9 a.m. on 16 April, leftist activists formed a human roadblock along Putali Sadak, the main road to Singha Durbar, to prevent the prime minister from reaching his office. It turned out he had entered Singha Durbar an hour earlier. Enraged, the leftist activists burned twelve government vehicles in a rampage.

Three days later, they held a mass rally demanding that G. P. Koirala step down.

G. P. Koirala had decided, by then, that even the Armed Police Force were not up to quelling the Maoist insurgency; the army had to be mobilized. On 18 April, he ordered the deployment of both the Armed Police Force and the Royal Nepal Army for the first phase of the Integrated Security and Development Programme, a newly developed 'hearts and minds' operation targeted at Maoist strongholds. In so doing, G. P. Koirala came smack up against the army's resistance to civilian command. Two days later, the Chief of the Army Staff General Prajwalla Sumshere Jung Bahadur Rana publicly asked all the major political parties to reach a national consensus on the deployment of the army. This was unheard of. Was he questioning the Defence Council's orders?

This unleashed a storm. Or yet another storm. Kathmandu was once again shaken by rumours of a royal coup. Even G. P. Koirala got skittish. He skipped Kathmandu without informing anyone, and went to his hometown Biratnagar, near the Indian border. Word had it that he wanted to be able to evade arrest should the army come for him, as they had decades earlier for his brother BP. The UML and other left parties should have helped the prime minister to stare down the army; instead they announced another round of public protests against him. The UML General Secretary Madhav Kumar Nepal vowed to disrupt the next session of Parliament if G. P. Koirala had not resigned by then.

In the middle of all this, King Birendra received, from the Supreme Court, a bill that he had sent them for an opinion. The bench had unanimously found it in violation of the constitution. The bill had been passed on 26 July 2000 as the sixth amendment to the 1964 citizenship act. It allowed less xenophobic standards for establishing citizenship, and granted citizenship to men married to Nepali women (previously, only women married to Nepali men were allowed citizenship). It was the first bill that the king had not ratified immediately, as he was supposed to, but sent to the Supreme Court for an opinion. Now he ratified it, but with the Supreme Court's opinion attached. The king, too, was playing politics.

Meanwhile, one hundred policemen had deserted their stations in remote outposts, and armed Maoists had staged an attack in Sunsari District in the east. There was always one thing or another, if it wasn't one thing it was another. On 26 April, the Centre for the Investigation of the Abuse of Authority ordered the arrests of a former executive chairman and a former board chairman of the Royal Nepal Airlines Corporation. A Congress party member, a former minister of tourism and civil aviation, was asked to hand in his passport. The Congress party immediately deemed the investigation to be politically biased.

The UML crowed. The same day, left parties carried out a chakka jam, in the evening rush hours, demanding G. P. Koirala's resignation. This was followed by a blackout. Over the weekend of the 28th and 29th, leftist activists patrolled the streets and stopped government vehicles, including the car being used by the Speaker of the House.

The prospect of a coup was looming large, but the political parties were too shortsighted to see it. April ended with the deployment of the army to Rukum, Rolpa, Jajarkot, Salyan, Gorkha, Pyuthan and Kalikot Districts as the beginning of the Integrated Security and Development Programme. Army troops would reach the districts in two weeks to get the security situation under control. In the second phase of the programme, the army would be deployed to Kavrepalanchowk, Ramechhap, Lamjung, Dhading, Dolpa, Jumla, Sindhupalchowk, Sindhuli, Nuwakot, Dailekh, Baglung, Myagdi, Tanahun and Achham Districts, where it would build infrastructure like roads and bridges. In the third phase, there would be long-term work to alleviate rural poverty. The Integrated Security and Development Programme seemed to be handing the development responsibility of the civilian government to the army. But the political parties were not concerned. They only wanted G. P. Koirala's resignation.

Despite all this, sometimes for brief periods I thought everything would be all right. I would attend a lecture by an articulate intellectual, and suddenly see some light. A journalist would report bravely on what was happening in rural Nepal. A civil rights activist would say something pithy. One or another Nepali would achieve international success, or someone very young would climb Mt Everest. One day I went to Kathmandu's zoo and saw that the animals were kept in conditions that were more or less humane. I watched a particularly effusive chimpanzee and felt my sense of normality restored.

But then my view would grow cloudy again. On 2 May, the Centre for the Investigation of the Abuse of Authority asked G. P. Koirala for clarification of his role in the Lauda Air jet deal. By this time, even his own party members wanted him to resign. But GP sent back a three-page letter challenging the Centre's jurisdiction to question what had been a cabinet decision. The head of the rebel faction within the Congress, Krishna Prasad Bhattarai, publicly demanded GP's resignation. GP shot back: 'Bhattarai's job is to ask for my resignation; mine is to refuse the same.' Even the deputy prime minister and the foreign minister suggested that he resign, but at seventy-eight, GP wanted to keep holding on to power.

And I saw that terrible things would happen any day now, as the Congress leaders bickered among themselves—something nobody was prepared for—and everyone's lives would be given up to naked survival.

On 8 May, scores of members of a Maoist-affiliated student body, the All-Nepal National Federation of Student Unions (Revolutionary)—ANNFSU (Revolutionary)—attacked two 'bourgeois' private schools in Kathmandu, destroying their computers and photocopy machines and setting the furniture on fire. Brandishing khukuris and iron rods, the assailants demanded that the schools lower their fees, and—because the schools' principals were of Indian origin—they chanted slogans against India. One million children all over the country stayed at home as the Public and Boarding Schools Organization decided to shut down all 8,000 of its member schools for three days in protest.

The news was, meanwhile, filled with the deployment of the army in the Maoist-affected districts. Gorkha District, home to the Shah kings, was also home to Maoist leader Baburam

Bhattarai. It was, we now learned, to be a model district for the Integrated Security and Development Programme: The army would carry out forty development projects here, constructing bridges and irrigation canals, implementing drinking water and electricity schemes, and supporting the collection, processing and distribution of herbs.

The Maoists carried on unhindered, skirting the army. On 13 May, three Maoists were killed in Surkhet District, two of them women. Five days later, the Maoists looted weapons in Kaski and Parbat Districts. On 19 May, the Maoists killed three policemen and injured eleven civilians in an attack in Okhaldhunga District, in the east. On the same day, their cadres held a mass rally in Bhawang village in Rolpa District, and announced the formation of their 'People's Local Governments' throughout the district. This took place just weeks before army troops were due to arrive there. The People's Local Government consisted of a ten-member committee, including members of the ethnic rights group Magarat Mukti Morcha, members of the Dalit rights group Dalit Mukti Morcha, local intelligentsia, women and Maoist area commanders. The Maoists vowed to form similar governments in Rukum, Salyan, Jajarkot, Kalikot and Gorkha Districts, establishing a parallel government.

In Kathmandu, G. P. Koirala resigned as the general secretary of the Congress, only to appoint a relative. He also appointed two other relatives to the party's Central Working Committee.

Word had it that the Centre for the Investigation of the Abuse of Authority was going to announce, any day now, its findings on the Lauda Air jet deal. Before that could happen, though, the Public Accounts Committee of Parliament announced that it was charging both the Congress's and the UML's former ministers of tourism and civil aviation with corruption in another deal involving Royal Nepal Airlines Corporation's lease of a China Southwest Airlines jet. The UML suddenly lost steam; its leaders denounced this decision, though feebly. Days later, the Centre for the Investigation of the Abuse of Authority announced that it was prosecuting ten people in connection with the Lauda Air jet lease, including two foreign Lauda Air executives based in Italy and Austria. No mention was made of G. P. Koirala's culpability. I found myself wondering whether these prosecutions were politically motivated.

The UML rallied back and announced a three-day-long nationwide bandh from 27 to 29 May, demanding—what else— G. P. Koirala's resignation. No taxis or tempos or buses or cars ran for these three days, no shops or offices or businesses opened. So zealous were party activists in enforcing the shutdown that even the few vegetable vendors who defied other bandhs decided not to risk it this time.

During one-day bandhs, people generally cleaned their houses or caught up with chores. This time, though, they lost all will. They sat and watched Hindi movies and tele-serials. I did the same. On the first night I watched a ghost movie, though I didn't usually like those. I watched religious programmes the next morning, and a gleaming guru told me to keep Krishna in my heart. That day, two patients died in hospital because leftist activists had obstructed ambulances. On the third day, there was unrest throughout the country as people tried to defy the bandh. More than six hundred people—and a line of cars—took out a rally in Kathmandu in protest. Most people, though, just sat home and watched soap operas, police shows, sitcoms, docudramas—anything that was on.

One day sometime after that, I got into a conversation with the manager of my gym about Upstairs, a jazz bar that the man frequented. I had been meaning to go there for years, I said.

'I'm there every night after nine,' he told me as he did his abs. He also talked about a resort not far from Kathmandu where he had done some bungee jumping: 'It used to be the second-highest jump in the world, but the highest closed down, so now this is the highest.' Moving on to bench presses, he said he had attended a fancy dress party at which two men had shown up in drag. 'One really looked like a woman,' he grinned.

So surprised was I by all the fun he was having that all I could say was, 'Wow. That's great. That's cool.' I did not begrudge him his fun; I knew, after all, that I would not feel any more light-hearted dressing up for parties, or jumping off bridges with my life on a rope, or even dropping by a bar to hear jazz. But the man's appetite for fun got me thinking.

Later, at Himalayan Java, a hip new café in Thamel, I looked at the young people of Kathmandu—a blithe, carefree generation—and found that I did resent them. The café was filled with people of my economic class—the Kathmandu bourgeoisie, who were unaffected, in any real sense, by the failure of democratic politics. They got on with their lives despite it all. Close to me sat a young woman in a halter top, bell bottoms and platform heels, a navel ring showing on her sleek stomach. Her face was frozen in a come-hither expression as she listened to the young man across her. He had gelled, spiked hair, and earrings, and sleek clothes offset by a big-buckled belt and bulky Dr. Martins.

Why were these young people being so relentlessly hip? No, this was good. I sipped my iced mocha, thinking, here is a whole country writhing with youthful energy. There is an age, isn't there, at which one wants to smash all that is traditional, at which one wants to destroy the old and usher in the new? The youth were following the paths open to them. Those in Kathmandu were mimicking MTV VJs, and those in the villages were joining the Maoists. They were both, in their own ways, trying to force change.

Meanwhile, Amnesty International had begun to criticize the country's police for execution, torture and disappearances, and the Maoists for passing death sentences in their 'People's Courts' and recruiting children into their ranks. Nepal could soon have one of the highest rates of human rights atrocities. Panicked, more and more of the bourgeoisie began hoping that the king would do something, anything, to restore order. Most of the royal family was unpopular, but about King Birendra Bir Bikram Shah the bourgeoisie had always been addle-headed. He was such a pleasant fellow. Because he now did so little as a constitutional monarch, he committed few mistakes. Because he controlled so few public funds, he was not tainted by money. Because he spoke so little, what he said sounded sage. He shone in comparison to the coarse, bungling party leaders of the day.

Eternal dynasty. The hows and whens of a royal coup became topics of endless conjecture in Kathmandu. All of us were convinced that it would happen. It almost seemed like there was a Panchayat propaganda hex on us: Our political parties would muddle endlessly, and the king would return to power, claiming that it was for our own good. We did not want a royal coup to happen. But we felt helpless to prevent it. And so all we did, when we heard a fresh round of rumours, was to hunker down and brace for the worst.

On 30 May, just as the Lauda Air jet lease hearings began at the Patan appellate court, the jet in question flew to Bangkok for routine repairs, never to return.

The next day, the Maoists set off a bomb at an offset press in Kathmandu, accusing the press of printing 'obscene materials'. No one could figure out exactly what printed material had angered them so much. Local UML leaders in faraway Musikot village, in Rukum District, boycotted the chief district officer's all-party meeting on the army's Integrated Security and Development Programme. The country was in a shambles.

By now my interest in my work was petering out. It seemed to me that fiction couldn't keep up with our reality. Or I did not know how to make it. My friends were beginning to worry about their career prospects. Non-government organizations could no longer work in the villages without the fear of local Maoists turning against them. The cancellations in the tourism industry were affecting not just Kathmandu hotels and travel agencies, but also village inns and lodges. Businesses were closing. Artists were unable to find clients. The garment industry had declined in the last year, though the year before it had grown by 30 per cent. Eight people died of gastroenteritis in far-western Jajarkot on the last day of May.

As I walked through the Kathmandu streets late that afternoon, it occurred to me that all I ever did any more was worry. And if the way that Kathmandu's hip youth ignored their country's troubles helped nothing, neither did my anxious and burdened attitude. I thought: My life has become so aimless, so desultory, that I feel a compulsion to link it to larger, more compelling collective narratives. I am infusing my experience with an importance that is otherwise absent. I am trying to make my life interesting by linking it to bad politics. I had to do something to lift my mood. I might start by doing something small, I thought, something different to alter my days, or at least this day, or the next few hours. Perhaps being happy required nothing much: no marches or demonstrations, no political action, no grand gestures. Our lives are small, our problems are small, and maybe their solutions are also small.

On a whim I veered into a tandoori restaurant where my friends and I used to go when we were all feeling more upbeat

about life. It wasn't the kind of place where women went alone—
for a price the restaurant arranged girls. Most of the clients that
day were male, though at a few tables couples were huddled over
tea and snacks. I phoned a friend from there and said I'd come
over with some food, and he said all right, so it was a date. I
ordered a half tandoori chicken and naan, saag paneer and daal,
and asked the waiter to home-pack it.

As I waited, my eyes fell on a couple at a corner table. The
man was much older than his partner, who was another one of
those image-conscious young women. She was wearing tight
black pants and long, sharp heels. Her face was heavily made up.
She could not have been more than eighteen. The man was in
his forties, the age when men bore of their wives. I wondered
whether he was her lover or client.

As I looked on, something about the man struck me. The
width of his back. He was wearing a chequered jacket, and
was stooping slightly. I recognized the stoop. He had the same
frizzy hair as the psychiatrist I had thought of visiting months
ago. Most of his clients were young women who wore defeated
expressions. This woman was not like that. She was the kind of
woman that even insecure women warm to: bright, unapologetic
about her youth, happy to claim her due. The man, leaning into
her, wiped away a crumb on her lips. She laughed in a way that
was meant to be both girlish and sexy.

When my home-pack order came, I paid and went outside,
suddenly feeling confused. Evening was falling, and the first few
cars had turned on their sidelights. My friend's street was blasted
through with the sounds of car horns. The gap-toothed unevenness
of the sidewalk frazzled me as I pushed through the crowds.

I did not enjoy dinner that night. My friend was going
through a bad patch, and we talked awhile about the difficulty of
finding work, and then we gossiped about common friends. We

had dinner, then put on the television news. Once the headlines were over, my friend told me a joke that he'd heard that day.

'It's a little indecent,' he said, slightly embarrassed. Then he went on. 'There was a man on a crowded bus, and he was standing with his hands like this.' He cupped both palms, and said, 'No matter how much the bus jolted him around, the man wouldn't change the position of his hands.' He smiled in anticipation of the joke. 'After a while, the people around began to notice this. Every time the bus stopped, all the passengers would reach for a railing or a chair back to hold onto, but this man would just balance himself with his legs, never changing the position of his hands.

'Now one of the passengers on the bus was a policeman, who thought, This man is a Maoist. He's got explosives in his shirt, and the detonator is in his hands. Otherwise why would he keep from touching anything even when the bus turns?

'So the policeman followed the man when he got off the bus. Even on the streets, the man kept his hands cupped. The policeman was sure he had found a Maoist. As they neared a police post, he arrested the man.

'But even after he was arrested, the man wouldn't stop cupping his hands. The police thought, This man is a hardened Maoist, we'll have to beat him into confessing. So they took him straight to the investigation cell. But before beating him, the inspector said, Now we're going to beat you, but you can avoid that if you just tell us why you're holding your hands like that.'

My friend's face was flushed with glee. I was smiling along expectantly. Holding up cupped hands, my friend said, 'And then the man said, Sir, this is the measurement of my wife's breasts. I was going to buy her a bra!'

My friend burst out laughing, and I also laughed, because it was silly, the man walking around with cupped hands. But my friend found it unusually funny. 'It was just a man going to buy a bra!' he hooted, and began laughing so hard that he had to bend over to be able to breathe.

He was still bent over, his shoulders shaking, when I stopped laughing, and I looked at him, doubled up, convulsing, making a sound halfway between a sob and a squeal, and I realized that I hadn't seen him laugh this hard for a long time. He had been low for months on end now. When he lifted his head again he was still laughing, and his lips were stretched thin, his teeth were showing and his eyes were sparkling with tears. He looked like someone I didn't know. 'A bra!' he sputtered and bent over once more.

I laughed, uncertainly, to keep him company, but I was also thinking—for my mind was merciless—why was he laughing so hard at a joke that wasn't that funny? How rare laughter had become in our lives.

For his sake I should have laughed longer, but my breath would not carry false emotion. My mirth died completely.

'A bra,' my friend said again, weakly, then he finally sat up, and for a while we remained as we were, both facing the television, which was on sports news. My friend wiped away some tears and I smiled at him, but inside, I was pierced with sadness at the meagreness of happiness in our days.

I stayed on awhile, as my friend made a few good-humoured remarks about the sports news. But the sadness inside me kept growing till I could no longer bear to stay on. 'I'll go,' I said, and I left him still watching the news.

Barely twenty-four hours after this, King Birendra Bir Bikram Shah and his entire family succumbed to the massacre at the royal palace.

HISTORY TRIES TO REPEAT
ITSELF IN THE MANNER OF A TIRED CLICHÉ

If you were to effect a coup on a postmodern democracy, the coup would have to be a postmodern coup, a coup that doesn't look like a coup, but which has the outcome of one.

Horrifying though the 2001 massacre at the royal palace was, the events that followed were worse. As the Maoists escalated their insurgency, the party leaders continued to botch and bungle, and the new king, Gyanendra Bir Bikram Shah, took the opportunity to steer the government back towards an absolute monarchy. All as Nepal became one of the worst countries for war atrocities and human rights violations.

Just over a month after the royal massacre, in the first week of July 2001, the Maoists overran three police posts in Lamjung, Nuwakot and Gulmi Districts, killing forty-one policemen and making off with ammunitions. They also set off a rash of pipe and pressure-cooker bombs in Kathmandu, alongside 'banner bombs'—bombs dangling off red banners splashed with Maoist slogans. They had decided, it seemed, to raise the stakes of their war.

They followed with the largest attack to date, one which brought down Prime Minister G. P. Koirala: Around 19 July, approximately 1,000 Maoists surrounded a police station in the village of Holeri in Rolpa District, kidnapping seventy-one police and armed police personnel. The prime minister, in desperation, ordered the army to pursue the Maoists. This attracted shrill opposition from 'democrat' and 'progressive' intellectuals alike, who wanted the government to negotiate a political settlement with the Maoists instead of pursuing a military tack. Deputy Prime Minister Ramchandra Poudyal even resigned in protest. And for some reason India deployed troops along the border at this time, setting off jitters in Nepal about an imminent invasion.

But G. P. Koirala would not retract. The army, for its part, appeared to comply with his orders, surrounding Nuwa village, where the Maoists had taken the hostages. The media was not allowed into the area by either the army or the Maoists, but the government informed the public that the army was undertaking a 'cordon and search' operation there.

One day passed, and then another, with no further news. Then the Maoist leader Prachanda issued a statement that it was the Maoists who had surrounded the army, and not the other way around. Local villagers were providing food to the Maoists, he claimed, so that they could in turn feed the hostages.

The government issued a denial, explaining that the army had been prevented from capturing the Maoists by the heavy monsoon downpour.

As another day passed, then another, rumours began to circulate in Kathmandu that the government was lying. Word now had it that the army had never surrounded the Maoists at all. The government kept insisting otherwise, maintaining that the army would capture the Maoists as soon as the rains abated.

Then independent media sources reported that the army had withdrawn from Nuwa village. G. P. Koirala's government again issued a denial. Again, days passed amid uncertainty.

Eight days after ordering the army into action, G. P. Koirala abruptly resigned. He later cited the army's non-cooperation as his reason. Apparently, the army brass had lied to him about having surrounded the Maoists. What exactly occurred in Nuwa village remains unclear till today. But this much was obvious: The army would do as it pleased if drawn into the counter-insurgency.

Sher Bahadur Deuba became the eleventh and last democratic prime minister of Nepal in July 2001. Though the Maoists killed seventeen policemen in Bajura District on his first day in office, he was able to announce, the same day, a ceasefire between the government and the Maoists, beginning his tenure on an optimistic note.

Peace talks began. On the last day of August, government negotiators met with representatives of the CPN (Maoist) at a Kathmandu resort for a first round of talks. At day's end, both sides committed to solving their differences through dialogue.

Showing good faith, the government relaxed restrictions on the right to assembly (revoked by the Public Security Ordinance days after the royal massacre), and the Maoists began to hold public meetings in Kathmandu. The biggest of them all, an open-air meeting, would be held on 21 September, they announced. Over 2,00,000 of their supporters would show up in Kathmandu that day.

The Kathmandu bourgeoisie baulked. Everyone was saying that the Maoists would demand shelter in people's homes, marking them for retribution if they refused. A wave of panic rippled through the business community. Investment halted, and there was much cocktail-hour talk on capital flight and the collapse of banks.

As another round of peace talks neared, the Maoists whittled their forty demands (made back in 1996) down to three points: They wanted an all-party interim government to be formed; they wanted the all-party government to hold elections for a constituent assembly (a constituent assembly that Nepal had been promised back in 1950, but that everyone had forgotten about); and they wanted Nepal to become a republican state.

The government responded by accusing the Maoists of extorting money, raping women and enlisting child soldiers.

The second round of talks took place at a resort in Bardiya District on 12 September (Al Qaeda's attacks on the United States were overshadowed, in Nepal, by this). The government would not hear of the Maoists' three demands, but agreed to release information on Maoist suspects in police custody. It also asked them to cancel their 21 September open-air meeting in Kathmandu. The Maoists, in turn, demanded that the Armed Police Force be dissolved, that the army's Integrated Security and Development Programme be stopped and that the Public Security Ordinance be revoked.

After that, both sides stepped up the pressure. The government raided the Maoist centres that had come above-ground after the ceasefire, arresting dozens. The Maoists forced a five-day closure of schools throughout Nepal beginning on 19 September. They did, as a concession, call off their open-air meeting, much to the relief of the Kathmandu bourgeoisie. The government reciprocated by releasing the names of Maoist suspects in its custody.

But in the end neither side could sustain the peace talks. Sher Bahadur Deuba expanded his cabinet to include forty-one ministers, some of whom were notorious for past corruption. The Maoists too went back to business as usual: At the end of October, thirty-odd members of a militant ethnicity rights group, the Rastriya Kirant Mukti Morcha, killed two men in Solukhumbu District, adding a new ethnic dimension to the insurgency. Then two hundred Maoists attacked a police station in Kavre District, not far from Kathmandu, and Prachanda declared that the formation of an all-party interim government (to hold elections for a constituent assembly) was a precondition for further talks.

Then, days before the third round of talks, the Maoists made an ambiguous public statement suggesting that Nepal need not, after all, become a republican state; the king could stay (confirming, in the minds of some, that all they really wanted was to rid Nepal of democracy). Their leaders never confirmed this policy change, but it created an illusion of flexibility. Pleased, the government scrapped the Public Security Ordinance and released sixty-eight alleged Maoists from police detention.

So fast were events moving by now that in just a few months the massacre at the royal palace had begun to feel faraway. On 12 November, Princess Prekshya, the youngest sister of the late Queen Aishwarya (and the ex-wife of King Birendra's youngest brother, Dhirendra) died in a helicopter crash at Rara Lake in northwest Nepal. She had not been invited to the tragic 1 June family gathering, but now she too was dead. Bad luck? A wave of fresh conspiracy theories started...

Nobody had time to indulge them, though, because the next day, the third round of talks began. Again the government refused the Maoists' three demands. Constitutional monarchy and parliamentary democracy were non-negotiable, they said. The Maoists too took an inflexible stand. On 21 November, Prachanda ended the ceasefire, saying, 'Our bid to establish peace has been rendered unsuccessful by reactionary and fascist forces.'

Two days later, the Maoists launched nationwide attacks, setting off bombs in Surkhet, Rukum, Kalikot, Kaski, Makwanpur, Sankhuwasabha, Taplejung and Khotang Districts. In a move that dramatically escalated the war, they also attacked the army for the first time, ambushing a military truck in Ghorahi, in Dang District, to loot a cache of sub-machine guns. They followed up with raids on police and army posts in Dang and Syangja Districts, killing thirty-nine police and army men. Smaller attacks were carried out the same day in eleven other districts. They were intentionally drawing the army into the war.

By now the United States' post-9/11 rhetoric about the 'war on terror' had gained worldwide currency. On 26 November, Prime Minister Sher Bahadur Deuba deemed the Maoists to be 'terrorists' and declared a state of emergency, at the same time ordering the army into the counter-insurgency. The cabinet passed an accompanying Terrorist and Disruptive Activities Ordinance, authorizing arrests without due process. The media was directed to contact the defence ministry for any information on the counter-insurgency.

On the first day of the state of emergency, thirty-four people, including eleven army men, were killed in a clash between the Maoists and the army in Solukhumbu District. The next day, four policemen and twelve alleged Maoists (now called 'terrorists' by the government) were killed in Darchula District. A bomb went off in a carpet factory in Kathmandu on 3 December.

The state of emergency, which was to last ten months, would eventually leave nearly 4,300 people dead (as against 1,800 in the previous six years of the insurgency). Whereas earlier the number of people killed by the Maoists equalled the number of alleged Maoists killed by the state, now the ratio became one to four, with the state security forces responsible for 80 per cent of the killings. Of the alleged Maoists they killed, up to 40 per cent were innocent civilians, said human rights workers.

Given the nature of Nepal's army, these statistics are not surprising. The Royal Nepal Army claims in its official documents that since the king became its supreme commander-in-chief in 1950, it has been modernizing itself: 'Continuous training in most aspects of modern military technique and ideas as held the RNA to keep of with the rest of the world in terms of its capabilities to defend the sovereignty of Nepal.' But the grammar of that sentence alone is indicative. Of course their weapons were upgraded. Yet—though Nepal's Gurkhas were famously adept in the British and Indian armies, and though Nepal dispatched troops to UN peacekeeping units—the army at home had withered into a largely ceremonial body, good for adding pomp to state occasions. Of all government branches, it was the least touched by democratic changes. Even after 1950, it was headed mostly by members of the Rana family, as had been the case since Jung Bahadur Kunwar Rana's time, over a century and a half ago. Since Nepal's unification in 1768, all army chiefs have been from five clans of the ruling Chettri caste: twenty-six Ranas, four Pandeys, four Thapas, two Basnyats and two Shahs. The army's top brass embodied the traditional elite of Nepal, an elite in very slow decline.

The growing militarization of politics silenced intellectuals of both democratic and progressive persuasion. To begin with, they did not know what to believe any more. The defence ministry, the official source of information on the counter-insurgency, claimed impressive successes: seven hundred Maoists had surrendered in four districts; fifty to sixty Maoists were killed repelling an attack on a repeater station in Rolpa District; eleven Maoists had been killed in an encounter in Kailali District. The government fed the media one after another unlikely report; for example, not a single civilian was ever admitted killed, even by mistake. These reports were obviously false, at least in part. But it was impossible to ascertain what, then, the truth was.

After the Maoists bombed the Tumlingtar airport in the east, the army moved into 'search and destroy' mode, which, the public were told, was more aggressive than their earlier 'cordon and search' mode. In bald defiance, 2,500 Maoists stormed the town of Mangalsen, the headquarters of Achham District in the west, on 17 February 2002—exactly six years since the start of the insurgency. They attacked a garrison of fifty-nine army men, killing all but two. Many of them were later found with execution-style bullets to the head. The Maoists also burned government offices and destroyed a nearby airfield, killing twenty-seven policemen.

A mental paralysis crept over the intelligentsia in Kathmandu.

Militaries were rising: What was a mere thinker to do? To set right all that was wrong, one needed to do more than attend a few meetings, deliver eloquent lectures, sign a few petitions, march in peace rallies. Was the intelligentsia prepared to make a real difference?

The answer was, 'Not without the leadership of our political parties.'

But the political parties were still dithering.

On 10 April, the government re-enacted the expired Terrorist and Disruptive Activities Ordinance, which severely restricted civil liberties. According to some estimates, the Maoists now controlled up to two-thirds of the countryside. The state's presence was thinning, or altogether vanishing in the rural areas as the Maoists destroyed bridges, hydropower projects, water-supply systems, horticulture farms, forestry projects, telecommunications towers and government buildings. The damage to infrastructure had already mounted to billions of rupees when the Maoists blew up an electricity station in Kapilvastu District in early April. Then they bombed the control room of the newly built Jhimruk hydroelectric project which supplied electricity to three districts. Over one-third of the country's telephone links had also been severed.

In mid April, thousands of Maoists—as many as 8,000, according to some sources; around 2,000 according to others— attacked an Armed Police Force barracks in Dang District, leaving 150 dead, ninety-two of their own comrades among them. Barely three weeks later, they stormed an Army base in Gam village, Rolpa District. This encounter left another 150 people dead, including seventy army men.

By this time Sher Bahadur Deuba had been prime minister for nine months, which is as long as most of Nepal's prime ministers last. G. P. Koirala was pressing for his rival's resignation.

(This time around, the feuds that brought down the Congress were between Koirala and Deuba.) The prime minister had scheduled a special meeting of Parliament to extend the state of emergency for a third time, but G. P. Koirala convinced his party members to vote against this extension. Deuba retaliated: The night before the special meeting, he went to the Narayanhiti palace and met with King Gyanendra, and—without informing his own party's members—he dissolved Parliament, announcing a mid-term election for 13 November.

The local governments had already been dissolved by then, for their elected members' five-year tenures had ended, and fresh elections had been unfeasible due to Maoist threats. So, till the local and general elections could be held—and no one was sure when security conditions would improve enough for that to happen—the country would be governed by the prime minister and his cabinet at the national level, and by bureaucrats all the way down.

For dissolving Parliament, G. P. Koirala had Sher Bahadur Deuba expelled from the Congress. Despite this, Deuba convened a general assembly of the party on 16 June. Though the assembly quorum was lacking, it dismissed Koirala as party president, replacing him with—who else—Deuba. Koirala fought back by petitioning the Election Commission to recognize his faction of the Congress as the real Congress, and to grant it use of the party's four-starred flag and tree-shaped election symbol. Deuba's faction refused to concede these.

In a time of deep gloom, as the political parties were failing again and again, new leadership for the Kathmandu intelligentsia emerged, slowly, from two professional groups—the human rights lawyers and the journalists.

The human rights movement had begun in the early 1980s,

under the leadership of the historian Rishikesh Shaha. After
1990, human rights organizations proliferated, though work took
place somewhat fitfully, with most organizations only criticizing
governments formed by parties not to their liking. The Romeo
and Kilo Sierra 2 operations jolted them out of their partisan
biases. Now, regardless of which party helped to perpetrate
violations, activists such as Mandira Sharma and Krishna Pahari
were focusing on the remedies, helping to salvage amid war a
measure of rule of law.

Journalists, too, were speaking out with increasing boldness:
Kathmandu-based reporters like Gunaraj Luintel, Sudhir Sharma
and Mohan Mainali, as well as other field-based reporters from
the private media houses were bringing back first-hand accounts
from the war-torn hinterlands. This, despite the fact that—by the
count of Reporters Sans Frontières—more than one hundred
journalists were jailed during the state of emergency, making
Nepal the most repressive state against the media.

But both these professional groups were young, and they
could only do so much for the cause of justice. Krishna Sen's
case demonstrated how flagrant the state's violations could be.
Sen, a CPN (Maoist) central committee member who worked
as a journalist, was arrested on 20 May 2002 by the police.
Weeks later, the vernacular *Janaastha* reported that he had been
tortured and executed in police detention. His body had been
shown to his family, then secreted away by the government.
A few international human rights workers had also seen Sen's
body. Yet—in response to the *Janaastha* report—the ministry of
home affairs issued a statement denying that Sen had even been
arrested, let alone executed. Taken unawares by the unprecedented
outcry by Kathmandu's galvanized intelligentsia, the government
finally set up an investigation committee. But the committee's
findings were never released. And so, despite the best efforts of

the human rights lawyers and journalists, Krishna Sen's murder in police detention went unpunished.

The impunity with which the state security forces operated was enabled by the see-no-evil, hear-no-evil, speak-no-evil spirit of Kathmandu's frightened bourgeoisie. Why protect the civil liberties of Maoists who want to kill us? What are the political affiliations of these human rights activists? And these journalists—are they Maoists?

For the bourgeoisie, it felt as though the heathens had reached the gates: 'The state security forces *must* kill the Maoists for the protection of you and me' was the gut response. Rules of engagement? Rule of law? Civil liberties? Human rights? No, no, no, only a strong army could protect us. Right-wing political parties like Save the Nation began posting banners exhorting King Gyanendra to take over. Royalist intellectuals waxed eloquent on the glory that was the monarchy. The business community started pressing for the king to intervene: Tourism had ground to a halt, and all the other industries were suffering heavy losses. The country had reported the lowest GDP in twenty years.

In all this, Kathmandu's international community—the diplomats and heads of international aid agencies, who, because they supply 60 per cent of the national budget, have always exercised great power—were also turning towards the king. Lacking historical knowledge of Nepal, they were unable to sympathize with the aspirations pinned onto democracy here. And, unable to understand the Nepali language, and limited in their social interactions to hobnobbing with the traditional elite, they could not understand what the intelligentsia was jabbering on about. Instead of using their clout to help save democracy, they dismissed it as the dysfunction of the political parties. 'It is lucky for you Nepalis that you have a king,' they said at Kathmandu's cocktail parties, wilfully ignoring King Gyanendra's lingering image problem following the royal massacre. Munching hors d'oeuvres and canapés, the diplomats, aid workers and expatriates of Kathmandu said to the Nepalis, 'Only your king can save you from turning into Cambodia.'

The political parties obliged them with more bad behaviour:

The Congress split in two when the Election Commission announced, after great delay, that the party's name, flag and election symbol would remain with G. P. Koirala's faction. Prime Minister Sher Bahadur Deuba, bereft of a party, quickly formed the Nepali Congress Party (Democratic) with members of the 'rebel' faction. The deadline for elections was looming. But prospects were bleak: The Maoists threatened to kill all candidates, and even followed through with the grisly beheading of a UML candidate and the murders of several Congress activists.

If a new Parliament could not be reinstated through elections, the country would enter a constitutional crisis; and the 1990 constitution granted the king limited discretionary powers under Article 127. Hoping to prevent King Gyanendra from exercising his powers, the political parties finally—momentarily—halted their bickering to agree on a postponement of elections by six months.

On 4 October, Prime Minister Sher Bahadur Deuba went to the king with this request.

But the king swiftly dismissed him and his cabinet on grounds of incompetence, and took power into his own hands.

The royal coup was announced on Nepal Television around 11 p.m., as most of the country slept. On the crisp autumn morning of 5 October 2002, the Nepali people awoke to the news that King Gyanendra had relieved them of their sovereignty. Royalists rejoiced in victory, and democrat/progressive intellectuals raged. Yet most people—including the Kathmandu bourgeoisie—remained addled as always: The party leaders had squandered their chance, the Maoists were getting stronger, and the king had no choice but to step in and save us. Like his father had done in 1960, he would make it all better now.

THE
MASSACRES
TO COME

LEAVING KATHMANDU

King Gyanendra's first royal cabinet, headed by a hand-picked prime minister, the Panchayat-era politician Lokendra Bahadur Chand, reached a ceasefire agreement with the Communist Party of Nepal (Maoist) three months after the royal coup, on 30 January 2003.

Three weeks later, a friend and I were in the unsightly clump of wooden houses of Chupra village in Dailekh District, west Nepal. We were here to begin a trek through the war-torn districts of Dailekh, Kalikot and Jumla. It was eight in the evening when we reached Chupra after a day-long drive, but the lodges in the bazaar were filled to capacity. There was a festive air about town.

A local man explained that the regional volleyball championships were on. Young people from all the nearby villages had come to watch. He threw us a significant look. 'Even the Maoists are competing this year,' he said.

'Is that right?'

'All the region's big players are here.'

My friend, Malcolm, very tall and very pale—which made him an exceptionally conspicuous foreigner in a land full of short, dark people—was a British human rights expert interested in seeing whether the war had been, as most independent reports had it, high in violations. I was desperate to leave Kathmandu, to stop being a politics junkie and to see what war had wrought in the countryside. The government and the Maoists had agreed on a code of conduct for the ceasefire, which bound them to allow people to move freely through the countryside. Otherwise we would have felt too endangered to take this trip.

After hunting through Chupra village, we eventually found a lodge with two free rooms. In its neat, clay-swept dining room, the portly lodge owner was standing about doing nothing in particular. His wife, cooking at a wood stove, nodded us towards a table. Our driver and a friend of his joined us as well.

Three men were eating at the table, downing glasses of milky white chhaang with their food. One, a young man with long, greasy hair, was eating with special gusto, shovelling handfuls of daal-bhaat into his mouth, then licking his fingers clean before sucking noisily on chicken bones. Malcolm and I consulted the three maps we had brought from Kathmandu. All three marked different villages, rivers, hills and passes. Their scales were inconsistent. We had no idea what lay ahead. But we both shared a basic confidence that rural Nepal was negotiable; we would find our way through somehow.

His noisy meal over, the man with greasy hair turned to us with an inebriated smile. Slowly he slid over to examine the maps, saying, in English, '*Don't mind.*' He then pointed at Chupra with a food-stained hand. 'Here we are. If you don't *mind.*'

I decided to venture a conversation. 'So there's a volleyball tournament going on,' I said.

'Hunh? Yes. There are games tomorrow.' He blinked, then blinked again. He slid closer, till I could smell the booze on his breath. 'You don't *mind* my sitting here, do you?'

'I don't mind,' I lied. 'Are you going to watch the games?'

'Hunh? No. I have to drive back early in the morning.'

He was a bus driver. Originally from Sindhupalchowk District, near Kathmandu, he had come on a whim to these parts years ago and had never gone back. He usually plied this route once a week, but nowadays he had been coming every other day. 'All the people who left their villages are returning now that there's peace,' he said.

We asked how many people were coming back.

'Five hundred a day.'

'Five hundred?'

He blinked. 'Nobody knows how long the peace will last. They're visiting their families while they can.'

The other men, who had finished eating, vacated the table so that we could eat. The bus driver stayed on. As the lodge owner's wife served us steaming plates of daal-bhaat, I asked him whether the Maoists had given people any trouble here.

'They don't bother people like us,' he said cheerfully, making a gesture that included us all. 'They hitch free rides on the buses, so sometimes the police or army accuse us of supporting them. But how can we turn the Maoists away? They'll punish us if we do.' Punishment amounted to public apologies, fines, physical torture or forced labour.

'And they don't punish you if you drink alcohol?' I said, looking at his empty glass.

He grinned sheepishly. '*Don't mind,*' he said, using what was clearly his favourite expression.

'I don't mind,' I said. 'But don't the Maoists mind?'

'Not with people like us. They say, You are the labouring classes, so you can drink. But don't make trouble afterwards.' He grew serious at the thought. 'They do punish men who get drunk and beat their wives. They also punish you if they catch you playing cards or—if you don't *mind* my speaking like this—and I never do this—but if they find out that you have made physical contact with a woman, they will punish you. The Maoists will make you marry her. But otherwise,' he said, growing cheerful again, 'they don't make trouble for people like us.'

We chatted a bit about the volleyball game as we ate, and later, went to our rooms, which were all adjoined. We had to share a cramped den with walls covered by splotchy betel stains. I

kept all the doors open so as to prove—to anyone who cared—
that I was sharing the room with men strictly for convenience. I
crawled into my bed, a window ledge just my size, as Malcolm
lay with half his legs dangling off a pallet half his height. Our
driver and his friend were down to their underwear in their beds.

I was unsure about this trip. In the past months I had turned
to non-fiction writing as a means to find out how Kathmandu's
bad politics was playing out in the countryside. I had asked
journalists who had written about the insurgency, 'How do you
go to the insurgency-affected areas?'

'You just go,' they had said.

'Just like that?'

'Just like that.'

The next morning, the lodge owner arranged us a porter—we
were to pick him up across the river that ran through Chupra
village. We were looking to hire another porter as well. Outside
the lodge, a short, stocky man came up to us. In his hands
he had a jute rope of the kind used to tie loads. 'You need a
porter?' he asked.

We told him that we needed someone who had been to
Jumla District before.

'I've been there twice,' he said. 'I know all the routes.'

We fixed a daily rate with him, and were about to pile into
our pickup truck when the lodge owner took me aside.

'I don't know about this man,' he whispered urgently.

'Why?' I asked, looking back casually at the porter. His clothes
were tattered and he wore a wool cap in the subtropical heat.
He looked like a nice enough man.

'He's of the lower castes,' the lodge owner whispered.

'Oh,' I said, taken aback, though I probably shouldn't have
been, 'that doesn't matter to us.'

'You have to keep an eye on him,' he hissed.

The porter—his name was Chitra Bahadur Sunwar—surely understood what was going on. He was looking hard at us, grinding his teeth in a way that made his eyes widen and his chin jut out. 'I know all the routes to Jumla,' he called out again.

'Let's go,' said Malcolm decisively.

We got into the pickup and took off down the road.

We had to ford a river that looked shallow at first but got worryingly deep when the pickup was midway through it. Relieved to get across, we stopped at the house of the porter whom the lodge owner had arranged for us.

As it turned out, the man was not up for the work.

Chitra Bahadur offered help: 'I have an uncle who is also a porter.'

We saw no reason not to hire his uncle, so he went off to fetch him. The man he returned with, though, did not inspire confidence: Padam Bahadur Sunwar had a wrinkled, folded face, and salt-and-pepper hair, his eyes were milky and his back was slightly stooped. 'This is my mama,' Chitra Bahadur said, addressing him as his maternal uncle. 'He's very strong. You can carry big loads, can't you, Mama?'

Mama nodded weakly.

Chitra Bahadur ground his teeth. His eyes widened. 'Mama has to reach a bundle to Dailekh bazaar, then he'll join our group,' he said.

The two of them hoisted a sack onto the back of the pickup before climbing on themselves. An urchin boy showed up from nowhere and scrambled onto the back as well. The rest of us piled into the front of the truck. The driver made to start the engine, but didn't. Instead he groaned. Further ahead were two girls, heading our way. 'Maoists,' the driver muttered.

The driver's friend, who had taken to explaining things to us, helpfully said, 'All Maoist girls dress like that.' The girls had on plain kurtha-surals in the place of the usual colourful lungis. Instead of woven baskets, they had rucksacks strapped to their backs. Most tellingly, they were wearing closed shoes in case they had to run. Most women here went barefoot, or wore cheap rubber sandals.

The driver groaned again. 'They're going to ask us for a ride.'

One of the girls had a green bandana covering her face. The other, whose face was not covered, came to the front window. She was clearly the older of the two.

'Dai, what do you think they'll do if they see us?' she asked the driver in a singsong voice, without preliminaries. She scanned us all before resting her eyes on the side mirror to check her dark, freckled face. 'The army will recognize us if they see us.' She turned back to the driver. 'Both sides have said they won't do anything to each other, but what does that mean?'

The driver said, 'There's a ceasefire—they won't do anything to you.'

'That's what they say, but do you think it's true?' The girl glanced through the back, eyeing an empty seat beside Malcolm. Then she asked the driver, 'Will you take us past the checkpoint?'

Asked point-blank, he could not say no. He told the girls to get into the back of the pickup.

They did so. Then, just as we were about to set off, the older girl jumped off the back and came in to sit beside Malcolm.

She had easy, affable manners. Over the next hour, as we jolted along the rough road to Dailekh bazaar, we plied her with questions. How old was she? What did she do for the party? Did she really think a violent insurgency would liberate the masses?

She did not mind our questions, and even welcomed them. 'I'll tell you everything I can,' she said, smiling at how much of a curiosity she was for us. Her fingers toyed girlishly against the window as she spoke.

She was, she said, seventeen years old. 'Though I'll be eighteen soon. I'm almost eighteen.' Her friend was fifteen. They worked as 'motivators' for the party, going from house to house in neighbouring Surkhet District, talking to people about the Maoist movement. Now that there was a ceasefire, she was coming back to visit her family.

She hadn't been home in the entire year since she joined the party. She was her parents' only daughter. 'None of my brothers have joined the party,' she said.

Had she taken military training, Malcolm asked.

She shook her head. 'The party only trains those in the army wing. And those who request it.'

Did she carry weapons? Was she carrying one now?

She laughed and said no. During the state of emergency, between November 2001 and August 2002, all the party's cadres had carried socket bombs. 'We were trained how to pull out the pin,' she said, her voice lilting in excitement. 'You have to throw the bomb and run away. It's only four seconds before it explodes. We all had one bomb each. I carried mine with me and almost used it once against the army, but in the end I didn't.' She said that at the end of the state of emergency, most of the party's cadres stopped carrying these bombs. 'Now there's no danger. But things were hard during the state of emergency.'

We asked if the party paid her for her work. 'No!' She laughed at the idea. She got 150 rupees a month for soap and emergency expenses, but otherwise she had to support herself by eating and lodging for free at the houses of ordinary people.

We knew, from newspaper reports, that this was how most of the party cadre operated. We were more interested in the lingering mysteries of the insurgency: Where did her party buy weapons?

She said that the bigger weapons came from some of the communist parties in India. 'But some of the parts for the socket bombs are available in Nepalgunj. A lot of Nepalis living in India support us, you know. What are they called?' She answered herself: 'Prabaasi Nepalis.'

Did the Revolutionary Internationalist Movement supply them with any weapons?

'The who?' She had not heard of the RIM, a coalition of radical leftists around the world which held the Nepali Maoists in high esteem for leading what was currently the world's most successful Maoist insurgency.

The driver's friend, who had met many Maoists before in these areas, began to hector the girl about the hardship that they subjected ordinary people to. 'What's the point of destroying bridges and telephone towers?' he said. 'What's the point of killing people? Ordinary people have suffered the most. Why don't you tell your leaders to stop the violence?'

'The people have suffered,' the girl conceded, easily enough. Then, looking out the window, she sat at alert. We were approaching an army checkpoint. Her face darkened. 'Shall I get out? What shall I do?'

The driver stopped the truck. 'Take a back road,' he said, wanting her to leave.

More to herself than to us, the girl muttered, 'They say they won't do anything, but what if they arrest us?' She turned to her friend at the back and signalled to her to take off her bandana. 'It'll be safer for us to stay in the truck,' she said.

The driver sighed and started the truck again.

As we reached the checkpoint, the girl kept her head down. Her hands were curled into tight balls in her lap. An army man strolled over to the truck and looked us over, his gaze lingering on the girl, who sat very rigidly, more or less giving herself away. The army man went to the back of the pickup and asked the porters where they were going. Then, looking the younger girl over, he ambled away.

I felt sorry for the girl who was sitting with us. To put her at ease, I asked her name.

'I'll tell you later,' she hissed.

'It's all right, he's gone,' I said, but she would not budge.

It was only after we were moving again that she lifted her head. She asked the driver, 'They won't stop us again, will they?' When he said no, she turned to me. 'My name is Binita. That's my party name, Comrade Binita. My family name is Durga.'

Then she went back to answering our questions in her amiable, pleasant way.

Was it hard for her as a girl, I asked, to live such a rough life?

'There are lots of women in the party,' she said. 'There's even an all-woman company.' She explained that a company consisted of three platoons, and each platoon consisted of forty-five armed personnel. 'Even the commissars and commanders of the women's company are women,' she bragged. She had never seen this all-woman company, though. It was stationed in another part of Surkhet District.

'Ask her if she's ever killed anyone,' Malcolm said to me in English.

'I can't ask her that,' I protested.

'Go on, ask.'

So I asked her.

Comrade Binita grew serious. 'I've never done anything like that.'

'Would you, if the party told you to?'

She fidgeted with the windowpane. 'Most likely I won't ever have to.' She said she had never seen her party members killing anyone, and had never recommended that anyone be killed. The greater danger, according to her, was that her party cadres might be killed by the security forces. She had once sprained an ankle while fleeing them. 'Three army men were shooting at us from above, and I came across a ditch, so I jumped.' She smiled, recounting the incident. 'You know, when you see them, you think it's better to die than to fall into their hands, so you run. And what happens when you run is, the bullets land in front of you or behind you, but they don't hit you. The important thing is to keep running.'

And if she were to be wounded, there were doctors in every platoon of the party. The party sent those who were seriously wounded to the nearest district headquarters for treatment, or even to India, she informed us proudly.

'You enjoy working for the party,' I remarked.

'The movement is changing so many things,' she said brightly.

'You have no regrets at all?'

She didn't. Then she said that the one thing she regretted was that she had left school after the ninth class. 'My parents were saying I should at least pass my SLC,' she said. School Leaving Certificate exams took place at the end of the tenth class.

'If the peace holds you could go back and complete your SLC.'

She frowned. 'I'll have lost a year, though.'

'Does that matter?'

'It'll be embarrassing,' she said. 'I'll be older than everyone else.'

Her childishness struck me. Did she feel, I asked, that girls like her were being used by her party? From what we could tell—given that the party was underground—the CPN (Maoist)'s leadership was, like all the other political parties, dominated by Bahun-caste men. 'If there's a Maoist government tomorrow,' I asked Comrade Binita, 'won't the men of your party capture the top posts?'

Confidently, she shook her head twice. 'It's not like that any more.'

'That's happened in the other parties,' I said.

'But women and men are equal now,' she said simply.

I asked her why then there weren't any women in the negotiating team that her party had just set up. 'Couldn't they find any women?'

She suddenly grew sombre.

'Why didn't they put any women in the team?' I persisted.

'I don't know,' she said, scowling.

We all fell silent.

Dailekh bazaar was a row of buildings along a sunny, rolling ridge. People were going about their daily lives, milling about, carrying firewood, bargaining at shops or loitering in groups, drinking tea. This modest bustle had started up only after the ceasefire. Before that, with the army and the police manning the bazaar, people from the outlying villages were loath to come here, lest they be taken for Maoists. Now even known Maoists were roaming about openly.

After Comrade Binita and her friend headed off with thanks, we took leave of our driver and his friend. Chitra Bahadur and Padam Bahadur reached the sack that they had brought with them to a nearby shop, and then they presented to us the urchin who had hitched a ride with us. Bharat was Chitra Bahadur's son of eleven. He would be coming with us, the father announced.

Malcolm protested: 'The boy will slow us down.'

'He's walked to Jumla before,' Chitra Bahadur countered. 'Besides, how can I send him back? He doesn't know his way home.'

We said that we couldn't hire a child.

'He's just walking with his father,' Chitra Bahadur said.

'He's not going to carry any loads.'

'No loads,' he conceded.

We had no choice but to agree.

The urchin let out a thuggish laugh. 'Ba,' he said, tugging at his father's shirt. 'Tell them I want to eat noodles.'

'The boy wants to eat noodles,' Chitra Bahadur said.

They set about buying him noodles.

Nearby, the annual passing-out ceremonies were taking place at the local high school. A skinny graduating boy was warbling a plaintive song by the Nepali singer Fatteman—'I made the mistake of loving someone'—as rows of bored students listened on. A man watching from the side told us that even some Maoist students had come to attend the ceremonies. Did we want to meet them?

We were hoping to leave the bazaar as soon as possible, though. Before that, we wanted to visit the office of the human rights organization INSEC. I knew a prominent poet in Kathmandu who had said I should look up his brother, who lived here. We asked around till we found the brother's house. He then dispatched a neighbour to take us to INSEC's office.

The neighbour led us straight into a district-level meeting of the CPN (UML), taking place in the fusty, sunless first-floor room of a modest stone house. We suddenly found ourselves in a circle of officious-looking men. We stood awkwardly, puzzled about what we were doing here. They looked equally puzzled. One man, in a natty suit and sunglasses, introduced himself as Rajendra Pandey, a former member of Parliament. We introduced ourselves. Then everyone told us their names. An awkward pause followed.

The former parliamentarian put us at ease with an impromptu speech. 'This is the first time we've been able to gather from all over the district for a party meeting,' he said. 'Before the ceasefire, the Maoists wouldn't let our party members leave their villages to attend our meetings.' The party had recently held a public rally here, the first of its kind in years. 'We're reclaiming our political space again,' he said. He, who usually lived in Kathmandu, had come on a tour to conduct party meetings in two districts; other party leaders were doing the same all over the country. 'In all seventy-five districts the UML is entering the villages again.'

This was wonderful, both Malcolm and I said, still wondering why we had been brought here.

It turned out that the INSEC human rights worker was also at the meeting. Relieved, we excused ourselves, and took him to a side room so that we might talk.

Surya Bahadur Shahi was a slim, soft-spoken man on whom fell the unenviable task of recording wartime atrocities. His work was very risky. 'The Maoists didn't like me coming to their villages, and the state security forces would think I was a Maoist if I strayed outside the bazaar,' he said. He was vulnerable to threats from both sides.

Even after the ceasefire, human rights violations continued. A fourteen-year-old boy had recently been arrested by the security forces and detained as a Maoist. The security forces had also shot two girls point-blank in a neighbouring village. Two unidentified bodies had turned up in a nearby jungle, and six bodies had been found in a cleft elsewhere. 'The violations aren't at the earlier scale,' Shahi said, 'but both sides are still committing them.'

Another man then joined us in the room. Raj Bahadur Budha was the head of the Teachers' Union in Dailekh District. 'The teachers have it the worst,' he said to us. 'The Maoists force us to join their party and donate five per cent of our salaries to them. They'll kill us if we don't agree.' The Maoists had in fact killed a disproportionate number of teachers throughout the country, teachers who had refused to go along with their agenda. But teachers also fell victim to government reprisal. When the district education office found out that they were donating part of their earnings to the Maoists, it froze their salaries. 'Now we can't even support our families,' Budha said.

Most importantly, the war was devastating the lives of an entire generation. 'The older students have all fled to the district headquarters for fear that they'll be recruited by the Maoists,' Budha said. 'Or they're afraid the security forces will kill them, taking them for Maoists. Those who can have migrated to India. A whole generation of children have seen their education destroyed. They're facing the basic question of how to survive.'

After these meetings, we had a sober lunch at a local lodge. Dailekh was famous throughout Nepal for its curd: the herbs in the pastures made the curd fragrant and green. But the curd we ate was sour and watery, and of no merit at all.

Along with Chitra Bahadur, his urchin and his uncle, we then headed out of Dailekh bazaar, hoping to reach the village of Dullu by nightfall. Thanks to our three confusing maps, we did not know if this was possible. Chitra Bahadur seemed to think not.

'If we weren't carrying packs, maybe. But we're carrying packs,' he said. His uncle, whom we too took to calling Mama, grunted in agreement, weighted down with his load. 'Anyway,' Chitra Bahadur said, 'why go to Dullu? There's a shorter route to Jumla.'

'We have to go to Dullu,' I insisted. Dullu used to be the winter capital of the Khas kingdom of the twelfth to fifteenth centuries. At one point one of the largest kingdoms of the Himalayan belt, the Khas kingdom had contributed such things as the Khas language, the precursor to modern Nepali. I was set on going there.

But the sun was fierce, and we were slow, and both Chitra Bahadur and Mama stopped often to rest in shady spots. The urchin Bharat was grating on Malcolm's nerves by pointing at him and making such observations as, 'Yah ha ha, how big his feet are!'

Eventually we left the porters behind, and fell in with some children heading home from school, and a skinny woman from Dullu village who had come to the bazaar to buy oil and spices. The long trek was routine for her. She and her equally skinny teenage son were both bearing packs on their heads. 'Here, I'll carry your bag,' she said to me. 'You're from Kathmandu, you won't be able to walk in the hills.'

I said no.

'I'm used to carrying loads,' she said, patting her own pack. 'Put your bag on top of this.'

Again I said no. I did not believe that villagers were more inured to physical labour than we fleshy townsfolk. Chitra Bahadur and Mama—by now lagging far behind us—were proof enough that a lifetime of deprivation offered, in fact, no advantage at all.

Bharat soon tired of laughing at Malcolm, and he fell behind, waiting for his father and uncle. As we walked, we met a group of men who were also going to Dullu. One of them said he was a JTA, an agricultural technician. 'If you keep up with us you'll reach there by nightfall,' he assured us. Another man—taciturn, bearded—threw odd, dark glances over us, unnerving me, for he looked very much a caricature of a Maoist. I directed my conversation at the JTA, bandying the term 'human rights' liberally in the hope that the other man would not…what—behead us for being the class enemy?

We reached the bottom of a steep hill, and waited at a flyblown tea shop for the porters to catch up. Malcolm wowed the tea shop owner's family—and a bevy of local women—by taking pictures with his digital camera. 'It's like a TV!' one girl squealed. 'Look!' she pointed at the monitor. 'That's me!'

Chitra Bahadur showed up over half an hour later, alone.

They had taken another route and had waited for us elsewhere. 'That route is faster,' he said. 'It goes straight to Dandibandi.'

We had no idea, of course, where Dandibandi was. 'But does it go to Dullu?' I asked.

He said, 'You *have* to go to Dullu?'

'We *have* to go to Dullu.'

He sighed. 'I'll go and fetch Mama and the boy. Wait for us at Siristhan. We'll all walk together from there.'

'We have to get to Dullu tonight,' I said crossly.

He ground his teeth. 'Let's see.'

Malcolm and I went ahead, fording the wide Katia Khola, its pebbly shore echoing with the drumbeats at a nearby cremation. We took a meandering path through a breezy, broadleaf forest. Siristhan was at the far edge of the forest. Instead of waiting there we decided to walk on, confident that we could reach Dullu. The porters were slowing us down on purpose, we muttered to each other. We were, after all, paying them by the day. If we went ahead, we'd force them to catch up. Soon we were in another forest.

Past the forest we arrived at a temple complex. An immense, rustling peepal tree towered over it. A grassy expanse in the centre of several buildings was studded with Shiva lingams, tridents, stone carvings smeared with teeka and wooden totems with flower offerings. A few cows were grazing nearby.

An emaciated, ancient-looking man in a red vest and orange lungi came out of one of the buildings, staring at us with open curiosity. We asked him if this was, by any chance, Dullu village.

'No. This is the holy shrine of Nabisthan,' he said, speaking with a lisp. When he spoke we could see that all but one of his top teeth had fallen out.

He was the temple's kothari, or caretaker. Assuming we were here to worship, he said, 'You can go into all the buildings except that one'—he pointed at a shrine with a cloth covering its doorway. 'Go and get your blessings, then I'll put teeka on you.'

Obligingly, we took in the main shrine—a sooty room with a blue flame, smelling of petroleum—but our minds were on the porters. We decided to wait for them here. As we sat on the grassy expanse near the cows, the caretaker returned with tea. It proved undrinkable, with pungent, foul-smelling herbs, and sugar, salt and pepper.

'It's delicious,' I said, putting it aside.

He flashed me a one-toothed smile. 'I used special herbs.'

Perhaps it was the single tooth that gave the caretaker a daft look. Or the red vest and orange lungi. He was also wearing striped hoop earrings that looked like they were made of plastic. We made small talk with him, telling him we had lost our porters.

Where were they, he asked.

'We don't know.'

He looked puzzled. 'You should always walk with your porters.'

Then he suddenly leaped up and went running, in a stiff, old man's way, towards the cows, which were nearing one of the buildings. 'Dears,' he called out plaintively, 'I always tell you not to go into the house, but you're so frisky, you always disobey me.'

Malcolm and I tossed our tea into the grass.

Evening was falling. The caretaker's nephew, also an elderly man, had arrived to cook the old man's evening meal. We made a quick recce back along the forest, but did not find the porters. So we returned to the Nabisthan temple, with no option but to spend the night there—with no sweaters, no sleeping bags, no soap, no toothbrushes, no change of clothes.

'I'll cook you a meal,' the caretaker offered graciously. 'I don't have any blankets, but I'll build you a fire in the stall to keep you warm.'

His eyes fixed on a headlamp that Malcolm was taking out of his day pack. 'You know,' he said, apropos of nothing, 'there is a kind of torch that you put on your head. I have seen them.'

Malcolm humoured him by fixing his headlamp on his head.

The old man cackled in glee.

Chitra Bahadur, his urchin and his uncle did not show up. Morosely, we realized that it was our fault for not waiting for them at Siristhan. As the sky darkened, the caretaker went about his duties, sweeping the grounds with a twiggy broom, then sitting down in one corner of the temple complex to blow on a conch shell. From another corner, his elderly nephew beat a flat drum. The night erupted in a racket of atonal shrieks and beats: *Pyaan! Pyaaaan! Dyang! Pyaan! Dyang! Dyang! Dyang!* It was as though the two men were making noise for noise's sake, to prove to the gods—or to the neighbouring houses along the surrounding hills—that they were earning their keep.

They finally stopped, and went into the house that the caretaker lived in. From outside it was pretty, a whitewashed brick structure of spacious, elegant proportions. But when we went in for our meal, we saw that its rooms were filled with thick grey smoke from a sacrificial yagya fire that burned permanently in one corner of the house. Our eyes filled with tears, and we could hardly see anything through the kitchen's feeble oil lamp.

We ate daal-bhaat and some kind of meat, grateful for the food. As we blinked back our tears, the caretaker and his nephew discussed the various routes our porters might have taken, tossing about the names of villages that meant nothing to us. 'They probably went by Gamauri,' the nephew said. The caretaker nodded, then shook his head: 'Maybe they went via Moursyang.'

They decided, eventually, that we should just walk on to Dullu village in the morning. The porters would probably be there, the caretaker said. 'Unless of course they've taken off with your bags.'

After dinner we went to an abandoned goat shed where the caretaker had laid out straw mats for us. We lay down, waiting for him to come and light us a fire.

He came bearing two sheets. 'I've given up all material possessions, but these might keep you warm,' he said. Squatting next to a stone hearth, he piled up twigs, branches and logs, and had a fire crackling in no time. Then he settled across from us. We, rare guests, were to be his evening's entertainment.

He was, he said, seventy years old. He spent all his days alone; his nephew only came in the evenings, to cook his meals. The caretaker had no parents, no wife or children. His nephew was his only family. 'After me, my seed dies,' he said with a tinge of pride.

By the leaping light of the fire the caretaker's face took on ghoulish contours as he continued his life story. He had given up the worldly life at a young age, going to India to live the life of an ascetic. 'I spent twenty-seven years there, in the pilgrimage sites—Haridwar, Rishikesh. I even attended the Kumbh mela.' He grinned, and his tooth glinted. 'Oh, the pot I smoked,' he sighed. 'Ganja! Hashish! I was always high, always. I spent twenty-seven years in bliss.'

Why had he come back?

'Oh, I walked all the way back,' he said, not understanding the question. As he neared home, he had spied a marijuana field. 'So thick! Like this!' He waved his fingers to mime luxuriance. He smacked his lips in the darkness. 'So I said to my fellow travellers—you go on ahead, I'm going to stay here awhile. And I picked a leaf and crushed it like this'—he rubbed his palms together vigorously—'then I smoked it, sssss, taking full pleasure.' He sighed. 'Twenty-seven years I spent smoking pot!'

Not sharing his passion for pot, we just murmured politely.

'But I had to stop smoking five years ago,' he went on. 'It was bad for my asthma.'

The permanent yagya fire in his house sprang to mind, but before either of us could say anything, he continued: 'They didn't recognize me!' He was suddenly wrathful now. 'My nephew's wife—she didn't recognize me! I spoke only Hindi at that time, you see. Over the years I had forgotten Nepali. So they thought I was an Indian ascetic, and told me they didn't have any money for alms.'

The return home had obviously disappointed. So the caretaker had left his village to tend cows at this temple complex. At the time, another caretaker looked after the temple. When he went to India, this caretaker took over.

I had been confused that the caretaker had eaten meat at dinner, and asked him what his caste was.

He was a Yogi, he said.

'A jogi? An ascetic?'

'No.' He was a Yogi. A jogi was a renunciate, something that anyone could become upon abdicating from worldly matters. Yogis, though, were a separate caste that one was born into, like all castes. 'This area is a stronghold of the Yogis,' he said. 'Siristhan, Nabisthan—there's another shrine nearby—these are all Yogi strongholds.'

He saw that I was lost, and mentioned Yogi Narahari Nath. I immediately grew wary. Yogi Narahari Nath had, in the 1950s, led right-wing peasant revolts against democracy, helping to generate mass support for the 1960 royal coup. In Panchayat times he had become a national politician, and after 1990 he had been nominated by the king as a member of Parliament's Upper House. He had died just a few weeks before.

The caretaker asked me whether, since we lived in Kathmandu, we had attended his funeral at the Pashupatinath temple.

I said no.

He looked surprised. 'But do you know if his soul was seen departing his body?'

'No.'

Now he grew worried. 'His soul surely would have departed his body.'

'I'm sure it did,' I said, just to put him at ease.

He gave me a hopeful glance. 'Did the newspapers mention this?'

'No.'

For a while he fell silent. Then he began, once again, to go over all the routes that the porters might have taken—Moursyang, Gamauri, Satthumba.

I was not keen on this topic, so I asked him if the Maoists had given him any trouble.

He gave me a blank look. 'Why would they bother an old man like me?'

'Well, I don't know. They don't like religion, do they? Haven't they... I don't know—desecrated the shrine?' In other western districts the Maoists had taken menstrual rags—considered ritually impure—into temples.

The caretaker suddenly pulled a sullen expression. 'You know, I don't like the people of these areas,' he said. 'You were lucky to find me tonight, but be very, very careful with other people. Folks in this area, you can't trust them.' Then he grew melancholy. 'I sometimes think of leaving,' he said.

'Oh?'

He said, 'I wonder if I should go back to India.'

Then, out of the blue, he said, 'There is a kind of blanket that you can wrap around yourself and button up, so that only your face is showing.'

'Sleeping bags?'

'I have seen them.'

'Yes, they exist,' I said.

He smiled widely, and there was his tooth.

Finally he stood up to leave, reaching, for some reason, for the lungi wrapped around his waist. 'Do you need more covers to keep warm?'

I assured him not.

We spent a sleepless night groaning in discomfort, scratching bug bites, and every now and then getting up to stoke the fire.

IN THE PEOPLE'S REPUBLIC

Dazed by lack of sleep, at a loss about how to find the porters, and wondering if we would have to call off the entire trip, we arrived in the lush, sun-drenched village of Dullu the next morning to be greeted with hammer-and-sickle banners welcoming the Maoist People's Liberation Army. In my strung-out state this caused me extreme jitters. But oddly, as we stood by the gate, a man came running up the village's one narrow road, screaming hoarsely against the king and the Maoists: 'Gyane and the Maoists are conspiring to end democracy,' he cried, waving his hands madly as he sped past us. 'Death to the monarchy! Death to the Maoists! They're working together against democracy!'

I worried that the Maoists would kill him. But I alone looked worried. A few village men sitting nearby just guffawed to see the man.

It was the day of the Hindu spring festival of Holi, we realized: The man was high on dope.

We were desperate to find the porters. On the walk up from Nabisthan, we had stopped along the trail, telling everyone we met that we had been separated from porters of such-and-such description; had they seen them? Nobody had, but everybody had loved our tale: 'You spent the night where? Did the old man have any blankets? Did he feed you anything?' And without exception they had advised us to go to Dullu, because the porters would surely be there.

'Based on what logic are people giving us this assurance?' Malcolm had asked me at once point. I couldn't tell. But we were both banking heavily on local logic.

We made our way to the Sundar Hotel, said to be the finest in Dullu village. The hotel yielded no porters. We sat in its neat, stone-paved courtyard and once again explained to the hotel owner what had happened. The JTA from the day before dropped by and listened with great sympathy. 'Your porters probably wouldn't have stolen your bags,' he assured us. 'But they might have abandoned them and gone home. I could tell yesterday they were lazy bastards.' He laughed, and we laughed along with him, in a freaked-out, mirthless way.

There was little to do but wait. As we did, the man ranting about the monarchist-Maoist conspiracy against democracy ran past the hotel several times, screaming himself hoarse. Finally a young man with a stern face stopped by, complaining to the hotel owner.

'What can one do, it's Holi,' the hotel owner replied with a good-natured laugh. But in the end, the screaming man was taken, by village men, to be locked up in his home.

The stern-faced man stayed on, talking to the hotel owner. Something about him—his controlled bearing, his calibrated speech—made me think he might be a Maoist. On a whim I introduced Malcolm and myself. We had come to see how the ceasefire was holding, I said. Would he talk to us?

Comrade Ribbon was his name, he said.

'Comrade Ribbon?'

'Reben,' he said.

'Reben?'

'Bidroha,' he said in Nepali.

'Oh.' I turned to Malcolm. 'His name is Comrade Rebel.'

Malcolm rolled his eyes.

'Don't do that,' I hissed.

We went to one of the hotel's rooms to talk. A short, bearded man with glittering eyes joined us without a word, and sat through our entire interview. He was, I assumed, a Maoist, though the fierce red teeka on his forehead—to mark the Holi festivities— made him look like a Hindu zealot.

Comrade Rebel was the local area secretary of the CPN (Maoist). By my guess he was in his late twenties, and of either Bahun or Chettri caste. He was wearing slacks and a shirt of the kind that any city man would wear, and closed leather shoes. He sat perfectly upright and spoke not a word in excess.

The area that he served extended from Chupra village to the Paduka River, he said. He explained his work in terms that I did not understand: 'I relay the party's rules to the people, and see to the give and take between the party and the people. It is my job to mobilize the party's forces and to teach them how to communicate effectively with people.' He received no salary for his work.

We asked: How did the party workers look upon the prospect of a peaceful settlement?

'We welcome the talks,' he said. 'The war has been hard on people; people want relief. But the government must follow the rules of the ceasefire.' He then talked about an exchange of fire that had taken place during a rally in Dullu only a few days back. The Maoist People's Liberation Army had amassed here, when, according to him, army troops had infiltrated the rally and fired in order to create the impression that the Maoists had fired upon them. 'We didn't fall for it,' he said. 'There were three, four hundred of us, and ninety-eight of them, but we were so disciplined that we didn't fire a single bullet.' Nobody was shot, but he and other Maoists were beaten by the army. Even a comrade of his who approached the army with his hands up was beaten, he said.

At this he sat forward and said forcefully, 'If the army wants to move about freely, they should stop carrying guns. We've put down our weapons, why shouldn't they?'

For him, the state's military forces were equivalent to the Maoist army.

We asked about the situation before the ceasefire, and Comrade Rebel effortlessly listed atrocities committed by the state: Two girls, Laxmi Shahi and Laxmi Risal, had been killed in Dandibandi; an eleven-year-old boy, Karna Bahadur Rana, had been shot; the houses of two or three party members of the district had been set on fire by the security forces. He rattled off the names of six bodies found in the Totke Lohorey area: Surad BK, Hari Bahadur BK, Indra BK, Bal Bahadur BK, Dambar BK and Jhuse Sarki. They had been participating in a Maoist programme for Dalits, he said, when they were summarily killed.

And what about the atrocities his party had committed?

He nodded gamely. 'We took up violence out of necessity, not out of desire,' he said, repeating what was obviously a well-rehearsed line. 'We try to change people, but if we find that the deeds of one person endanger a thousand of our comrades, then killing such a person is not an atrocity.'

Malcolm asked, 'What if you kill the wrong person by mistake?'

'We haven't so far,' he said. 'We're not like the state. They've shot a six-month-old baby in this area, they've killed innocent people. We kill only those who commit crimes against the people, or those who inform on us. The people support us in these killings.'

Both Malcolm and I pulled sceptical faces.

Comrade Rebel smiled for the first time. 'Otherwise why would we have so many party members?' he asked.

But surely there were some bad eggs in his party?

He accepted this. 'We take action against those who break party rules.' He mentioned a politburo member—a Comrade Alok—who had been forced out of the party for 'cultural degeneration'.

There had been rumours that two Maoist politburo members, Badal and Pampha Bhusal, had had an affair, for which they had faced disciplinary action. I thought of asking Comrade Rebel if that, too, was 'cultural degeneration', but out of fear of offending him, did not.

On our way up to Dullu, we had seen a bombed-out Village Development Committee building. Why, we asked, had the Maoists destroyed government infrastructure?

'We destroy bridges in order to protect the local people from army patrols,' Comrade Rebel said matter-of-factly. 'We destroy telephone lines if people are informing on us through the phone. If we're holding a meeting somewhere and someone calls the security forces—that endangers our comrades' lives.'

He said it was the army, and not the Maoists, who cut Dullu's telephone lines in April 2002. 'We had destroyed the telephone tower of Dailekh bazaar in order to give the government a shock,' he said. 'To retaliate, the army cut the phone lines in Dandibandi and Nawamulya villages.'

As for Dullu's VDC building, the party had destroyed it because it had been housing the police, as well as the staff of the United Mission to Nepal, a Christian aid organization.

By this time Comrade Rebel had eased a little. I was curious to find out how he had fallen in with the Maoists, and asked him. He had joined the party two years ago, he told us. Before that, he had been with the UML. 'I was born into a poor family,' he said. 'The chairman of our Village Development Committee was feudal and arbitrary. And even the UML respected the feudal king. People just don't understand,' he said, suddenly growing passionate. 'Even a dog can feed its own litter, can't it? We are human beings. We should feed the children of others. We must take care of the poor.'

His show of emotion emboldened me. 'But what if your party sells out its ideals, just like the UML did?' I asked. 'In the peace talks—what if they compromise with the king?'

He immediately stiffened, and his earlier restraint returned. 'We won't obey the negotiating team if they sell out,' he said. 'We don't follow Baburam Bhattarai. Prachanda is our leader. We follow only him.'

We asked whether it was true that his party had given up the demand for a republican state.

'We'll have to find a place for the king,' he said, evading the question. 'Maybe he could be the president. What we need to do is take the army away from him and put it towards national service. We want these things to work out,' he said. 'We want the peace talks to succeed.'

Just then, Chitra Bahadur staggered into the room, his face beaded with sweat. Mama and the urchin Bharat followed, and suddenly the world, which had begun to look like a murky pond, turned bright and sparkling again.

'You didn't wait for us,' Chitra Bahadur snapped as he put down his load.

'You didn't show up,' I shot back defensively.

'We told you to wait for us.'

'We waited an hour!' Then I said, 'It doesn't matter. Seeing you is like seeing the face of the gods.'

Chitra Bahadur would not be placated. 'We kept the load

at Siristhan, then went up one trail, then another, then another. Finally we found out you'd stayed the night at Nabisthan. We carried the loads there. But you had already left. So we came here not knowing whether we'd ever find you again.' He took off his woollen cap and wiped his face. 'From now on,' he said crossly, 'we always walk together.'

We agreed. Bharat took this chance to ask for a new pair of pants, and was promised one.

Comrade Rebel took leave.

The hotel owner's wife began to prepare the porters their meal, and Malcolm and I went on a tour of the village. The short, bearded man who had sat in on our talk with Comrade Rebel tagged along, his eyes glittering all the while.

Dullu was breathtaking in the way that only well-off villages can be. It stood atop a hill, circled by teeming terraces of wheat, the soil rich and the water abundant: This was the stuff of agrarian dreams. Further off in the distance we could see jagged, dry peaks, but here, in this rare village, was a feel of plenitude. Plum trees were in flower, their blossoms quivering in the wind.

This kind of terrain any hill king would want to lay claim to. From the twelfth to the fifteenth century, the Khas kingdom had been at its height, extending from Lumbini, the birthplace of Siddhartha Gautam, across the Sivalik mountain range, north to the steppes of Mustang and across to Garhwal. Some scholars maintain that it encompassed Ladakh and Mount Kailash as well. The kingdom controlled an important pilgrimage route, and was powerful enough to raid Nepal valley several times over the centuries. Sinja village—several days' walk north from here, in Jumla District—had been the Khas kingdom's summer capital. Dullu was where the Khas kings had built their winter palace.

Remnants from those times were scattered around the area. On our walk up to Dullu, we had passed the Patharnauli, a mandala-shaped building of stone blocks that dated back to the thirteenth century, when Buddhism had swept over this land. It was now flooded with water and served as a village well. The old palace of Dullu had been burned down by the Maoists, but there was, I had heard, a stone pillar in the village dating back centuries. I wanted to see it.

The short, bearded man led us to the centre of the village, where the pillar stood in an enclosure. It was more of a slab than a pillar, with a chaitya etched into it, above a column of indecipherable Khas script. The man watched as we examined the letters. They listed, I knew, the seven Challa kings who had ruled over the Khas kingdom from the twelfth to the mid-thirteenth century, and the twelve Malla kings who had ruled after that, till the kingdom broke into three smaller kingdoms in 1404, eventually to be defeated by the kingdom of Gorkha.

'Hello, hello.' From a tea shop next to the pillar, some local men waved at us. 'Hello, namaste. Brother. Sister. Come.'

From their wide, senseless grins it was obvious that they were stoned.

The bearded man muttered, 'It's not right,' his gaze glittering over the men. He tried to lead us away, but the men were not to be refused. 'Hello! Namaste! Brother. Sit. Here. Here. Here.' They came to the pillar and dragged us back to the tea shop and plied us with bitter, boiled tea. The short, bearded man stood outside the tea shop, glowering.

One of the men patted Malcolm on the knee. 'You like Nepal?' as the others engaged us in their village English: 'Where you from? Why you come?'

After they realized that I was Nepali, one man said to me, slurring his words, 'Sister, you go and tell them in Kathmandu... tell them that we need a plus-two programme in our high school. Tell them that. Tell them that. Will you tell them that?'

'I'll tell them that,' I lied.

'Please tell them that.'

Just then, a young man, succumbing to a fit of paranoia, broke into a cold sweat. The others attended to him as he began to rave inchoately, and we made our escape.

The bearded man tagged along to the hotel with us. 'The people in this village are no good,' he muttered. 'See how they misbehave, even before outside guests.'

'We didn't mind,' I said.

'They are no good.' He hissed, 'It's not just today. They drink all the time, Sister, even when we tell them not to. They never obey us.'

'Is that right?'

'It is insufferable. We must take action against them.' I was worried that this grim, muttering Maoist would follow us out of the village, possibly all the way to Jumla, condemning the heedless locals to dire consequences. But he dropped away as we left the village—Chitra Bahadur, his son and uncle right next to us, as was our agreement.

Instead we had for company a plump, precocious boy, from a well-to-do family if his girth and high-neck sweater were any indication. He had taken it upon himself to guide us through the sights. 'The air is refreshing in these climes,' he said, sounding like an old pedant. 'The farming is bountiful. See these ancient stone lions that date back to the Khas kingdom? Those are the ruins of the old palace. Nepal,' he said, 'is the only Hindu kingdom in the world. This is the heart of our national heritage. The potential for tourism is tremendous. Observe the resplendent scenery.'

Finally he too dropped away, and we set out in earnest to reach as far as possible in the remaining daylight hours, which were few.

It was not long, though, before we fell in with another Maoist, a dark, twenty-something man with thick, fierce brows that only became fiercer when he smiled. He was wearing a photographer's jacket with many pockets, all of them bulging prominently.

He greeted us with extra-firm communist handshakes. He worked, he said, in the Farmers' Front of the CPN (Maoist). The party had several such fronts for women, teachers, students, Dalits and intellectuals. These fronts operated independently, he said, but in a way that supported the party.

He turned out to be very personable. I asked whether the area was as agriculturally rich as it appeared to be, and he said no, because of unequal land distribution patterns. He explained that the Farmers' Front had ranked the region's farmers into five classes. Of the lowest class were 'landless farmers', who worked as tenants on others' lands.

'Like the halis?' I asked. Halis were bonded labourers who worked for so little that over the years they accrued debts they could never pay off, which effectively forced them into slavery.

'Including the halis,' he said. The landless farmers were those who either had to work for others or migrate to India for work. They couldn't survive otherwise.

The man went on: The second class were classified as 'poor farmers'. There were, he said, two subclasses of poor farmers. One consisted of those who could live off their land for three months, and the other of those who had land enough to feed them for half the year. Poor farmers worked others' farms in the lean seasons, or else they too migrated to India.

Better off than they were the middle-class farmers. These were farmers who could live off their land through the year. The fourth class consisted of rich farmers, those who earned surplus off their land. And finally, at the top, were the feudal farmers. 'We've classified every farmer in our area,' he said with a flourish.

I found this interesting, and told him so, and he flashed me a fierce smile. I asked, hazarding a guess, whether he had been in the UML before joining the Maoists. With an even fiercer smile, he said yes.

Malcolm asked if he had ever killed anyone.

'That is not the kind of work I do,' he said, growing solemn.

'Do you carry weapons?'

He shook his head.

'Then what's in your pockets?' Malcolm persisted, pointing at the bulges in his photographer's jacket.

At this, the man burst out laughing, and emptied his pockets one by one. Out came a handheld radio, a camera, an orange, a notebook, a torch. 'No weapons,' he said, still laughing as he put his stash away.

He then took an interest in Malcolm. For the rest of our walk, he asked him about the US invasion of Iraq, which was imminent. Why was Britain supporting the US when the rest of the world was against the invasion? 'In my opinion America is only after oil,' the man said. 'And I feel that Britain is trying to control America by bringing it under the purview of the UN system. Is that correct?'

When our paths diverged, we parted amicably, with another round of extra-firm handshakes.

When the man left, Chitra Bahadur came up to me. 'Was that man a Maoist?'

I said yes.

He frowned. 'What did you talk about?' he asked. 'What did he say?' He listened to my answers carefully. I couldn't quite tell what he made of it all.

WE HAVE TO GO TO MANMA

There were two passes that we could cross to reach Kalikot District, but one of them—the shorter route—bypassed Manma town, the district headquarters. Manma was one of the more inaccessible district headquarters of the country, lacking even road access. We definitely wanted to go there.

Chitra Bahadur was not pleased to hear this. 'You *have* to go to Manma?' he asked again and again.

We replied, each time, that we did.

Then he said, 'But the path to Manma goes straight up, straight down, straight up, straight down. The other path is faster.'

'But does the shorter path go through Manma?'

'You *have* to go to Manma?'

'We *have* to go to Manma.'

He ground his teeth. 'Well, then what can I say.'

We spent the night at the village of Dandibandi, extravagantly partaking of soap, toothpaste, hand cream, face cream, lip balm—all the comforts we had missed last night. The house we stayed at had the smallest outhouse in the world: I had to crouch to fit in, and even then my head touched the ceiling. On which, I was distressed to see, there was a very large spider.

That night we were too tired to talk to anyone. The following morning, though, we asked a man who was drinking tea at the lodge whether it was true that two women had been killed here by state security forces.

He nodded. One of them had been a teacher at a local school and the other a student, he said. 'Their names were Laxmi Shahi and Laxmi Risal.'

A teenage girl sitting nearby joined in, saying that the two Laxmis had been arrested here, then detained at the Dailekh bazaar garrison for two weeks. They were then brought back to fields just outside the village and shot dead. 'I heard the gunshots myself,' she said. 'I saw the army. There were many army men, and just the two of them. They passed the fields. And then I heard the shots. Other people in the village actually saw them being shot.'

After a pause she added, quietly, 'They weren't Maoists, you know.'

'It wouldn't be legal to kill them even if they were,' I said.

'They were like any of us,' she said.

We were in a sober mood as we left the village. We knew that stories of such atrocities would multiply as we entered Kalikot. It was the fifth most insurgency-affected district in the country. According to statistics from INSEC, 3,681 people had lost their lives throughout Nepal during the state of emergency. Dailekh District had lost thirty-four people; by contrast, Kalikot had lost 147. Allegations of other violations—disappearances, rapes, illegal detention and torture—abounded here.

Tellingly, only five of the 147 killings here had been perpetrated by the Maoists. Of the 142 people killed by the state security forces, all were alleged to be Maoists killed in combat. Amnesty International and other human rights groups were saying that up to half of those killed by the security forces were not Maoists engaging in combat, but unarmed Maoists and innocent civilians.

The path from Dandibandi wound uphill along a ridge to a one-lane village. Malcolm was walking ahead, with wraparound sunglasses and a CD player that made him even more conspicuous than he already was. A man at a tea shop call out after him: 'Hello, namaste, laal salaam!' Unable to hear him, Malcolm walked right past him.

Alarmed, I ran forward and brought Malcolm back to the tea shop.

The man greeted us with a raised fist. 'Laal salaam!' The red salute. He was, he said, Area Committee Member D. P. Rizal. He asked, in a proprietorial, slightly haughty way, why we had come, and nodded on hearing the words 'human rights' and 'writing'.

We took a dislike to him, but afraid to cross a Maoist, we sat with him over tea, during which he subjected us to a long, jargon-laden speech about his party's fight against the semi-feudal, semi-capitalist comprador bourgeois rent-seekers, foreign imperialists, informers and capitalist roaders. On and on he went. We were both familiar with Maoist rhetoric—the CPN (Maoist) website was chock-a-block with it—and it did not sound any less pat and formulaic when uttered in a village. D. P. Rizal had learned his lines well.

To change the topic I asked him to explain how his party had reconfigured the boundaries of the state's districts, Village Development Committees and wards. Pleased, he obliged with this explanation:

The CPN (Maoist) had divided Dailekh District into twelve areas, each governed by an Area Committee, headed by an area secretary and an area commander. The twelve areas were further broken into Village People's Committees which were in turn divided into wards. The smallest political units were cells, which reached every neighbourhood. None of these boundaries corresponded to those of the Nepali state. Parts of what the government considered to be in other districts fell in the CPN (Maoist)'s demarcations for Dailekh District.

This explained, D. P. Rizal went back to railing against comprador bourgeois rent-seekers, foreign imperialists, informers and spies and capitalist roaders.

'We must be going,' I finally said, standing up.

He looked disappointed. 'But don't you want to know about all the people the army has killed here?'

'We want to spend more time in Kalikot, actually.'

'Yes, Kalikot has suffered much.' He nodded, and raised a fist. 'Laal salaam.'

Awkwardly, I said, 'Namaste.'

Malcolm, who had had quite enough of him, said, 'Keep it real, man.'

Chitra Bahadur looked distinctly unhappy that we were running into so many Maoists. As we headed on, he asked me, 'Was that a Maoist too? What did he want?'

'Aren't there Maoists in your village?' I asked.

He said no. His village, Guranse, was a high, misty settlement of twenty-odd Sunwar-family houses in a clearing in a rhododendron forest. We had passed it on our drive to Chupra, on the first day. A few of the villagers had left to work for the Maoists in other parts of the district, but the village itself was Maoist-free.

I realized that perhaps Chitra Bahadur was worried that we were, ourselves, Maoists. So I explained to him Malcolm's human rights interest, and my interest as a writer. He listened attentively, but did not respond.

Soon, he and his urchin and his uncle fell behind us. We had intended to walk together, but weighted down with loads, they could not keep up with us. And we were too impatient to wait. As the trail steepened, Malcolm and I passed several small, parched settlements where villagers immediately gathered around us, gawking openly and asking where we were from and why we had come.

We stopped for lunch at the ridge-top village of Ghumnekhali, where the urchin Bharat chased a rooster around till he trapped it amid an orgy of flutters and squawks. The woman of the lodge swiftly beheaded the bird, dunked it in boiling water, plucked it, gutted it, chopped it into pieces and curried it. We ate the meat along with staggering quantities of rice.

After lunch, our path led up through rocky scrubland where

the air cooled and the fields became droughty. Mama—Padam Bahadur—had thus far been a man of few words. As we passed by a dry patch of fields, he was finally moved to observe, 'This is not good land.' He stopped along the trail and eyed the land with sorrow. 'This is not good land.'

It got tiring explaining ourselves to curious villagers at every settlement that we passed. In one village, as we waited for the porters to catch up, I stood around mutely, pretending to be foreign. The village looked wretchedly poor; the men were dressed in tattered shirts and pyjamas, and the women in lungis stained with earth. As little boys in traditional daura-suruwals and half-naked babies and old grandmothers and grandfathers gathered around, I heard an old man say, in a lilting local accent, 'The times must really be improving if their kinds are coming back to our village.' Unwilling to tell them no, peace was precarious and could end at any time, we walked on.

Soon we crossed a forest of gnarled rhododendrons and whispering pine trees dappled by the golden light of the setting sun, and before dark we reached the scrappy hillside settlement of Bajhangeneta. Evening fell as we made our way through the rocks and boulders of the village and asked for lodging at almost the first house, a mean raw brick hovel. Two other men were also lodging here. The woman at the hearth said she could put us up if we were willing to share a room with them.

The night grew cool and misty. We piled on our warmest clothes—Malcolm outfitting Chitra Bahadur and Mama in matching down jackets—and sat in the front porch, sheltered from the elements by a low thatch roof. This was by far the poorest village we had passed yet. There was not a trace of government here, not a single sign of what the Nepali state had done in all its centuries of existence. Beyond the scrappy village was a vista of inky hills high on the horizon. Crickets trilled in the surrounding forests, and owls hooted and shrieked. An occasional voice floated over from a nearby house and dissipated, leaving in its wake a forlorn silence.

The woman at the hearth put rice and daal to boil. We exchanged introductions with the two other lodgers. One of them had been a ward chairman till the tenure of all local elected officials had lapsed. He used to be a member of the UML, he said, but now he wasn't politically active.

'It isn't possible to be,' his companion explained.

At this, the former ward chairman smiled thinly. 'Even those of us who belong to other parties have to join the Maoist committees now.'

We figured he might orient us to the politics of the region, so we asked him which parties were popular here: 'If there were to be an election tomorrow, who would win?'

The former ward chairman mulled over the question awhile. 'If the Maoists put down their guns, the UML will win,' he said finally. 'But if they don't put down their guns, they'll win.' Then he smiled just as thinly as before.

'Would it be possible to hold fair elections here?'

'Not unless the Maoists put down their guns.'

We fell silent, and he turned to the woman at the hearth. He wanted, apparently, to sell her some milk. There was a buffalo tethered outside the house, which kept turning its queer gaze at us. He had bought it in Dandibandi village, and was walking it back home. Along the route, he was selling its milk in exchange for his and his companion's meals.

Tonight was proving to be a problem, though. The woman at the hearth was refusing to buy his milk. 'We already have our own supply,' she said. 'Why would I need to buy milk from you?'

The former ward chairman's thin smile vanished, and his forehead furrowed in anxiety. 'If I could just sell you a little bit of milk,' he pleaded, 'I could buy a handful of rice, and cook some rice pudding to eat.'

The woman was not moved. 'You go and ask anyone in the village, nobody will buy your milk.'

The man fell silent, facing the prospect of drinking only milk as his evening meal.

When I translated what was going on for Malcolm's benefit, he looked aghast. 'Tell him I'll buy his milk,' he said to me.

'The foreigner has said he'll buy your milk,' I said to the former ward chairman.

This only embarrassed him. 'No, no,' he said. 'I want to give him some milk as a gift.'

'He wants to give you some milk as a gift,' I said to Malcolm.

'Oh, for Christ's sake.'

From an aluminium jar, the former ward chairman began to pour a cup of milk for Malcolm.

Speaking slowly, Malcolm said to him, 'I. Will. Buy. Your. Milk. You. Use. The. Money. To. Buy. Dinner.'

Sweetly, without any guile, the former ward chairman said to me, 'After all, when will we ever meet again? Please tell the foreign guest that the milk is a gift.'

'What's wrong with him?' Malcolm hissed, as the man poured more milk for me, Chitra Bahadur, Bharat and Mama. 'Tell him to eat a proper meal.'

'It's Nepali graciousness,' I said. But with some effort, we finally prevailed on him to let Malcolm buy him and his companion their night's dinner.

Afterwards, the two of them, our party of five, and the woman of the lodge and other members of her family piled into the house's one room, fitting snugly into five creaky beds and several floor mats. The squalor of the house was disheartening. My arms rubbed against a pile of potatoes and a rickety shelf boasting a few packs of Khukuri cigarettes and Maggi noodles. The porters slept in utter silence, without so much as shifting. Malcolm tossed about, trying, in vain, to sleep. In one corner of the room, the woman of the house was whispering to another family member, filling the darkness with murmuring.

The next day's walk took us up the Haudi pass into Kalikot District. Here the path became arduous, an endless pile of stone steps leading past rocky clefts jammed with dirty, leftover winter snow. The air grew frosty as we climbed up.

We overtook several donkey trains heading for Jumla District. One, led by a young man in tattered jeans, was transporting sacks of sugar. Another was carrying kerosene in plastic jerry cans. The donkeys heading south were carrying sacks of deodar wood and fragrant herbs. We saw many people also heading south, including whole families. One man, speaking a Nepali that sounded antiquated, said his family was heading to India for work. His wife, behind him, had a basket slung over her back. An infant of only a few months lay on top of the basket, jiggling about as his mother skipped from step to step.

A three-hour climb later, we reached the Haudi pass, from where we could see a horizon of arid, scabrous wastelands and rocky hills: Kalikot District. Manma was a spot on the edge of a faraway hill.

'Will we get there today?' I asked Chitra Bahadur.

'Maybe in three days,' he said.

'Three days?'

'The Maoists blew up the bridge along the direct route,' he said. 'So we'll have to take a longer route. Or we could skip Manma and go straight to Jumla District.'

'No, we *have* to go to Manma.'

'Well if you have to go to Manma...' He pointed out our

route—along a far-off ravine in the east, which then backtracked west.

Dispirited, we headed down along a treacherous slope with a slick, icy path cut into the snow. The urchin Bharat was springing ahead at great speed, but he never once lost his footing. The rest of us proceeded at a crawling pace. Every now and then Mama cast a milky gaze over the snow-capped peaks and said, in his saddened way, 'This is not good land.'

We stopped for lunch at a clearing below the snowline. The lodge—if the shack we stopped at could be called that—was run by a man who cradled a baby in one arm the whole time he cooked our meal.

'We spoiled her early on,' he said to us, about the baby. 'She was born in the winter, so we kept her by the kitchen fire. Now she can't sleep without heat and smoke.'

He was a chatty fellow, and he told us that he had just come back from Lucknow, India, where he worked as a cook at a restaurant. His wife farmed the family fields in a nearby village; without this lodge, they had no cash earnings. He hadn't really wanted to return from India, he said, but his parents were getting old. He talked wistfully about all the dishes he used to cook: 'Chicken masala tikka, vegetable shahi korma, paneer, naan—all the Indian dishes. What is it called? Boti kabab. I used to cook boti kabab.'

The meal he served us did not, though, bear witness to his skills as a chef. Our plates were heaped up with clumps of overcooked rice, watery daal and potatoes slathered liberally with chilli.

'There aren't any spices in a place like this,' he said, noting our dismay. 'In this place,' he laughed ruefully, 'there are so few ingredients, it gets depressing to even try to cook well.'

A two-hour walk down from there, we arrived—our legs trembling from effort—at a filthy cluster of clay-and-thatch houses amid dry, desiccated fields.

'This is not good land,' Mama said again. 'The land in Dailekh District was better.' This time, we all agreed. This would surely count as one of the all-time worst places in the world to have to live in. There was no water for irrigation, and hardly any way to make a living. And it was days of arduous walk from anywhere.

We rested at a tea stall manned by a dark young woman whose blouse was pulled all the way up above her breasts, exposing her brown milk-swollen nipples. She had a sleeping baby in her lap; presumably she had been feeding it.

She asked us where we were going, and I said Manma.

'The furthest you'll reach today is Haudi village,' she said, not bothering to cover her breasts.

'Will we reach Manma tomorrow?' I asked, training my eyes on her face.

'If you take the ropeway you will.'

Chitra Bahadur quickly piped in, 'The ropeway is dangerous.'

'What ropeway?' I asked the woman.

The government had just constructed a ropeway in Raraghat, she said, exactly where the old bridge had stood. She pointed at four surly-looking young men at another tea shop nearby. 'Those boys just came that way. I myself crossed the ropeway a few days ago. We transport all our goods on it.'

I asked her if the ropeway would support Malcolm's weight. She assessed him up and down. 'The Shahi man from ward number eight crossed over yesterday. He's bigger than this foreigner.'

After another hour's walk downhill, the path finally flattened past a clear, bubbling brook. By this time my legs were shot, and I was almost hobbling. Malcolm, too, was walking slowly. Chitra

Bahadur, Bharat and Mama had fallen far behind.

The trail wound along the side of a hill, through a small but hearteningly lush stretch of wheat fields. We stopped in exhaustion at the first house we saw. Seven or eight men—all dressed in traditional daura-suruwal—were sitting in the front courtyard, chatting among themselves. Was there tea, I asked, and one of them went into the house to prepare some.

The men were looking at us with frank curiosity, so we introduced ourselves. A teenage boy with a soft, girlish face came up to us, listening carefully. He was wearing a modern shirt and pants, and carrying in his hands a folded-over notebook, and for some reason this made me think he was a Maoist.

'This village has seen the worst human rights violations,' he said, when we mentioned human rights.

It turned out that he was a student. We asked him to tell us what had happened here. He sat down beside us, and began to talk in a low, intent voice. 'Last year they shot the ward chairman, Dilli Prasad Acharya,' he told us. 'He wasn't even a Maoist. He was in the UML. It was about three in the afternoon, and he was washing his hands at a house before having a snack. It was this kind of courtyard.' The boy pointed around him. The other men had fallen silent to listen to him. 'The army shot him,' the boy said. 'He died on the spot.'

'His wife was pregnant,' one of the older men added. 'She gave birth to their son three days later.'

'Why did they shoot him?' I asked. 'I mean, why him in particular?'

Troops from the Manma army garrison were on a week-long patrol to the area, the boy said. 'They just shot anyone who was outdoors in those days. They didn't know who they were shooting. They didn't care. They shot Dilli Sir from across the village. From that distance, how could they know if someone is a Maoist?

'That's not all,' he continued, urgently. 'Two days before that, a student—like me, he was of my age—was studying a guess paper for his exams on the roof of a house. He saw the army walking by on a patrol, so he decided to go inside. In his room, he was looking at himself in the mirror, like this'—he patted his hair, mimicking the boy—'when the army came into the room and asked him why he'd gone indoors. They took him to the stone tap below the village and shot him dead. His name was Takka Bahadur Shahi. He studied in class ten, at the Sri Mahadev Uccha Madhyamik Vidyalaya in Rarakatiya.'

I was taking notes and Malcolm was recording him. The boy went on speaking, as though in the grip of a trance: 'A teacher in the same school was shot as well. His name was Ratan Bahadur Shahi. He was a simple man, like Dilli Sir. He wasn't a Maoist. The army came to the staff room at the school and asked for the names of all the teachers. They were looking for a Maoist from another ward, a man named Ratan Bahadur Bam. They mistook Ratan Bahadur Shahi for him, although he said—No, I'm Ratan Bahadur Shahi, not Ratan Bahadur Bam. But they didn't believe him. They took him down to the river, along with a student whom they suspected of being a Maoist. They blindfolded the teacher and shot him dead. The student escaped with a beating.'

All this, said the older men, had happened on 1 March 2002, mere weeks after the Maoist attack on neighbouring Achham District's headquarters, Mangalsen. That attack, led by a 2,500-strong Maoist force, had left all but two of the fifty-nine army men in the barracks dead. Many of them had been shot point-blank. The Maoists had also killed twenty-seven policemen in the attack, and destroyed a nearby airfield. The government buildings of Mangalsen had all been razed to the ground.

Pursuing the Maoists who had staged this attack, the state security forces had come here. These villages were—they obviously felt—helping to hide the Maoists, who had quickly disappeared into the civilian population. Their pursuit had been especially savage in Sukhatiya Village Development Committee, under which Haudi village fell, and in the adjoining Bharta Village Development Committee.

'Tell them about the Badi fellow,' an old man said to the boy.

'Sahadev Badi,' said the boy. 'He was killed on the same day. He was originally from Dailekh District, but he had settled down here, marrying a local woman. The army thought he was a Maoist. They think everyone from outside is a Maoist, you see. They took him from his house, down to the river.' His face spoiled and he paused briefly. 'They made him dig a pit. Then they made him sit inside it, crouching, like this.' He curled into himself. 'Then they poured kerosene on him and set him on fire.' After another pause, he said, 'They buried him in the pit that he himself had dug.'

An older man said, 'The army also shot another local man, Hasta Cholagain, accusing him of being a Maoist.'

'And there was Ravi Bohora,' said the boy. 'From ward number nine. He was just a simpleton. He went to where the army camp was when they came on their patrol. They thought he was a Maoist spy, so they shot him.'

More than thirty houses had been burned by the army throughout this area, the men in the courtyard told us. 'It's only now that we're able to sit around in the open like this, it's only now that we're eating proper meals,' said one man. 'It's only since the ceasefire that we've even returned to our homes. We were living in terror before then. Every time the army came on patrol, all of us men would flee our homes, lest we be killed.'

And what of the Maoists, I asked. Hadn't they killed anyone in the village?

The boy nodded. 'There was Raj Bahadur Shahi,' he said.

'They took him to the jungle and made him confess that he had informed on them to the security forces. They made him say that he had helped to have Maoists killed. Then they cut off his hands and feet and shot him dead.'

'That's the only case of Maoist violence?' I asked.

He nodded. The other men confirmed that this was the only case.

'What about the bridge that the Maoists destroyed?' I said. 'That must have made life hard for you.'

The boy shook his head. 'It's been a relief since the bridge was bombed. Before that, the army used to come here on weekly patrols. The later patrols weren't as bad as the ones after the Achham attack, but even then, the army would beat men and boys, they'd speak roughly to women.' He hesitated. 'They'd call the women whores.'

Who led these patrols, I asked. 'Were there majors and captains with the soldiers?'

An older man let out a short laugh. 'We can't tell who's a major or a captain or a soldier,' he said. 'But the problem was, they saw no difference between ordinary villagers and Maoists. And they'd act on information people gave them out of personal or political rivalries. If someone had a dispute with someone else, he could lie to the army and have his enemies killed as Maoists.'

Bitterly, the boy said, 'Our government betrayed us. Our member of Parliament didn't come even once during the entire state of emergency to see how we were faring. The government left us to fend for ourselves against the Maoists and the army.'

An old man said, 'Right now there's peace. But if the war starts again, we'll all have to leave our village.'

'We'll have to leave,' the boy said, 'or be ready to die.'

We left the gathering haunted by the urgency with which the

boy had spoken. The older men, too, had talked with a strange compulsion, needing, it seemed, to tell somebody—anybody— what they had been through. We were perfect strangers, yet they could not help but unburden themselves on us.

When we reached the place where we were to rest for the night, the lower part of the same village, we were immediately surrounded by a crowd of adults who, unbidden, started to talk—in the same compulsive manner.

'You are the first outsiders to come here since the state of emergency,' said one woman. 'Nobody cares about what we've been through, nobody.' She spoke at a fast clip, hardly pausing for breath. One year back, the army had come searching for the Maoists who had waged the attack on Achham. 'They told us— You're all Maoists,' she said, her eyes flashing with rage. 'They beat anyone they met on their patrols—men or women. They beat at least fifty, sixty people in this village. Even I was almost shot.' She put a hand to the back of her neck, where a graze wound was visible. 'I was at home when the army came by on patrol. My niece, a child of six, ran into the house in fear. They chased after her, firing at my house. They even came to the door, and thrust their SLRs inside, firing. My mother was shot in the knee. My niece was shot near the stomach.' She said, 'All because a child of six had run from them! They came in later, and searched up and down for weapons. When they didn't find any, they told us we shouldn't run when we see them, and they left.'

Other villagers confirmed all the stories we had been told in the upper part of the village. They went over each case, and repeated the same details.

I was again struck by their candour. They didn't, after all, know who we were; who was to say we weren't going to pass along their information to the security forces? This thought did not seem to worry them. Or their need to talk was so strong, they could not stop to worry about the consequences.

I asked the woman about how the state security forces treated the village women.

She said that one woman, of twenty-two, had been raped here. Sometime later, another, twenty-four, and a third, twenty-five, had also been raped. 'They were all married, with little children,' she said. 'The army raped them when they came to search their houses. How could they save themselves? Their husbands have all accepted them, because they weren't to blame. But imagine their shame.'

One man said, 'Tell them about the helicopters.'

'Yes, the army dropped bombs from a helicopter,' the woman said. This, according to her, took place on 9 April, over a month after the first reprisals following the attack on Achham. A helicopter flew over the village, hovering over the stretch between its upper and lower reaches. An eleven-year-old boy was standing close to his house, near his front porch, when a bottle-shaped explosive fell out of the helicopter. It landed in the fields near his house, exploding, and shrapnel struck the boy in the back. The helicopter went on to drop four more explosives in different parts of the village, the woman said.

'All the crops were burned,' said one man. A boulder not far from where we were talking had also been hit. It had white explosion marks at the top, and a jagged crack down the centre. Our lodge for the night stood less than twenty feet away.

'Why would the state security forces drop bombs from the air, deliberately targeting civilians?' I asked.

'The army wanted to punish us,' said the same man. He had a sharp, keen expression and nervous mannerisms. He said that only eight villagers had joined the Maoists—and they were all working in other parts of the country. 'There's not a single Maoist here,' he said. But the Maoist military often came to the village, two to three hundred strong, collecting food from all the houses to cook in a collective mess. Before the Achham attack, five hundred armed Maoists had stayed here overnight. 'We weren't in any position to refuse them food and shelter,' the man said. 'But the army wanted to punish us.' Another helicopter returned on 10 April and dropped more explosives in the village, he said.

I was curious about the villagers' political affiliation. Had Congress and UML activists returned to the village after the ceasefire, I asked.

'The Maoists won't let them,' the man said.

If there were elections here tomorrow, who would win?

'Not the Maoists,' he said. 'Not if they have to put down their arms. Whatever support we give to the Maoists, we are forced to give. The government thinks we're all Maoists, but the fact is nobody likes them. Nobody.'

Surprised, I asked what the villagers thought about the prospect of peace talks.

'We don't care about whether we have a king or whether the country is a republic,' the man said. 'These issues don't matter to us. We want peace. That's all.' Then he asked me, 'What are people in Kathmandu saying? Will this round of talks succeed?'

'Nobody knows,' I said, 'whether the Maoists are sincere about coming to a peace settlement.'

'So there's no sense if all this can be settled?' The man's eyes fixed hard upon me. 'Surely you in Kathmandu know which way things will go.'

'We know just as little as you,' I said.

'So there's no indication if the peace will last?'

'There's no indication.'

He broke out in an odd grin. 'If the fighting starts again, we'll all die,' he said. 'We'll all die.' He let out a high, erratic laugh.

KINGDOMS PAST AND PRESENT

The next morning, as we made our way past the wheat fields in Haudi village, Mama declared, 'Now this—this is fine land. That land near the pass—that was not good land. This land is better.'

No doubt, Mama held more complex views on a variety of other matters. But to talk to him we would have had to walk at his pace, which was plodding. Chitra Bahadur, who was stronger, slowed down to keep him company. Bharat sometimes walked with them, and sometimes sped up to catch up with us.

Past Haudi, the path led through a small settlement perched precariously on a hillside. The houses had holes for windows and doors, giving them an incomplete, gaping look. As we rounded a corner, we crossed a group of men playing carom. I stopped to ask, out of curiosity, whether the Maoists took action against carom players. Board games were, after all, as unproductive as card games, which the Maoists had banned. The men admitted, with sheepish smiles, that if the Maoists were around today, they would not be playing in public.

The walk from there led through desperate-looking villages strung along dusty fields. At one house, a white-haired crone, blind in one eye, called out to us and asked if we had any medicine for her eyes. The eye drops I was carrying would be of no help to her, so I said no. Further along, another group of elderly men asked if we had come to conduct an eye camp. We found out that the army had recently conducted an eye camp at a nearby village. Again I said no. What were we here to do, then, the elderly men asked. We were not here to do anything, I said, feeling suddenly embarrassed. We were just walking through. They waved us past.

In time we arrived at a clutter of fly-ridden houses befouled by the stench of rotten hay. The men of this settlement looked old and weary, and the women had wild, matted hair and soiled clothing. A disproportionate number of them were elderly. The bellies of the children were swollen, and there was a red tint of malnutrition to their hair. We went to the village's only tea shop, but were told by an old man that there was no tea. So we just sat before the tea shop, trying to regain our strength in the scorching midday sun.

'Why,' Malcolm asked me, 'is this village so filthy?'

I had been wondering the same thing. Haudi had been very clean, but here the streets were littered with dung, and the adults and children alike had dirt-smeared faces. A tap was running nearby, but nobody seemed to use it.

I tried a variety of explanations: the lack of soap, the lack of leisure time, the general difficulty of maintaining personal hygiene in a life of toil...

We were getting ready to move on when a wisp of a teenage boy came up to us.

'What are you here for?' he asked in a bullying tone.

Unlike the other men of the village, he was wearing a shirt and pants.

'Are you a party member?' I asked in an equally bullying tone, not wanting to be intimidated.

'I'm a cell member,' he said.

'Well, we've been talking to your party's area secretaries along the way,' I said, trying to pull rank.

'But did you get the party's permission to come?'

I shot back, 'You don't need permission, Bhai. There's a ceasefire now. The code of conduct, which your party signed, says everyone can move freely.'

This seemed to confuse him. He flicked his hair out of his eyes and stared back with some hostility.

I suddenly lost my composure. 'I have one question for you,

though,' I said. 'Where are your party's women? I'd heard that you had a lot of women in the party, but I haven't met many. Can I meet some here?'

Uncertainly, he shook his head.

'Why?'

'We don't have women in this area,' he said. Then he corrected himself: 'We have them, but they've gone. Out.'

'Out?'

'For programmes.'

I turned away with a snort. To an old man who was looking on, I asked, 'Will we be able to cross the ropeway?'

'The ropeway?' He blinked, bewildered.

'The ropeway at Raraghat.'

At this the Maoist boy stepped forward. 'You're going to Manma?' he asked.

I turned to him reluctantly.

With a suddenly helpful tone, he said, 'The ropeway is handmade, but it's strong. All of us use it to cross the river.'

I pointed at Malcolm. 'Will the foreigner fit onto it?'

To my surprise, the boy giggled.

The old man said, 'The man from ward number eight crossed, and he's bigger.'

The boy assured us, 'Take the ropeway. That's what we all do. You'll reach Manma today.'

Confused by his sudden transformation from a bossy Maoist to your average, sweet village boy, I thanked him, at which he grew abashed. The boy watched us for a long time as we walked away, and I felt sorry for him, for the scant options in his life.

In the parched, barren village of Raraghat, where we stopped for lunch, Malcolm went to bathe at a village tap, baring his ghostly pale torso, much to the delight of Bharat. 'How white he is, yah ha ha,' the urchin roared, then tossed off his own shirt and ducked under the tap alongside him. I, sitting at a lodge at some distance, heard some village men speculate among themselves. 'It's the milk that foreigners drink that makes them so white. The whiteness of their milk. And their special medicines.'

I fell into conversation with a man at the lodge, who was wearing—amid a grimy population—a dandyish white shirt, red waistcoat and tailored pants.

He was, he said, from a nearby village, and had come to reach his wife to her maternal home. I asked about peace here, and heard, again, about the cases that had been described to us in Haudi village. He pointed at a hill across a deep ravine. 'The army would just shoot from distances like this,' he said. 'You and I would be sitting here. The army would shoot from there. How would they know if we were Maoists?'

Though the man was not fond of the state security forces, he also disliked the Maoists. 'If there were an election tomorrow, they'd lose,' he said. Then he laughed dryly. 'Unless they're still armed, of course. Then people would have to vote for them.' After a while he said, 'Our place never had anything going for it, you know. We were always as you see us now—living off nothing. But with the state of emergency last year, it turned into hell. Now, everyone is saying, We don't need the government, and we don't need the Maoists. Just let us go back to the way we were. We just want to go back to living off nothing. Just let us be poor. You know?'

When Malcolm and Bharat came back from their baths, we sat down to a meal of daal-bhaat sprinkled liberally with pubic-looking goat hair.

Afterwards, the dandyish man, who was also heading for the ropeway, took us along a shortcut through terraced fields. Along the way we met a contractor who had been working on the

Karnali Highway before its construction was halted. The Maoists kept stealing explosives from the construction site, the contractor said, and the state security forces accused the construction staff of selling it for profit. Had work on the highway not stopped, it would have already wound past Raraghat, north towards Jumla District.

Avoiding patches of stinging nettles, we descended the terraced fields till we reached the bridge that the Maoists had bombed. It was a coil of glinting metal submerged in the Tila River's blue-green rapids. I looked with great longing at the metal, for no such strength was in evidence in the ropeway that the government had built. Its ropes were of rusting metal and jute, and the pulley that passengers sat on was hand-fashioned out of bits of wood, wire, aluminium and iron.

The dandyish man offered to ferry us across. He was of slender build, but then the man who usually ferried passengers across was skinnier. So the man sat in the front part of the pulley, as, one by one, we sat behind him, holding on for dear life to the bars that pinned the pulley together. The pulley would leave one shore, plunging at bracing speed halfway down to the centre of the river, to dangle there forlornly. Then—his slender arms bulging with effort—the dandyish man would pull on the jute rope to reach us to the other shore. There he would fasten the pulley to a side hook.

Back and forth went the pulley, ferrying us and our bags, and villagers with sacks of grain, kerosene drums and even, once, a panicky goat. For each trip the man earned ten rupees. The other man, who usually ferried passengers, said he went back and forth over fifty times a day. The work was hard, but the money, he said, was good.

From there began our ascent to Manma, an ascent that often felt endless. The word Kalikot comes from two words, kalo (black) and kot (fort). The hill we were climbing was just this, a mass of black rock glinting with schist. Up and up we walked, reaching, after an hour and a half, stone steps that did not make it any easier to proceed. Not seeing Manma anywhere, we began to worry.

'Where,' I asked everyone we passed, 'is Manma?'

'It's just there,' they would invariably say, pointing to the sky. 'You'll reach it soon.'

But the steps wound on and on, and at times disappeared altogether, forcing us to scramble up, on all fours, along rocky cliffs. Exhausted, I began to feel like we were journeying to some mythical land—a land said to be under government control, a far-off hilltop bastion of the Kingdom of Nepal.

The landscape took me back to the wars of ancient times. How had the Khas kings from here ever laid siege to Nepal valley over six hundred years ago? They had done so six times, the kings themselves leading the troops, and camping out for months at the edge of present-day Kathmandu. The longest of these sieges had lasted six months. The Khas invaders overran the kingdom of Bhadgaon, but found that Bhadgaon's Malla king had fled to a nearby fort. They were unable to break the fort because the people of Bhadgaon would not cooperate with them; the villagers preferred to abandon their homes in passive defiance. Unable to feed and house themselves without local support, the invaders came all the way back here, defeated.

Resting unhappily on a ledge—for Manma was still nowhere in sight—we saw the snaking contours of the abandoned Karnali Highway far across the hill, where we had eaten lunch. How this area could transform if a highway cut through it! I had never, in Nepal, seen villages as destitute as those we had passed through on this trip. If it was a crime for the state to violate its citizens' political liberties, I thought, it should be equally a crime to violate their economic rights.

Walking on, we eventually reached a shrine built of stone topped off with bamboo poles. Inside, a line of jagged stones stood in, cursorily, for deities. From the shrine we could see Manma bazaar.

I asked an old man idling by the shrine how long it was to the bazaar.

He lifted his hand, checked his watch, and said, 'One minute.'

'One minute?'

'Ten maximum.'

It took us forty minutes.

It was near five o'clock when we reached the entrance to the bazaar. We were stopped there at a police post, and questioned by a policeman about the purpose of our trip. We gave him the same answers we had given Maoists along the way. Malcolm wanted, if possible, to meet the chief district officer. He said he would escort us into town.

Manma bazaar stood atop a hill that was equally inaccessible from all directions. An endless hillside of terraced fields stretched along the southern slope. Beyond, to the west, was the Karnali, the largest river of western Nepal. A portion of Kalikot District lay on the river's far shore. Kotbada, the site of the district's yet-unbuilt airport, was also across the river. I scanned the hills to see it. This was where, on 24 February 2002, the security forces had shot dead more than thirty-four workers, including seventeen who had come here all the way from Dhading District, near Kathmandu, to find work. Thanks to the reporting of the journalist Mohan Mainali, this incident had found wide coverage in the Kathmandu media, jolting the intellectuals to rethink their habitual complacency. Like the atrocities we had heard about in Haudi village, this one had taken place as the security forces hunted down the Maoists who had staged the Achham attack.

The policeman who was escorting us was a garrulous fellow.

'I don't know if the CDO Sah'b is in his office,' he said. 'The Maoists held a programme today.' All government officials, as well as the heads of the political parties, had been invited for round-table talks in Tadi village, he said, pointing at a distant cluster of houses with his walkie-talkie. 'I don't think CDO Sah'b attended, though. The party leaders probably boycotted it too.' He grinned. 'Their leaders in Kathmandu haven't been invited for round-table talks by the Maoists, so why would they attend round-table talks here?'

His walkie-talkie buzzed: 'Where are the visitors now?'

He replied, 'We're just reaching the post, Sah'b.'

As we reached the bazaar, he made us sign in a register at the District Police Office. It was the rule that everyone entering Manma had to identify themselves, and obtain passes for the duration of their stay. That this was in violation of the code of conduct was no matter. The district authorities were keeping Manma in a state of siege. This was apparent also from the large numbers of policemen manning the bazaar's main street.

In the CDO's office grounds, two policemen were playing badminton, one of them bearing a rifle in his free hand. They stopped when they saw us, and led us to the office.

The CDO met us in his capacious room with water-stained walls and mildewy carpets. He was a middle-aged man—obviously from the southern Tarai plains—with a guarded, wary expression. He sat stiffly in his chair, as though we had come to conduct a spot check, and had caught him off guard. The assistant CDO was also at the meeting, as was an army officer, who took out a notebook and pen when we began to speak.

Malcolm conducted some official work, and then we talked informally, trying hard to draw out the CDO, who was hesitant.

So, there had been a round-table talk in Tadi village?

'I didn't attend it,' the CDO said.

'The Maoists invited party leaders as well?'

'I don't know about that.'

How was the security situation, we asked.

'Everything's fine now that there's peace.'

So there was no threat from the Maoists now?

'No.'

The conversation kept halting abruptly.

Nevertheless we went on with our questions.

It emerged, eventually, that the CDO had been posted here just over a month ago, immediately before the announcement of the ceasefire. Before that, his post had been vacant for seven or eight months, for much of the state of emergency. Given the security threat to government officials, the CDO had not been able to venture outside Manma to the rest of the district. 'Now, with the ceasefire, we'll go,' he said, though without conviction. 'We must go. We must.'

The CDO relaxed only when I asked him how he thought the insurgency could be countered. 'To solve the Maoist problem we must alleviate poverty,' he said, easing into his chair. 'First we must improve the education sector. And we must create income-generating opportunities. For that, we need a road.' He lamented the halt in the construction of the Karnali Highway, and went on about the imperative of development, becoming quite animated.

But when I told him of the atrocities that we had heard about in Haudi village—the beatings, the killings, the rapes, the explosives dropped from the air—he again stiffened. 'I can't speak on things that happened before I came here,' he said.

'Oh, of course,' I said, thinking: Why ever not?

And what was an army officer doing taking notes on our meeting with civilian officers?

The conversation finally petered out, and we stood up to leave.

Outside, in the grounds, I felt I could breathe again. The CDO, too, looked glad that we were leaving. His was not, certainly, a job that I coveted—defending this hilltop government outpost with the Maoists all around. We took leave from him.

On the bazaar's main street, we passed the district offices of the Congress and the UML, their flags fluttering gaily in the wind, in what was, for me, a strangely moving sight. The 1990 People's Movement had made it possible for Nepalis to enjoy pluralism in politics. Now that pluralism was under threat: The headquarters was the only place in the district where the political parties could now be present.

The street ended at an odd, artless bust of the late King Birendra, more parody than memorial. Out of a marble platform jutted a torso, clad in a black, lumpy coat and thick black glasses. The bust's eyes were cast up in an expression of shock as it looked out from before a sandbagged and bunkered police post, in what seemed an apt enough image for the state of the monarchy. We wanted to look up a journalist, Tula Ram Pandey, who worked as a correspondent for *Kantipur*. He was the district's sole journalist. It proved easy enough to find him, given how small Manma was. We had only just invited him to our lodge when the six o'clock curfew fell. Blasting tinny whistles, two armed policemen cleared the streets, shouting for everyone to go home. Men who had been ambling about picked up their pace. Mothers called out for their children. Waifs scampered off yelping. If we were to talk to the journalist, he would have to stay in the lodge tonight. With a smile he said he was used to being caught out by the evening curfew.

We moved into our room—the lodge's one free room—and were about to talk when the army officer who had taken notes at the CDO's office came by.

He wanted, he said, to talk to us. 'I want to respond to some of your earlier questions.'

We wished he had not come. He would not, after all, admit to any of the atrocities we had heard about along the trail. And we were not up for propaganda. But we could not really refuse him. The journalist left and we sat down with the officer.

Speaking fluent English in the manner of the Kathmandu bourgeoisie, Captain Ashok Khand introduced himself. The major who headed the Kalikot garrison was on leave, he said; it was the first time in ten months that he had been able to leave his station. The captain, meanwhile, was second in command.

He was young, and gave off a sharp, professional air. Taking out his notebook, he denied the atrocities we had mentioned at the CDO's office. 'We may have made a few mistakes,' he said, taking a line that the army was officially to take in a few weeks' time, a line that for the first time acknowledged that not all was going well in their counter-insurgency efforts. But none of the beatings, killings or rapes had taken place, he said. Neither had explosives been dropped from the air.

We steered the conversation towards other grounds. The Kalikot garrison had two hundred men, the captain said. This amounted to one company. Before the ceasefire they used to go on weekly patrols to the district's outlying areas, in situations fraught with danger. 'We're lucky not to have lost a single soldier,' he said. One soldier had lost an eye in one Maoist ambush, and another had lost a foot. 'But these are the only casualties we've sustained so far.' He took a lot of pride in this.

From his poise, Captain Khand looked set to go far in life. His job, too, I did not covet, I thought as I listened to him. Neighbouring Achham District's garrison had lost all but two men in a Maoist attack. The garrison of neighbouring Jumla District had also suffered heavy casualties in another attack. The Kalikot garrison obviously operated under great threat. Two hundred men—from families of ordinary means—were fighting daily to save the government, but more immediately, their own lives. They were no richer than the Maoists. They were only doing their jobs. The captain was responsible for them.

I could not help but ask how old he was.

He took some offence at the question. 'Old enough to do my job well,' he replied with a tight smile.

But my curiosity got the better of me. 'How old is that?' I persisted.

'Older than you,' he said.

'Surely not,' I shot back.

He finally said, 'Thirty-two.'

'Two years younger than me,' I said, and thought: Hell, he shouldn't have to shoulder such a heavy burden.

We fell into a more personal exchange after that. It turned out that our family houses in Kathmandu were in the same neighbourhood. And he knew a cousin of mine, also a captain in the army, young and smart like him. He asked, amiably, about our route, and assured us that we'd reach Jumla District's headquarters, Khalanga, in three days.

I had quite warmed up to the captain when he began to speak in ways that again set off my qualms: Since the ceasefire, he said, the army had begun to conduct health camps, so as to win the hearts and minds of the people. These camps were proving immensely popular. The army was also thinking of taking up other development projects, primary among them the construction of the Karnali Highway. 'We recognize that the people of this area need development,' Captain Khand said. 'We must alleviate poverty.'

I could not help but think: If that was the army's job, what then was the job of the civilian government?

We parted politely enough.

Manma was publicly said to be a dry zone. For a decade now,

the government had imposed a ban on the production and consumption of alcohol, as public drunkenness had caused much local mayhem. But in the privacy of their homes few observed this ban. Over dinner, offering Malcolm some chhaang, the lodge owner explained, 'We don't get to buy bottled alcohol, but everyone brews their own drinks.' He laughed, 'Even the government officials and the army and the police have their own supplies.'

After dinner, as Chitra Bahadur, Bharat and Mama slept—in their still, dead silent way—and Malcolm, drowsy on two glasses of chhaang, drifted in and out of sleep, I resumed the interrupted conversation with the journalist.

Tula Ram Pandey was a lean, tall man with a quizzical expression magnified by thick eyeglasses. When I said that it felt to me as though Manma was under siege, he told me that things had in fact improved since the ceasefire. The rule that all visitors obtain passes was, he explained, aimed at keeping the Maoists out. 'If ordinary villagers have any work in the bazaar, they can at least come and go now.' Even this had not been possible before the ceasefire.

He worked under considerable constraint here. Government officials often told him he was too soft on the Maoists. Yet the Maoists thought that as an independent reporter he favoured the government. 'Now, the atmosphere has eased somewhat,' he said. But during the state of emergency, his job had proved very trying. Till a few weeks back, the only functioning telephone line in town was at the CDO's office. He had to dispatch all his reports through this phone. At one point, even this phone line was down, so he was reduced to waiting for stray helicopters to come—ferrying government officials or state security forces or non-government workers or foreign dignitaries. He sent his reports to *Kantipur*'s Kathmandu office via the pilots. But his

reports often went out of date because there were no helicopters
to send them on. 'I kept writing,' he said, laughing. 'Every day, I
wrote, not knowing whether I could ever dispatch my reports.'
And even when his reports did reach *Kantipur*'s office, there was
no saying they would be printed. He rarely found out what
became of them, as newspapers rarely made it to Manma.

As we talked we heard a volley of gunfire, not far away,
from some training that the army were giving to the armed
police in the use of their relatively more sophisticated firearms.
We went to a balcony to look. Outside, the hills surrounding
Manma were pitch black. The army garrison occupied one dark
hilltop to the northwestern side of the bazaar. As we talked, the
rattle of gunshots continued, and to me it seemed that the army
were announcing to the Maoists, who were not far beyond the
bazaar: Look, we've got lots of ammunition, don't attack us. And
again Manma struck me as an ancient kingdom, with soldiers
defending the fort from outside marauders. At one point a flare
went off in the sky, lighting up the hills in a lavish display of
military might.

THE WILL OF THE YOUNG

The next morning I woke up desperate to leave Manma. I would
have left the whole district if I could have. The poverty of the
villages, the compulsive, haunted way that the villagers had talked
to us, the besieged feel of the district headquarters and the loss
of civilian rule had all sparked off a sudden panic in me. Bad
politics had made a wreck of the countryside. It would take
great wisdom to set things right. Did Kathmandu's politicians
and intellectuals and bourgeoisie have this wisdom? I did not
see that we did.

We set off early, hoping to get to Khalanga in three days. We had a plane to catch on the morning of the fourth day. There was, however, no consensus as to whether we could catch our plane. Chitra Bahadur, for one, thought it impossible. 'It will take five days at least,' he said. But a man whom we met just outside Manma told us he had left Khalanga the day before, after his morning meal. 'If I can reach here in a day, you can definitely reach there in three days,' he said.

We walked as fast as we could. The path was thankfully flat, along a wide, meandering 'highway', as the locals called it, which passed through the cactus-dotted village of Tari. Here, the winter before, the state security forces had burned down a house belonging to a Maoist. It stood, a sooty wreck, by the side of the trail. We did not tarry to look at it. We walked on past a series of squalid, fly-infested settlements till we reached a wayside village where we stopped for lunch.

Our lodge gave off the stench of goat stalls. A band of young men with hard, unfriendly gazes were eating at the same lodge. They kept throwing glances at us, but we did not talk to them. I for one was sick of the Maoists. Given that—over the decades—the state had done so little for them, they were justified in demanding their rights. But what did their violent methods achieve? The powers that be—including donor countries funding the government—would not tolerate a Maoist victory. So, unless the present peace talks succeeded, the security forces would continue their brutal campaign, and all civil liberties would be lost. By adopting violence, the Maoists had enabled the king's royal coup in Kathmandu, and in the district headquarters, military rule.

The path was flat from here, but it wound around every slope, making us walk for miles and miles just to put a single hill behind us. Khalanga lay beyond an endless fold of peaks. The land grew dry and desert-like. We met nobody for hours. Then, suddenly, we came upon a swarm of anxious, fretting villagers at a health post, a humble clay hut with no signpost or board announcing it at all. Some of the villagers had walked hours to come here, carrying children or ageing parents on their backs. The man tending to them—the health post's sole attendant—was too busy to pay us any notice. Of all the state services, the Maoists had let only the health post operate, as cutting off medical services would prove too unpopular.

There was no doubting that we were back in Maoist territory. We passed several gates emblazoned with hammer-and-sickle signs, and houses with slogans painted on their stone walls: *Long live the Nepal Communist Party (Maoist)! Laal salaam to brave martyr Chankhe BK!* A sign on one abandoned house read—*Do not make washing foreign dishes leave the country to find employment!* Despite the garbled grammar, its sentiment was unmistakable. The government was not respected here.

We stopped for the evening in the village of Daha, a lush oasis of fields supported by gurgling irrigation canals. Here, the village lanes were neat and paved with stones, and the houses were washed with bright red clay. Each courtyard boasted a few goats or chickens. The villagers looked unusually well fed. They also looked as though they belonged to a bygone era: The men wore traditional daura-suruwals and the women were decked in elaborate fineries, bearing necklaces strung with coins on their chests, and showing off gold jewellery in their ears, on their noses, wrists and fingers. They wore patterned skirts and blouses, and their hair, cut in fringes, gave them a Tibetan look.

Disoriented by this sudden exoticism, I asked two young women at our lodge about the village. It was, they said, a Chettri-caste village. This in part explained its relative wealth. Both women were cradling infants in their laps. I assumed, patronizingly, that they would have been child brides. But when I asked, one said that she had been twenty-two when she had her first baby, and the other said she had married in her twenties.

As night fell a young Maoist man showed up at the lodge, asking for a meal. We were surprised to see the lodge owner, a man in his fifties, brusquely send him off to another house. But as we sat down to a meal of fragrant red rice and mustard greens, the Maoist returned, saying that he could not find food anywhere else. The lodge owner served him without a word, though his displeasure was evident.

It was dark in the lodge, and I could not see the Maoist's face. Or I did not bother to look carefully. I wasn't up for chatting with him. He asked the usual questions and we gave the usual answers. I had hoped, I said, to meet Maoist women on the trail. 'Your party keeps saying that thirty per cent of its cadres are women, but everyone we've met is a man.'

'You'll meet the women in Jumla District,' he reassured me. 'They'll be everywhere along the trail.'

He was a motivator. He seemed to think we were interested to know more about him, so he went on: 'It's hard work, walking through the jungles come sun or rain or wind, begging for food in the villages, sleeping anywhere. And people don't want to change their ways, they don't want to listen to us.' He sighed. 'But that,' he said, 'is a sacrifice we have decided to make.'

Perversely, I felt like telling him to take responsibility for a choice he had freely made, and not to expect the sympathy of others. But of course I didn't.

After our meal we left him and went upstairs, climbing a stairway of a hewn tree trunk to the attic. In a spacious clay-washed room, the lodge owner had laid out large woollen mats. We spread our sleeping bags and blankets on top of them and were hunkering down to sleep when the Maoist came upstairs.

He wanted, apparently, to motivate us.

Malcolm would not cooperate; he kept tight in his sleeping

bag, pretending to have fallen asleep within seconds. I did the same, hoping that the motivator would not take offence and subject us to a 'struggle session' and 'speak bitterness' about our bourgeois proclivities.

Chitra Bahadur, Bharat and Mama, though, sat up in their bedding, having no choice but to listen to the motivator. Or this is how I saw it. It could be that they were interested in the speech that he launched on, a speech that went along the following lines:

'Our movement is aimed at toppling the feudal monarchy. We are not against poor, simple folks like you. Our goal is to end the rich people's oppression. Won't it feel good to be liberated? It will feel good. You know the rich people, they've been oppressing us historically—for many, many generations. Our party is very scientific. It will lead the proletariat revolution. Do you know who proletariats are? Proletariats are people like us. And labourers. Proletariats and labourers. Also peasants. And who are the rich people? You've seen them. They drive big trucks and eat meat even in the morning. They live in mansions made of glass in Kathmandu. Now you may think that what I'm saying is like a tale or a made-up story. But the fact that we will succeed has been proven by revolutions that took place earlier in China, the Soviet Union, Cuba and Cambodia. Our victory is historically inevitable because our party is scientific.'

This was the gist of what the motivator said, except he took more than an hour saying it, repeating every line several times, and returning time and again to each point till I, still feigning sleep, was sick to death of him. If his party were so scientific, it would not let him loose on exhausted labourers, keeping them awake deep into the night. A foot massage might better motivate them…

But then this lecture was not meant for the Kathmandu

bourgeoisie like myself; I would obviously require extensive re-education to come around to Maoism. Chitra Bahadur and Mama, however, seemed won over by the motivator's logic.

'Poor people—how hard they have to work,' the motivator said at one point. 'You. How hard you have to work, carrying loads.'

'Carrying loads,' Chitra Bahadur murmured.

'Going to India to work.'

'Going to India,' said Chitra Bahadur.

'Going to India,' Mama joined in.

The motivator said, 'The revolution is going to destroy the feudal monarchy.'

'Destroy the feudal monarchy.'

'The feudal monarchy.'

'Our party is not like the others', the motivator said, 'because it is scientific.'

'It's scientific.'

This went on and on—till finally, a bit abruptly, Chitra Bahadur said, 'It's late, the foreign sir has to sleep now.'

'You know, I too am someone's son, someone's brother,' the motivator said. 'But I've decided to dedicate my life to this kind of work.'

'Oh it's good work,' Chitra Bahadur said.

'It's for your liberation.'

'It's for our liberation.'

'You must think of us as we walk the hills for the cause, as we dodge bullets, staying in the jungles at night, begging for food. Think of us, fighting for you. Keep us in mind, consider us your own family, love us.'

'We'll think of you,' Chitra Bahadur said.

Finally, the motivator left.

Bharat, who had been listening raptly, immediately asked his father, 'Was he a Maoist, Ba? Was he a Maoist? Was he a Maoist?'

'Go to sleep.'

They all settled into their bedding amid long sighs and murmurs.

Mama let out a sigh. 'That was a fine talk,' he said in the darkness.

Chitra Bahadur hmm'ed.

'That boy taught us a lot,' Mama said. 'He taught us a lot about history.'

The only thing the motivator did for me was turn me off the Maoists. The next morning, as we walked out of the village, I said as much to a local man who fell into our company.

The man could barely contain himself. 'It's not one day, it's not two days, it's not three days,' he spat out with vehemence. 'They show up all the time. We may not have enough to feed ourselves, but we have to give them food, because if we refuse them, they'll come back with even more of their comrades, and they'll force you to feed all of them. They say they're working for our sake, but they're just giving us trouble.'

I realized that of all the people we had spoken to on our trip, only Maoists had spoken well of their party.

This was very much on my mind when we stopped for lunch at the village of Pakha. The Tila River ran past the small settlement; we could hear the swish of the water. The man of the house we had stopped at said trout was on sale for sixty-five rupees a kilo. We decided to have some.

A group of men were gathered to one side of the house. Not wanting to meet any more Maoists, we tried to ignore them. But one of them, a twenty-something, was casting us inquisitive glances.

Unenthusiastically, I asked, 'You're in the party, Bhai?'

He nodded.

My heart sank.

He was an Area Committee member, he said. His name was
Comrade Kopila. His face had a soft, fresh look, and he was
dressed surprisingly neatly, in a clean shirt and tailored slacks.

Already regretting the conversation, I asked how things had
been since the ceasefire.

'The army's been poisoning people,' Comrade Kopila said.

I sighed.

'They conducted a medical camp in Pakha VDC, and they
mixed poison with the medicine!' Something about the way
he was speaking—the loudness of his voice—made me think
he was saying this more for the benefit of the other men than
for us. 'Two children got sick,' he went on. 'The army poisoned
people in Gela VDC also. We told people not to go to the camps.
Anyway, they don't want to go. They say—The army first comes
and kills us, and now they want to treat us? We're not going
to go to their camps. But the army's been forcing them to take
poisonous medicine.'

'Is that right?'

He went over a list of atrocities that the government had
allegedly committed during the state of emergency: In Dahale,
he said, a seventy-year-old man had been killed because villagers
had told the security forces that he was a Maoist. In the same
place, two Dalit children had been shot from across their family's
house. They still had shrapnel in their bodies, he said, though
Maoist doctors took out the bullet.

'You have Maoist doctors?' I finally took interest.

'Yes,' he said, but he went on listing other atrocities: Dan
Bahadur Singh, a teacher, and Dil Bahadur Singh, Rata Bahadur
Singh and a man named Jite in Odanakhu VDC had been made
to dig a large hole. Then they were all shot dead and buried in
it. In Dahale again, five houses of suspected Maoists had been

set on fire by the security forces. In Pakha VDC, three women had been raped. In Chappre VDC, a student was made to wear a sign that read 'terrorist' and then was shot point-blank. One Maoist worker was chased off a cliff by the army...

I did not doubt that these events may have occurred. But Comrade Kopila was being silent about the fact that his party, too, was violating human rights here, sometimes in brutal, medieval ways, hacking the limbs off people before killing them, or sentencing them to forced labour. Neither was he acknowledging the Maoists's responsibility for initiating the war.

Among the others listening on was a squat middle-aged man. He now spoke up. 'If you go to Malkot VDC—that's near Kotbada, where the airport was being built—you'll find eighteen children who were born to local women raped by the army,' he said.

His statement was calculated to rattle me. It did.

He introduced himself as Comrade Sandesh, the area secretary. He had a bearish, big-brotherly way about him, and he reminded me of several Kathmandu politicians I knew. Something about him unnerved me. I asked Comrade Kopila to tell us about the Maoist doctors.

The party had, he said, fifteen or sixteen doctors, who used medical supplies bought in India. They weren't actually doctors, but trained medical personnel who performed the tasks of doctors. 'They've already conducted six or seven eye and teeth camps since the ceasefire,' he bragged. 'People come to our camps because they know that we're working for them. They don't go to the army camps. At one army camp, the villagers even chanted against the army, saying—We don't need medicine when we can't get justice.'

Noticing, maybe, that we tended to glaze over at such propaganda, Comrade Sandesh spoke up again. 'Now that there's peace, our party is focusing on development,' he said. 'Our comrades are teaching in the schools, filling in for missing teachers. We're conducting clean-up campaigns. We've already built eight or nine bridges. Fourteen in Pushpa VPC.'

'VPC?'

'Village People's Committee.' Comrade Pushpa, he said, was one of the party's martyrs. The party had named an equivalent of a Village Development Committee after him.

'We're also planning to build the highway,' Comrade Kopila chimed in.

'The Karnali Highway?'

He nodded.

I grew sceptical. 'Your party has the means?'

'Yes.'

It turned out that the villagers were being made to put in free labour for all this work.

I became querulous. Turning to Comrade Sandesh, I asked, 'Are you going to allow the other political parties to come back now that there's a ceasefire?'

He laughed. 'We won't stop them from coming,' he said. 'But they should be prepared to return all the money they looted in the people's name.'

I wanted to ask why his party was so bent on destroying the other parties—by doing so, weren't they just helping the king maintain absolute rule? I was too scared to, though. Instead I asked how their relations were with the army.

According to Comrade Sandesh, the captain from Manma had come to Ratadab village for a few days; the army and the Maoists spent two days talking. 'The captain asked us: What is an interim government, what is a constituent assembly, why were we negotiating with the king and not with the democratic government?'

I asked, 'Why *are* you negotiating with the king, when you say he's not legitimate?'

He laughed again. 'Because the only people who command

power in this country are the king and Comrade Prachanda.'

Somehow this logic seemed to have convinced him. I was still hung up on the fact that the Maoists had, more than anything, disabled democracy. I said, 'You know, you say your party is popular. But everyone we've spoken to who isn't a Maoist says they're only supporting you out of fear.'

At this, Comrade Sandesh grew serious. 'That's not true,' he said.

I said, 'I haven't met a single person who isn't a Maoist who supports the party.'

He turned to the other men, and said, 'Well, brothers, you tell them for yourselves whether or not you support us.'

'We support the party fully,' one man said.

The other men nodded.

Comrade Sandesh turned back with a smile.

I got slightly scared. 'I understand that your party has worked a lot for social reform?' I said, to placate him.

'We've eliminated caste discrimination,' he said proudly.

'You've eliminated it?'

Of course, he said. The party had forced people of the so-called upper castes to attend the funerals of Dalits, who were traditionally considered untouchable. And the party had held community meals in order to break the taboo against the 'upper castes' sharing food and water with the 'ritually polluted' castes. 'In the beginning, people resisted these programmes,' Comrade Sandesh said, 'but now they all go along.'

Then he said, 'We've also eliminated discrimination against women.'

'You have?'

'Yes. After giving birth, women used to have to stay outside the family house because they were considered impure. For seven days nobody would eat anything that they had touched. Now we've brought them into the house. And we've done the same for menstruating women. Why, just next door there's a woman who had a son yesterday. Today she's preparing our meal.'

'She gave birth yesterday and you're making her cook today?' I was aghast. 'Don't you think she should rest?'

He chuckled, but then grew serious. 'It's important to free women from traditional feelings of pollution,' he said in the tone of a reprimand.

I had to agree.

'We've brought many positive changes. We've opposed witch doctors and put an end to superstition. We've entered temples at inauspicious times to prove that there's no god.'

'And people don't mind?'

'They used to, but not any more. Two or three years ago, everyone stopped believing in god.'

I rolled my eyes.

'It's true,' he said, laughing. He turned again to the others. 'You tell them for yourselves, brothers: Do you believe in god?'

The men all shook their heads.

One said, 'I stopped believing in god about two or three years ago.'

The others murmured in agreement.

It was enough to turn me into a theist. 'What happens if someone persists in believing in god?' I asked. 'What if someone tries, but can't stop believing in god?'

'Whenever someone makes a mistake,' said Comrade Sandesh, 'they're asked to acknowledge this in front of the people. If they refuse, they're put to labour.'

'What kind of labour?'

'They have to wash dishes for people, or build toilets for them.'

Malcolm asked whether the party had labour camps.

Yes, he said, the party had twelve labour camps in the Kalikot and Jumla Districts.

'Whereabouts?'

He guffawed. 'Now I can't reveal that to you, can I?'

My stubbornly bourgeois proclivities had apparently rankled, though. Comrade Sandesh finally took me on. 'It's important to transform society,' he admonished me. 'I noticed that when you walked into the village, you called our brother here'—he pointed at Chitra Bahadur—'Bhariya dai. But you mustn't call them porters. That's demeaning. You must call them helpers,' he said, using the English term.

'*Helpers*?'

'We are all human beings.'

'Indeed,' I said, feeling like a child.

He asked what we were paying the helpers, and we told him. He seemed satisfied with the rate.

Our lunch arrived, and with it, the fish that the woman next door had cooked. Comrade Sandesh offered everyone a piece, saying, 'Sharing whatever we have is the culture of the communists. We may not have much, but we share everything we have. That's what communism is about.'

To me, the fish cooked by the woman next door tasted bland, as though its flesh were spent and exhausted. By contrast, the fish that we had ordered was succulent and tasty. We failed, however, to share it with anyone.

As we ate I fell into conversation, again, with Comrade Kopila, who wanted to impress upon us, at this point, that he wasn't the mindless propagandist he had come off as, but a regular guy, one of us. He was a member of the party's Intellectuals' Front, he said. He had passed his intermediate-level exams, and had also trained as an assistant health worker in Kathmandu, going through an eighteen-month course. One of his brothers worked at the Danish aid organization DANIDA in Kathmandu; he had married a Danish woman. 'My other brother also married a

Danish woman,' he said. 'He's a medical doctor.'

It surprised me that someone with his bourgeois links should join the Maoist movement instead of looking for a job. 'You never worked as an assistant health worker?' I asked.

'No.'

'But you'd easily find work in an NGO.'

He shrugged. 'I just…fell in with the party,' he said. 'And once I was in, I thought—I might as well stay on. Till there's peace.'

He returned to the topic of development, boasting about a power plant that his party had made in the village of Dillikot. The party also published a fortnightly magazine, *Kanjiroa*, by desktop technology near the Rara Lake in Jumla District. They had electrified their office there. He said, 'The magazine's editor, Naresh Bhandari, is BA-passed.'

I thought I might press him on social issues. Were his party's women really equal to men? 'If so, why aren't there any women in the party's negotiating team?'

'Well, it's not enough to be a woman,' he said. 'You also have to be qualified. Most of the women aren't as educated…'

Comrade Sandesh poked him at this point, none too discreetly, and he fell silent.

But I pounced on what he had said. 'Are you saying that women like Hisila Yami aren't qualified?' She was the wife of the Maoist leader Baburam Bhattarai, an architect, who was now underground.

'Comrade Hisila holds a very high post in the party,' Comrade Kopila said.

'Yeah? What post?'

He hesitated. 'One day it will become public.'

I shrugged.

'You won't be disappointed when it becomes public,' he insisted.

I shrugged again.

That, then, was how the party worked: Comparatively savvy, ideologically educated thirty- and forty-somethings held the higher posts, guiding little-educated or uneducated twenty-somethings and teens. This was the pattern we had observed so far. The younger cadres were patchy in their knowledge—'Rich people drive big trucks and eat meat, even in the morning'—but what they lacked in knowledge, they made up for in numbers.

Not all the younger cadres were fun to meet. We headed off after lunch, passing another village along the Tila River, where sun-glassed, suited and booted hooligans stopped us, demanding to know what we were doing there. What are *you* doing here, I wanted to ask. Instead I politely introduced ourselves, and said, 'We need to reach Khalanga today,' and walked on, hoping they would not stop us. Luckily, they did not.

From there the path led up a sparse conifer forest, where the air sounded with the thunk-thunk of axe against tree trunk. High up on a pine tree shorn of its lower branches was a woman cutting firewood. She was wearing, impossibly, a sari. Why, I thought, were the hooliganish Maoists down the hill not helping her out?

We walked and walked, but walk as we might, we seemed to be making no headway. Every passer-by gave us different estimates. We reached the lonely village of Ranchuli as night fell, fearing that our trek would never end. We also feared, a bit, what we would find upon reaching Khalanga. On 15 November 2002, a 3,000-strong Maoist force had attacked the town in a midnight raid, killing twenty-seven policemen and four army men. The Maoists had shot the district superintendent of police and razed every government building, not even sparing buildings merely rented for government work. They had lost twenty-seven of their own cadres that night. This attack, combined with another attack carried out in Gorkha District on the same day, had forced the government to the table, to hold peace talks.

The next morning we set off at six, in darkness, our torches feebly lighting the way as we put behind us one shadowy settlement after another—dogs barking to alert the villagers—till finally, as daylight broke, we crossed over a metal bridge spanning the Sinja River into Jumla District. From here the land was sandy, the heat of the sun shimmering off the schist.

The urchin Bharat, who had all these days scampered along gaily, got tired all of a sudden. No promise of biscuits, noodles, eggs, fish or meat would induce him to scamper today. He began to lag behind us, grumbling volubly, and two hours into Jumla District, he was nowhere to be seen on the trail.

His father seemed unfazed. 'The boy will catch up,' he said.

'What if he's lost his way?' I asked.

'The boy,' he said, grinding his teeth, 'will catch up.'

Chitra Bahadur had five children; four of them were boys. Bharat was the second-born. His brothers all went to school, but Bharat was too lazy. 'He just won't go,' Chitra Bahadur said.

'Can't you force him?'

'I tell him—If you don't study, you'll have to carry loads, like your father. He says he doesn't care.'

'He will later.'

'I know.'

Our path led past a bridge decorated with a crudely hewn wood carving of the late King Birendra atop a phallus-shaped horse. One of the bridge's posts was carved into the shape of a green-uniformed soldier standing at guard. He even bore a wooden rifle in his hands. A third pole resembled the late Crown Prince—no, late King—Dipendra in a white daura-suruwal and black jacket. The Maoists, we thought, had obviously not bombed these poles because they were so subversive in their ugliness.

All of us had been affected, in various ways, by our trip. Over the days, Chitra Bahadur and Mama had conquered their initial fear of the Maoists. They were maybe even impressed by them. Mama had stopped commenting any more on the quality of the land—depressed, perhaps, by all the sand and schist. Malcolm and I, upset by all we'd seen and at the end of our physical and emotional resources, were having strange, freaked-out exchanges. He told me, as we walked, about a family dog that went on a long, long walk, and when it reached home, flopped down and died. 'This much walking can't be good for us,' he said. I snapped back, 'Are you saying you're having a nervous breakdown?'

In the village of Kudari we all snacked on crisp, juicy local apples, waiting for Bharat to show up. The buildings here were in the Tibetan adobe style, with flat mud roofs and colourful doors and windows. The fields were all oases supported by glistening irrigation canals.

Bharat did finally saunter into sight, pouting. The apples cheered him somewhat, but he was never again restored to the thuggish cheer with which he had launched on the journey.

We met some female Maoist cadres near the wayside settlement of Raka. At first we did not recognize them as Maoists, though. They walked past us, a few scattered girls, talking in high, tittering tones. We took them for schoolgirls on an outing—till one pumped her fist and exchanged a 'Laal salaam' with another.

I hesitated to talk to them. They were at most in their early teens; they weren't old enough for the kind of questions I wanted to put to Maoist women.

But they might be the only female Maoists I would meet in this region. I stopped three girls who were heading towards me. One was a teenager, and the two others were children. 'Can we talk awhile, Bahini?'

'Talk?' The teenager had her hair done up in braids, and was wearing a simple kurtha-sural. Her wide eyes fluttered uncertainly.

'We wanted to meet some women working for the party.' I hesitated. 'You are, aren't you, a Maoist?'

She nodded.

'We'll just ask a few questions.'

She glanced at the two younger girls. They glanced away, looking just as unsure as she.

But they followed us to a nearby log that served as a bench. Seeing us, some women from the nearby houses came over to listen in. And a boy in a smart green uniform strode over and stepped in between us, shaking hands firmly with all of the girls in turn. 'Laal salaam.' 'Laal salaam.' They all pumped their fists after their handshakes.

The boy turned to us with a stony look.

'I want to talk to these girls,' I explained, unnerved by a child of not more than fourteen.

He stood by glowering.

I turned to the oldest girl and asked her her name.

She gave me another wide-eyed look. 'You want my real name? Or my party name?'

'Your party name,' I said.

'Jamuna.'

'Have you been working long in the party, Jamuna bahini?'

She had joined only four months ago. The other girls had joined only two months ago. I asked them what their names were.

'What's my name?' One turned to the other, and then they both turned to Jamuna. They couldn't remember the names the party had given them. For a while the three girls whispered among themselves. Then Jamuna turned to us, and told us that the girls' names were Pragati and Sangeeta.

I could not bring myself to question the younger girls, so I directed my questions at Jamuna. Why had she joined the party?

This she answered confidently. 'I want to work for the party revolution,' she said. 'I want to fulfil the responsibilities the party gives me. I'll do anything for the party.'

This sounded earnest, if rehearsed. 'You liked what the party was doing?' I asked.

She nodded. 'And there was nothing to do at home.'

'You weren't going to school?'

Her parents had never enrolled her in school. 'My elder brother is a graduate, though,' she said, as though to let us know that she was not unworldly. 'My other brother is in class seven. Even my sister-in-law has passed her SLC exams.' She, however, was put to housework. She used to cut grass, work in the fields, gather firewood. 'There was nothing to do at home,' she repeated.

'So you joined the party?'

She nodded.

I asked her how old she was.

'Fifteen,' she said. Then, 'Eighteen.'

'She's fifteen,' piped in one of the village women.

'I'm eighteen,' Jamuna said, hotly.

'You were born a month after my son,' the woman shot back. 'And he hasn't crossed fifteen.'

When I asked the other girls their ages, the village woman answered for them: 'They're twelve and thirteen.'

'Is that right?'

The girls nodded.

Jamuna was from a nearby village called Nuwakot. She no longer lived with her family. When I asked what work she did for the party, she said, vaguely, that she worked in a team consisting of one male cell member. 'We all call him elder brother,' she said. There were three other girls in their cell. She alone among the girls was a cell member.

'But what does your team do?'

'We rear chicken and sheep.'

I was not a little surprised.

'And we grow potatoes,' she added.

One of the other girls said, 'Also corn and some green beans.'

'But isn't this exactly what you were doing for your family?' I asked.

Jamuna nodded. They farmed, she said, on fields that belonged to people who had left the village. 'Some people even give their fields to the party,' she said with pride. 'In fact a lot of people do.'

'Doesn't your family mind that you joined the party?' I asked.

'Why should they mind? They're happy. My family isn't like most families. They don't think that a daughter has to get married. They agree that things should change. They're not old-fashioned at all.'

Then why didn't they educate her, I wanted to ask, but let it be. 'And do other villagers support you?' I asked. 'Do the village women support you?'

She nodded.

'So you're enjoying your work for the party?'

She nodded again.

Just to see how she would respond, I asked whether she felt that girls like her were being used by the party.

She shook her head, fixing me with a confident look at last. In an exhorting tone, she said, 'We mustn't feel discouraged. There's no reason for that.' Her voice became low and intent. 'There's no reason to feel discouraged. We must realize—there's nothing to feel discouraged about.'

We reached Tatopani village an hour later. From here Khalanga was a three-hour walk: I knew this to be a fact, because I had read it in not one but two trekking books in Kathmandu. We had been on the road for ten hours already. We needed to eat quickly and leave at once.

Entering the village, though, we were immediately surrounded by a group of Maoist boys insisting that we speak to them.

'What,' asked one boy, 'are you doing here?'

We said we were here to have lunch.

'No, but what are you here to *do*?'

We mentioned human rights and writing.

'Many spies infiltrate our area in the name of human rights,' the boy said, narrowing his eyes.

We were not happy to hear this.

Luckily, another boy stepped in: 'No, human rights workers are on our side,' he said. But he, too, insisted we talk to them.

So we did. Or I did, as Malcolm lay down in imitation of his over-walked family dog.

The boy, who introduced himself as Comrade Jiwanta, complained that despite the ceasefire the army had not let off harassing his party members. 'Just the other day a patrol of about eight army men came by, and when Comrade Krishna and Comrade Sahara met them by one of our gates to offer them a greeting card, they beat them,' he said. 'And in Lamra village the army confiscated sixteen of our socket bombs and a hundred metres of wire.' They had also, he said, written 'I love you' on some Maoist banners calling for round-table talks.

I listened on, feigning interest.

'Before we waged our attack on Khalanga,' said Comrade Jiwanta, 'the people of this area lived in terror. When we captured Khalanga, everyone was thrilled.'

'I'm sure,' I said. Then I asked, 'But where are your women?'

'What?'

'Where are the women of your party?'

'Thirty to forty per cent of our party workers are women,' he said.

'But we haven't met any.'

'That's because they're busy.'

'Busier than you?'

'Yes,' he said. 'They have more work. They have to perform chores at home as well, you know.'

We broke away after an hour, and had lunch at a nearby lodge. An elderly woman served us as I, in my exhaustion, complained bitterly about the Maoists to another customer, a man from the same village. 'They shouldn't force people to talk to them if they don't want to—if they're tired, or in a rush, or hungry,' I complained, like the Kathmandu bourgeoisie that I was. 'There was this motivator the other night—he kept us up for hours! And along the way—all these men, asking what we came for. All these boys. They're like…children playing a game.'

The man agreed, with surprising anger. 'Most of them,' he hissed, 'are kids who can't find work. They wouldn't be given any money if they asked it from their fathers, so they join the party, and extort it on the strength of guns.'

'Yes, exactly,' I sputtered. 'Yes.'

'Only fifteen to twenty per cent of their workers are ideologically motivated,' he said.

'Really?'

'Most of them are in it for the fun. It's just something to do.'

Slightly restored by the meal—and a fragrant glass each of fresh milk—we set out in the blazing sun. I was flat out of energy, and the entire trip had become a blur in my mind. I could hardly remember Chupra, Dailekh bazaar, Nabisthan, Dullu, Ghumnekhali, Bajhangeneta…all these places we had passed through. The poverty of Kalikot District was my strongest impression. Everything seemed such a mess.

Along a high valley surrounded by snow-capped hills, I fell in with an aged woman. She was wearing a threadbare blouse and fariya, and her hair was wrapped in a shawl. A gold ring hung from her nose, decorating her leathery face. She said something to me in Jumli, which was incomprehensible to me. Not realizing this, she gabbed on awhile, then turned to me with an expectant look.

She had, I realized, asked me a question.

I assumed she wanted to know where we were coming from. 'We walked from Dailkeh District to Manma,' I said. 'And now we're going to Khalanga. We're originally from Kathmandu. Or I am. The man is from Belaayat.'

She hacked out a cough, and began, again, to talk, turning to me with another query.

For some reason I thought she had asked how many children I had. 'I'm not married,' I said.

She raised an eyebrow and babbled.

'Indeed.' If she could hold one end of an incoherent conversation, so could I. 'And how many children do you have?'

She said something. Perhaps that she had several sons and daughters. From her tone, she was not pleased with them.

At a fork in the road she blurted out a merry farewell, and trundled off to a stone hut not far from the path.

Was it that I was tired, I wondered. Or had the old woman been quite drunk? Well, if she was, that was one way to get by in the mess that we had become.

Not far along, we passed a group of young girls in kurtha-surals. Hell, not more Maoist children, I thought. They were all wearing bright red teekas on their foreheads, and tittering among themselves. Not one of them was older than fifteen or sixteen. I didn't want to talk to them.

We passed about twenty of these girls, till we reached their source: a gathering of Maoists at a roadside building. There were men here as well, but they weren't like any of the other Maoist men we had met. These men were taller, and brawny. They turned to us with combative stances.

Hell, I thought, we would have to talk. I saw, in their midst, a dark, small-boned older man who could not—at least with his bare hands—kill me. Nervously, I went up and introduced ourselves. He was, he said, the local area in-charge: Comrade Kanchan Sagar. Would he talk to us, I asked, purely to ingratiate ourselves to him.

Comrade Kanchan Sagar spoke in the measured manner of all the older Maoists we had met. 'We're taking the code of conduct very seriously,' he said. He pointed at a muscle-bound young man, glowering at us from nearby. 'He's in the military wing, but as you can see, he's not wearing his uniform.' Shooting us a bellicose look, the man slipped away, out of sight. Comrade Kanchan Sagar continued, 'We've put down our arms, but the army haven't put down theirs. Yesterday they conducted a patrol here, with sixty-six—no, sixty-seven—men. What purpose did that serve but to make a show of force?'

Insofar as he was in charge of younger cadres, Comrade Kanchan Sagar reminded me of Comrade Sandesh. But how small he was, and how militant were the youth he commanded! Some of these men, I realized, would have been part of the 3,000-strong force that had attacked Khalanga. Could their tiny little leader really manage them? Or was it they who steered him?

'We want the talks to succeed,' Comrade Kanchan Sagar said in his reasonable way. 'The people, too, want peace. They're very keen that the peace last. We won't let their hopes transform into disappointment.'

'So the party won't go back to violence?' I asked.

'We want to move from waging physical attacks to waging philosophical attacks,' he said.

I had no idea what this meant, but I nodded.

'The government is behaving treacherously,' he went on. 'But we're being as flexible as we can. We know that whoever presents an obstacle to peace will lose favour with the people. We want peace.'

Reassured, by this time, that we would not be killed, I said we had to be off.

He nodded, and we took leave, avoiding eye contact as we walked past the tough youths.

Beyond the gathering, we fell in with a Maoist girl. Her kurtha-sural, atypically, had flower patterns, giving her a soft, feminine look. On her feet were open flip-flops that made a slapping sound with each step. She talked easily, amicably.

The gathering we had passed was a wedding, she said, between two party cadres.

What, I asked, was a Maoist wedding like?

'First, the girl and the boy both have to like each other,' she explained. 'Then the party will hold a ceremony for them.' This entailed a simple exchange of garlands. There was singing and dancing afterwards. 'We've been dancing all morning.'

I asked her age, and she said she was sixteen. She was originally from Kalikot District, but she had been working in Jumla District throughout her year and a half in the party.

She was curious about me. She asked where my family was, and I told her: Kathmandu. 'You've walked more than we can,' she exclaimed when I told her that we had walked from Ranchuli today.

I asked if she was a motivator.

She shook her head. 'I'm in the army.'

Nothing about her would have made me guess this. 'You've taken military training?' I asked.

She nodded. 'They gave us physical training and taught us to shoot rifles. I've even learned how to shoot automatic rifles,' she said with a smile.

I asked if she had been involved in the attack on Khalanga.
She shook her head. 'I wasn't told to.'

'If you had been told to, you would have gone?'

She nodded yes.

Two other teenage girls had caught up with us at this point.
One of them asked me if I was married.

When I said no, she said, 'And your family allows you to
travel like this?'

'Women have to be mobile if they are to do the same work
as men,' I said.

'It's the same with us,' she said enthusiastically. 'We too have
to walk from village to village in the company of men. It's
something we *have* to do for our work.'

I asked the first girl—the girl in the military—what she was
doing before she joined the party.

'Nothing,' she said. 'I was at home, spending my days cutting
grass.' Then, with a blithe tone that belied the grimness of her
message, she said, 'You see, before, there were only sickles in
the hands of girls like me. Sickles and grass. And now there are
automatic rifles.'

All my irritation at the Maoists fell away with this. If I had
grown up in one of these villages, and were young, uneducated,
unqualified for employment of any kind, and as a female, denied
basic equality with men—hell, I would have joined the Maoists,
too. The other political parties had not offered better options,
and neither had the government. Join the Maoists is what any
spirited girl would do.

We walked a long way together yet, chatting about more
personal things. One of the girls asked me my age, and when I
told her, she asked me again why, at this age, I still wasn't married.

'What's in it for women?' I said flippantly.

All three girls laughed. 'I think the same way,' said one of them. 'I think that marriage only makes women work harder. I also don't want to marry.' She pointed at Malcolm, who was walking ahead. 'And is he married?'

'He's divorced,' I said. 'You know, foreigners do that. They marry, and if it doesn't work out, they get divorced, and marry someone else.'

She took this in, then asked, 'Is that good?'

'I think it's good.'

'I think it's good too,' she said.

As we passed a sparse settlement, a boy called out to the girls from the side of the trail. His voice was severe, and his tone had the barking quality of an order. The girls who had joined us later went off to talk to him. He said something clipped to them, and they followed him through some village fields.

The first girl stood, looking suddenly confused about what to do.

'Are you walking on?' I asked, hoping that she would keep me company.

She looked at her friends walking through the fields. 'I'll wait here,' she said.

As we parted, she just stood there, suddenly looking bereft, as though she had lost her direction.

Hell, hell, hell was the only thought I had from here on. If the insurgency was not resolved through peace talks, this girl, and so many of the people we had met on this trip, could die in the course of war: All the villagers, caught between the Maoists and the state security forces, and all the children and young, lost people who had joined the Maoists, wanting a better life. I thought of all the policemen and soldiers losing their lives for an unwinnable war, all to feed and clothe and shelter their families, who were no better off than the Maoists. I thought of

Durga, dodging army bullets, and Comrade Rebel, arguing that
there must be a difference in the conduct of dogs and of human
beings. The muttering Maoist of Dullu, condemning the locals
for getting high. The serious-minded man from the Farmers'
Front, rattling off his classification of landless, poor, middle-class,
rich and feudal farmers. Comrade Kopila, who should have been
working in a non-government organization, but had fallen in
with the Maoists instead. All the young rebel girls. They could
all die. As could many, many innocents caught in a war they did
not support, but could not avoid. How many political activists,
teachers, social workers and ordinary people were yet to lose
their lives in the massacres to come?

We staggered into Khalanga, sick at the thought of how
terror-struck the residents must have been when 3,000 Maoists
surrounded them in the dead of that November night. The path
to the town centre was endless. We trudged wearily, meeting, in
one lane, a pair of drunks stumbling about, yelling at the sky.
This seemed as good a way to cope with war as any. Further
on, we crossed a man passed out on the path, drunk, piss stains
all around him. Not far away we passed two more drunk men,
who tried to engage Malcolm in conversation, and ended up
roaring in glee.

Khalanga was a big town, its lanes lined with shops. The
houses looked relatively affluent, and were decked with electric
poles and wires. Every now and then, though, we would cross
the charred ruins of government buildings burned down in the
Maoist attack. All government offices here—even those housed
in rented buildings—had been hit. Some neighbourhoods were
entirely in a shambles.

We found lodgings easily enough, and took leave from Chitra
Bahadur and Mama and Bharat. Tomorrow, they would start the
six-day walk back to their village.

Our lodge was wildly luxurious: For the first time we had separate rooms, rooms with curtains on the windows and jute carpets on the floors and foam on the beds. Our minds were numb, though; our conversations were blank.

We slept heavily that night with the aid of crisp fried eggs and the better part of a hard-found bottle of whisky. Waking up bleary the next morning, we thought—hell, we should take in the gutted town. But our plane landed earlier than scheduled, and we got in a rush to leave.

THE
UNFINISHED
REVOLUTION

WE WANT DEMOCRACY

On 17 August 2003, seven months into the ceasefire, the government and Maoist negotiation teams were holding peace talks in Hapure village, in the western district of Dang, when radio reports came in that the state security forces had killed seventeen armed Maoists in Doramba village, in eastern Ramechhap District. Though there had been small skirmishes throughout the ceasefire, nothing of this scale had occurred in peacetime. The official reports claimed that armed Maoists had ambushed the security forces; but the Maoists immediately refuted this. The private media too reported aberrations in the official story. Then word filtered out that the Maoists had indeed been unarmed, and that the security forces had first captured them, then shot them execution-style. The Maoists pulled out of the peace talks.

Nobody wanted the war to resume; but the vast machinery of insurgency and counter-insurgency churned on again. Kathmandu convulsed in panic as the Maoists shot two army colonels on the streets, killing one. Rumours spread that the Maoists had regrouped over the period of the ceasefire, and that 7,000 armed guerillas were now poised for a final attack on the capital. Tales of a Maoist hit list made the nation's who's who shudder, and the government posted armed guards to the houses of high officials. The lesser government staff pored over security manuals issuing dire warnings: Treat everyone as a potential threat!

Why hadn't the peace held? The National Human Rights Commission dispatched a team of independent observers to uncover the truth about the massacre in Doramba village. Their report claimed that the security forces had captured nineteen unarmed Maoists. After marching them, with their hands tied behind their backs, to a nearby forest, the security forces had lined them in a row and shot them dead. The Royal Nepal Army was forced to open a new inquiry into this incident. Nearly two years later, the military court sentenced a major to three years' incarceration for this. Yet most observers agree that it is unlikely that he had acted alone. Who had really ordered the massacre at Doramba? It may forever remain a matter of speculation as to whether the army's top brass had intentionally scuttled the peace talks.

Events then followed a very bleak course. Having precipitated the constitutional crisis that enabled Gyanendra's takeover of October 2002, the political parties were slow to call for the restoration of democracy. When they did so, the call was guilty and half-hearted. In just as half-hearted a response, Gyanendra dismissed Lokendra Bahadur Chand and appointed another Panchayat-era politician, Surya Bahadur Thapa, as prime minister. He did not even bother to make overtures for peace talks. Instead he escalated the war, and the death toll rose, soon topping 10,000.

In 2004 the political parties reluctantly strengthened their call for democracy, clogging Kathmandu's streets with rallies and demonstrations. The government cracked down hard, injuring hundreds in a show of force; but this only inflamed anti-monarchy sentiment. Outdoing their party leaders, student activists became vocal about the need to abolish the monarchy. Even as stories circulated about a spate of brawls involving Gyanendra's son, Paras, the call grew for a constituent assembly and a new constitution. Democracy activists were taking up what had till then been the Maoists' main demands.

At this, Gyanendra dismissed Surya Bahadur Thapa and reinstated Sher Bahadur Deuba, whom he had sacked two years earlier. Some of the political parties—most notably Deuba's Nepali Congress Party (Democratic) and the UML—gladly halted their democracy movement and joined the cabinet. This, though the cabinet was still operating without legal legitimacy, under Article 127 of the 1990 constitution. Elections remained unfeasible, all laws were passed by cabinet ordinance, the king retained ultimate power, and the war was grinding on…

For those who stubbornly believed, against mounting evidence, that the country was still under the purview of the 1990 constitution, Gyanendra's military coup of 1 February 2005 proved a clarifying event. The coup was carried out amid high drama. The king announced his direct rule over live television, with an unintentionally funny backdrop that had a map of the country coming out of his ears, and khukuri knives sticking out of his cap, like horns. He banned free expression and suspended the right to assemble peacefully, the right to free association, press and publication rights, the right against preventative detention, the right to information, the right to property, the right to privacy and the rights to most constitutional remedies. Immediately after his announcement, all the telephone lines went dead. News spread that the military had rounded up thousands of democratic politicians all over the country and posted censors at the major media houses. Thousands of activists went underground over the following days.

Gyanendra had taken the final step in his staggered coup. Later, it emerged that he had long prepared for it. About a month earlier he had even informed the Indian, British and American embassies about his plans, sending them aflutter with panicky faxes to their home governments. They all later claimed that they had advised Gyanendra against taking over.

By then Nepalis had stopped saying 'It can't get any worse than this,' because we knew it could, and most likely, would. Declaring himself 'chairman' of a cabinet full of Panchayat-era

hardliners, Gyanendra set about trying to revive the Shah dynasty's
absolute rule. In this, his main ally was the military. Were it not
for the ultra-royalist top brass, he could not have exercised such
power. The reverse was also true: Were it not for the king, the
army's top brass would have also enjoyed little power. By some
accounts, the monarchy was but a puppet in the hands of a few
hawkish generals—the names of Generals Rukmangat Katwal
and Deepak Rayamajhi were generally bandied about—whose
ultimate goal was to establish military rule. Indeed, over the past
years the army brass had shown disrespect, even insubordination,
towards the democratic parties, to elected leaders, and to the
civilian branches of government. Under the king's absolute rule,
the army was in fact operating illegally, for the 1990 constitution
stipulated that the defence council, upon whose orders the army
acted, be chaired by the prime minister. But now there was no
prime minister, just an odd, illegal chairman/king.

For the Maoists, the king's coup proved a blessing. The
democratic political parties had been betrayed by the king and
military; they had nowhere to go but to the Maoists. And the
Maoists, too, needed a 'soft landing'—a way out of insurgency,
into politics. Refusing to talk to Gyanendra's government, they
invited the political parties to help them overthrow the monarchy.
They even offered to adopt a democratic platform; but so fierce
had the Maoists' war on the parties been, they were hard pressed
to trust them.

Ordinary Nepalis set the ground for a joint movement for
the restoration of democracy—the People's Movement II, as it
later came to be known. The movement began with low-level
defiance to Gyanendra's government, then expanded as journalists
began to ridicule, then break, censorship laws, and lawyers began
to activate the judiciary against Gyanendra's arbitrary dictates.
Members of civil society began to organize public gatherings,

defying the ban on free assembly. Poets, writers, artists, actors and singers withstood arrest, beatings and persecution. As the months passed, all of Nepali society went into open rebellion.

Still, the political parties hesitated to ally with the Maoists. They were helped to overcome their mistrust by the international community.

Over the monsoon season—when the heavy rains make public action unfeasible—the political parties opened up offices in exile in New Delhi, India. There, they began to confer among themselves and with the international community, who for a change proved sympathetic to their confusions, their quandaries. Upon much deliberation the political parties formed a 'Seven Party Alliance'. With the mediation of the Indian government, they met the underground Maoist leaders in New Delhi at the end of 2005. What resulted was a twelve-point pact in December: an agreement between the Seven Party Alliance to launch a non-violent movement for democracy, with the Maoists as allies.

Ordinary Nepalis threw their support behind this movement. In April 2006, millions of people poured out onto the streets of towns and villages throughout the country in an unprecedented show of people's power. They stared down the police and military, defied curfews and clampdowns, and overturned one after another ban on political freedom. Scores of people lost their lives; but faced with such crowds, the military proved unwilling to engage in mass bloodshed. Gyanendra's absolute rule ended swiftly. After nineteen days of demonstrations, on 24 April, he was forced to go on television and announce the reinstatement of the House of Parliament. It was not clear at the time whether the monarchy would survive his misadventure.

After the People's Movement II, the Maoists declared a ceasefire and entered a peace process monitored by India and the United Nations. In 2007 the Seven Party Alliance and the

Maoists signed a 'Comprehensive Peace Accord' and drafted an interim constitution. In 2008 came elections for a 601-member Constituent Assembly, which in a break from the past ensured the proportional representation of the excluded—women, Dalits, janajatis and the people of southeast Nepal, the Madeshis, who launched a late but forceful civil rights movement upon the start of the peace process. The Maoists won the elections, with almost 40 per cent of the vote, which nevertheless missed the majority mark. The question of who would form government remained open. Even as the political parties wrangled over this, the Constituent Assembly, in its very first meeting, abolished the 239-year-old monarchy. Gyanendra ceded with surprising ease in the end. Ram Baran Yadav of the Nepali Congress became Nepal's first President, and the Maoist's top leader, Pushpa Kamal Dahal (Prachanda), became the first prime minister of republican Nepal.

Now it is possible to decipher a pattern to what—since the mid 1990s—felt like a clutter of regrettable events. Now we can look back to that period and say, 'That was what it was like in the thick of the revolution.'

Halfway into the peace process, the revolution was still underway. It was not a Maoist revolution, but a democratic one, the liberal democratic revolution that began in the 1930s, a yet-unfinished revolution that brought us two short spells of democracy in 1950 and 1990.

The People's Movement II of 2006 was the latest stage of this revolution. Whether or not we complete the revolution depends on the constitution that is drafted. The stated goal of all the parties has been to draft it carefully, transparently, inclusively. But of course the less romantic imperatives of politics—the parties' deep mutual mistrust of each other, their clashing ideologies, their ongoing quests for domination over one another—have often overshadowed constitution-making. The peace process was set to be fraught from the start. The integration of the Nepal Army and the People's Liberation Army (the latter temporarily housed in UN-monitored cantonments) was bound to be explosive, as was the reform of the security sector, the need for justice for the victims of war, the need for rule of law and respect for human rights, and the delineation of boundaries for federal states. Halfway in, it was still hard to predict whether all this could be done successfully. On top of that, the Constituent Assembly had to draft not just any kind of constitution, but a constitution that established Nepal solidly, unshakeably, as a liberal democracy. The king exited the peace process vying for absolute monarchy. The Maoists came into the peace process dreaming of absolute communism. The Nepali people want neither extreme: We want both the extreme right and the extreme left to be contained by the political centre. Which is simply to say, we want democracy.

And for my birthday I want a rocket ship.

It has been symptomatic of the postmodern era to be embarrassed to say something as raw as 'We want democracy' or 'We want full democracy'—key slogans of the 1990 and 2006 movements. It is part of our zeitgeist to retreat from idealism into a knowing irony, and its source, despair. Yet nothing is more critical to Nepal now than attaining full democracy.

People's hope is that we can do so in peace.

Over the years, as I returned to the war-torn countryside to write about what was happening, I saw the majority of Nepalis yearn for legitimate, non-violent politics. They desperately want to avoid a resumption of war.

In one settlement in west Nepal, I met an old widow who said, in a daze, 'My truth has been destroyed.' Her elder son and daughter-in-law had been shot dead by the security forces after some neighbours reported them as Maoists, on a personal grudge. The villagers had then set the security forces after the widow's second son. He fled the village. Now the widow was living in destitution with a teenage daughter and a grandson from her slain son and daughter-in-law. Her entire world had fallen apart, in old age, she had lost all her certainties and comforts. After telling me her story she chanted, over and over, 'My truth has been destroyed. My truth, my life have been destroyed. My truth has been destroyed.'

ACKNOWLEDGEMENTS

The following books, writings and websites served as invaluable sources for research on this book: *The Rise of the House of Gurkhas* and *Nepal: Growth of a Nation* by Ludwig F. Stiller; *Modern Nepal: A Political History*, Volumes I and II by Rishikesh Shaha; *Jang Bahadur in Europe* by John Whelpton; *A Chronicle of Rana Rule* by Pramode Sumshere Rana; *Political Awakening in Nepal: The Search for a New Identity* by Prem R. Uprety; *Heir to a Silent Song* by Barbara Nimri Aziz; *Nepalmaa Communist Aandolanko Itihaas* by Surendra KC; *Aadhunik Nepalko Itihaas* by Deviprasad Sharma; *Indelible Scars: A Study of Torture in Nepal* by Bhogendra Sharma, Rajesh Gautam and Gopal Guragain; *People, Politics and Ideology: Democracy and Social Change in Nepal* by Martin Hoftun, William Raeper and John Whelpton; *The Challenge to Democracy in Nepal: A Political History* by T. Louise Brown; 'Day of the Maoist' by Deepak Thapa, *Himal Southasian*, May 2001; *State of Nepal*, eds. Kanak Mani Dixit and Shastri Ramachandaran; *The Kathmandu Post* reports from December 2000 to December 2002; *Nepali Times* reports from January 2002 onwards; *Understanding the Maoist Movement of Nepal,* ed. Deepak Thapa; the Informal Sector Service Centre's ongoing web count of those killed in the insurgency and counter-insurgency; and the National Human Rights Commission's reports on human rights violations.

My thanks to Ravi Singh, Isobel Dixon, Wayne Amtzis, John Bevan, Tej Thapa and Daniel Lak for their help in writing this book. Ben Schonveld was 'Malcolm', whose portrayal I had to curtail due to professional confidentiality concerns at the time. Over the past years he and many others have offered me their insights on Nepal, among them Seira Tamang, Mandira Sharma, Hari Roka, Khagendra Sangraula, Gopal Siwakoti Chintan, Kesang Tseten, Joel Isaacson, Judith Amtzis, Ashmina Ranjit, Pratyoush Onta and all the members of the Martin Chautari community. I would like to acknowledge my debt to them—without implicating them in the deficiencies of my vision.

Parts of 'The Massacres to Come' and 'The Unfinished Revolution' appeared in different forms in *Nepali Times* and *Himal Southasian* in Nepal, and *Biblio* in India. Some new parts of 'The Coup That Did Not Happen' and 'The Unfinished Revolution'— updated after February 2005—have appeared in different forms in *The New York Times*, *Tehelka*, *Hindustan Times*, *The Asian Age* and openDemocracy.net. My thanks to them all. My thanks, also, to Kunda Dixit at *Nepali Times* and Basanta Thapa at the Centre for Investigative Journalism for guiding me into the reporting which led me to write on the war.

My love, always, to my family, Bhekh Bahadur and Rita Thapa, Bhaskar and Sumira, Tej and the little ones: Barune, Maya, Siddhant.